# USING DATA
## TO IMPROVE
## STUDENT LEARNING
## IN ELEMENTARY SCHOOLS

VICTORIA L. BERNHARDT, Ph.D.
Executive Director
Education for the Future Initiative

Professor
Department of Professional Studies in Education
College of Communication and Education
California State University, Chico, CA

EYE ON EDUCATION
6 Depot Way West
Larchmont, NY  10538
(914) 833-0551
(914) 833-0761 Fax

For information about permission to reproduce selections from this book, write:
Eye On Education
Permission Dept.
6 Depot Way West
Larchmont, NY  10538

Library of Congress Cataloging—in—Publication Data

Bernhardt, Victoria L., 1952-
    Using data to improve student learning in elementary schools / Victoria L. Bernhardt.
        p.   cm.
    Includes bibliographical references (p. ) and index.
    ISBN 1-930556-60-8
    1. Educational evaluation--United States.  2. Educational indicators--United States.
    3. Education, Elementary--United States.  I. Title.

    LB2822.75.B43 2003
    372.12'00973--dc21

                                                                        2003044887

10  9  8  7  6  5  4  3  2

# Also Available from Eye on Education

**THE SCHOOL PORTFOLIO TOOLKIT:**
**A Planning, Implementation, and Evaluation Guide for**
**Continuous School Improvement (with CD-Rom)**
Victoria L. Bernhardt

**DATA ANALYSIS FOR COMPREHENSIVE SCHOOLWIDE IMPROVEMENT**
Victoria L. Bernhardt

**DESIGNING AND USING DATABASES FOR SCHOOL IMPROVEMENT**
Victoria L. Bernhardt

**THE EXAMPLE SCHOOL PORTFOLIO**
Victoria L. Bernhardt, et. al.

**THE SCHOOL PORTFOLIO:**
**A Comprehensive Framework for School Improvement, Second Edition**
Victoria L. Bernhardt

**SCHOOL LEADER'S GUIDE TO ROOT CAUSE ANALYSIS:**
**Using Data to Dissolve Problems**
Paul Preuss

**NAVIGATING COMPREHENSIVE SCHOOL CHANGE:**
**A Guide for the Perplexed**
Thomas Chenoweth and Robert Everhart

**BETTER INSTRUCTION THROUGH ASSESSMENT:**
**What Your Students are Trying to Tell You**
Leslie Wilson

**ACHIEVEMENT NOW!**
**How to Assure No Child is Left Behind**
Donald J. Fielder

**DROPOUT PREVENTION TOOLS**
Franklin Schargel

**STRATEGIES TO HELP SOLVE OUR SCHOOL DROPOUT PROBLEM**
Franklin Schargel and Jay Smink

**TEACHING MATTERS:**
**Motivating and Inspiring Yourself**
Todd and Beth Whitaker

**BOUNCING BACK!**
**How Your School Can Succeed in the Face of Adversity**
Patterson, Patterson, and Collins

# Acknowledgements

I am so lucky to have many wonderful, dedicated colleagues and friends all over the world who keep me going, and help me improve each day. I am particularly grateful for special colleagues from Arizona, California, Colorado, Georgia, Iowa, Indiana, Michigan, Missouri, Montana, North Dakota, Nevada, New Jersey, New York, Ohio, South Carolina, Vermont, Washington, Japan, and Brazil who have helped make this book factual and useful. These dedicated reviewers read a very, very drafty first draft and then encouraged me to keep going! They also gave me powerful information for making the content more useful and user-friendly. These reviewers were critical in the writing of this book for probably more reasons than they know. They gave me the confidence and sense of urgency to finish. The reviewers of *Using Data to Improve Student Learning in Elementary Schools* included (I apologize if I left anyone out):

> Carol Albritton, Jane Armstrong, Bob Birdsell, Becky Bogert, Martin Brutosky, Jane Bustos, Peggy Christie, Sue Clayton, Donnie Coggins, Cheryl Cozette, Bill Deeb, Marilyn Dishman-Horst, Laurel Eisinger, Judy English, Martha Fritchley, Randi Hagan, Elaine Hassemer, Rhonda Hays, Bill Johnston, Mike Kirby, Anita Kishel, Marcy Lauck, Sara Laughlin, Mary Leslie, Brownie Linder, Mel Lioi, Katie Lovett, Andy Mark, Terri Martin, Mark Maynard, Doug Miller, Sheryl O'Connor, Mary Parks, Paul Preuss, Virginia Propp, Chris Provance, Donna Rinckel, Maria Christina dos Reis, Joy Rose, Jo Seidel, Denise Shockley, Penny Swenson, Marlene Trapp, Zana Vincent, Judy Weber, Debbie Weingarth, Terri Whitehead, Cindy Wilcox, and Jody Wood.

Andy Mark gave additional time and energy by reviewing more than one draft, and for carefully looking over table and graph titles, labels, messages, and findings. Joy Rose read and edited the manuscript in every phase. Joy, as always, made herself available to help with any task, any time. Joy, my editor "extraordinaire," is unsurpassed as a supporter and encourager of high-quality work. The nature of her editing goes beyond the proper uses of verbs and commas—her knowledge of continuous school improvement provides insights and revelations that I do not always see. I know the final product is so much better because of her input. Thank you, thank you, and thank you, Joy.

A special thanks to the schools that gave me data to use in the case studies. In concert with our agreements, I will not reveal who you are or your real locations. We all appreciate the opportunity to learn from you.

I am appreciative and thankful everyday for my outstanding *Education for the Future* staff: Lynn Varicelli, Brad Geise, Alicia Warren, Sally Withuhn, Mary Foard, and Marcy Lauck. Brad Geise gives so much to *Education for the Future*—7 days a week, if necessary. Brad is continuously learning new software and hardware techniques while keeping our questionnaire services running. Brad managed the completion of the CD and graphics with his usual elegance. Alicia Hamilton, Mary Foard, and Sally Withuhn do amazing work, every day, to keep us operating and on the cutting edge. They also helped to make this book a reality. Alicia deserves special acknowledgement for help with the references and graphing, and Sally for graphing questionnaire results. Last, but not least, Marcy Lauck, serving as our depth charge in San Jose Unified School District, helps us know that it is possible to do this on a large scale and that it can be sustained over time.

Once again, I am awestruck and indebted to Lynn Varicelli, also an *Education for the Future* staff member, for her careful and artistic work on the book layout and CD files. Her dedication to supporting these publications is unmatched in the history of the world! Thank you, Lynn, for your stellar work, for your commitment, loyalty, and long hours over countless days without a break. These books could never be done without you.

I am also grateful to *MC² Design Group*. Brian Curtis and Rocky Campbell created the CD design, artwork, and cover—I highly recommend them—and Tom Devol (that's *loved* spelled backwards), our outstanding professional photographer (even if HE cannot spell backwards).

A special thank you to *TetraData Corporation* for being so helpful and encouraging of the work of *Education for the Future*. Your software and data warehouse is the best available. I am so honored to have the opportunity to work with you. Thank you for all you do for us.

I thank my husband, Jim Richmond, for again providing his brand of support for my work. He does a lot of what I should be doing around the house so I can pursue these publications and the work I can't not do—with few complaints.

A huge thanks to my publisher, affectionately known as *Cousin Bob,* Mr. Robert Sickles. I am grateful for all you do for us. Thank you.

This *Acknowledgement* section could not be complete without thanking you, the reader, and you, the school personnel working with continuous school improvement, who have believed in and tried *Education for the Future* products and processes.

I do hope this book exceeds your expectations and if it does, it is because of the continuous improvement that has resulted from your insights, direction, assistance, and support all along the way. Thank you.

In appreciation to all interested in continuous quality improvement, enjoy this first in a series of four books on *Using Data to Improve Student Learning*.

*Vickie Bernhardt*
*May 2003*

# About the Author

Victoria L. Bernhardt, Ph.D., is Executive Director of the *Education for the Future Initiative*, a not-for-profit organization whose mission is to build the capacity of all schools at all levels to gather, analyze, and use data to continuously improve learning for all students. She is also a Professor in the Department of Professional Studies in Education, College of Communication and Education, at California State University, Chico. Dr. Bernhardt is the author of:

▼ A four-book collection of using data to improve student learning—*Using Data to Improve Student Learning in Elementary Schools (2003); Using Data to Improve Student Learning in Middle Schools (2004); Using Data to Improve Student Learning in High Schools (2005);* and *Using Data to Improve Student Learning in School Districts (2005).* Each book shows real analyses focused on one education organizational level and provides templates on an accompanying CD-Rom for leaders to use for analyzing data in their own learning organizations.

▼ *Data Analysis for Comprehensive Schoolwide Improvement* (First Edition, 1998; Second Edition, 2004) helps learning organizations use data to determine where they are, where they want to be, and how to get there—sensibly, painlessly, and effectively.

▼ *The School Portfolio Toolkit: A Planning, Implementation, and Evaluation Guide for Continuous School Improvement,* and CD-Rom (2002), is a compilation of over 300 ideas, examples, suggestions, activities, tools, strategies, and templates for producing school portfolios that will lead to continuous school improvement.

▼ *The Example School Portfolio* (2000) shows what a completed school portfolio looks like and further supports schools in developing their own school portfolios.

▼ *Designing and Using Databases for School Improvement* (2000) helps schools and districts think through the issues surrounding the creation and uses of databases established to achieve improved student learning.

▼ *The School Portfolio: A Comprehensive Framework for School Improvement* (First Edition, 1994; Second Edition, 1999). This first book by the author assists schools with clarifying the purpose and vision of their learning organizations as they develop their school portfolios.

Dr. Bernhardt is passionate about her mission of helping all educators continuously improve student learning in their classrooms, their schools, their districts, and states by gathering, analyzing, and using actual data—as opposed to using hunches and "gut-level" feelings. She has made numerous presentations at professional meetings and has conducted thousands of workshops on the school portfolio, data analysis, and school improvement at local, state, regional, national, and international levels.

Dr. Bernhardt can be reached at:

Victoria L. Bernhardt
Executive Director, *Education for the FutureInitiative*
400 West First Street, Chico, CA  95929-0230
Tel: 530-898-4482 — Fax: 530-898-4484
e-mail: vbernhardt@csuchico.edu
*http://eff.csuchico.edu*

# Table of Contents

# Foreword

TetraData Corporation is a software and services company that focuses on analysis, assessment, and improvement in education. TetraData continues to be proudly associated with Victoria L. Bernhardt, one of the most dedicated, capable, and energetic leaders in school improvement today. Our firm shares a common passion, i.e., that fact-driven decision making can provide each district, each school, and each class with a reliable way to facilitate continuous school improvement. We also share a common vision of a world where education is moving toward increased knowledge, increased caring, and where we focus societal resources on our real future, i.e., the children of our world.

This book in the series of four, *Using Data to Improve Student Learning,* is an excellent addition to Dr. Bernhardt's preceding books that explain how to establish a data-driven environment and how to build the data warehouse to support the needed analysis of data. The four books in this series focus on what to do with a robust data warehouse, i.e., what analyses to prepare and how to interpret the analyses. In the several years that Dr. Bernhardt and TetraData have been building and using education specific data warehouses, the quality of the data and design of the warehouses has grown significantly. Now we have much of the data that we have been seeking to properly assemble, and the next step is addressed by this wonderful publication series.

What I enjoy immensely about these four publications is that Dr. Bernhardt has used real data from real life situations. This brings richness to the examples and the principles that Dr. Bernhardt provides since it is set forth in such a realistic environment. This realism approach has also enabled Dr. Bernhardt to provide both an insightful, as well as practical, description of how to prepare and interpret the analyses. Since there are four books, the publications deliver this information specific to the teachers and staff in elementary, middle, high school, and the district office. That was a wonderful decision by Dr. Bernhardt, as she provides very specific content for each portion of the education spectrum.

One of the major education issues that Dr. Bernhardt addresses is embodied in the word "Focus." One of the first results of the early education data warehousing and data analysis efforts was the *kid in the candy shop* syndrome. What I mean by that is the school data was finally available for examination, and educators started producing queries and analyses, many of which were useful, but not necessarily pertinent to the focus of their educational team. Dr. Bernhardt, in this work, brings focus to all of our data analysis efforts, a focus on what is important to bring about school improvement, a focus on what will bring results in our quality programs, a focus on the real challenges and opportunities, and a focus on what really can effect positive change.

This fine set of works touches the needs of numerous individuals in the education network, from the teacher who needs to understand the demographics and capabilities of her/his individual students to school principals, counselors, instructional coordinators, testing and data analysis coordinators, district researchers, and certainly the district executives. By virtue of her excellent skills, Dr. Bernhardt has given everyone in education, including the non-technologists among us, the opportunity to benefit from this fine edition. I encourage your reading of this newest edition to the library of Dr. Bernhardt's works and welcome you to embrace the passion of improving education by making objective education-enhancement decisions. Enjoy this wonderful rich material and let it drive all of us to focus on our future—our children.

Martin S. Brutosky
Chairman and CEO
TetraData Corporation
3 Independence Point, Suite 101
Greenville, SC 29615
Tel: 864-458-8243
*http://www.tetradata.com*

# Preface

When it comes to analyzing student achievement data, the first two questions educators ask are *Now that we have the data, what analyses should we make?* and *What do the analyses tell us?*

These questions are hard to answer on the spot, so I have taken up the challenge to develop a series of books with the purposes of showing what analyses can be made, describing what these analyses are telling us, and illustrating how to use these analyses in continuous school improvement planning. This series of books includes:

- ▼ *Using Data to Improve Student Learning in Elementary Schools*
- ▼ *Using Data to Improve Student Learning in Middle Schools*
- ▼ *Using Data to Improve Student Learning in High Schools*
- ▼ *Using Data to Improve Student Learning in School Districts*

I believe that most of the time we must look at K-12 data to ensure a continuum of learning that makes sense for all students. I have purposefully separated building levels so there would be ample space to do a fairly comprehensive job of data analysis at each organizational level and to make the point about needing to understand results beyond one school level.

Each of these four publications uses *two* sets of real data (with some slight alterations to blur identities and to fill gaps where data are missing) and shows the actual descriptive analyses I would perform if I were the person analyzing the data at that particular level. The first set of data shows a school, or district, that has state testing at relatively few grade levels. This set is shown in the chapters. For readability purposes, the second set of data, with consistent measures at every grade level over time, is shown in its own chapter, Chapter 9. You will see differences in what data analyses can be performed, and what they tell us when the measures are consistent and ongoing. You will also see that no matter how much or how little *data* your school has, the *data* can tell the story of your school. The study questions at the end of each chapter serve as guides for the reader. I have described what I saw in the analyses following the study questions for readers who want the feedback.

My goal with this book is for anyone to be able to set up these analyses, regardless of the statistical resources available. Therefore, in addition to showing the analyses in the text, the graphing templates, complete narratives, and supplementary tools appear on the accompanying CD. 

With the enactment of *No Child Left Behind,* every school and district in the country will need to analyze their data to ensure adequate yearly progress. Sometimes, looking at another's analyses makes it easier to see things you would not have seen while looking only at your own analyses. My hope is that you will find this book and the CD to be helpful as you think through the analyses of *your* data.

## Intended Audiences

This book is intended for school and district teachers and administrators who want to use data to continuously improve what they do for children; and for college and university professors who teach school administrators, teachers, and support personnel how to analyze school data. It is my belief that all professional educators must learn how to use data in this time of high-stakes accountability. I also believe that these practical and descriptive analyses are more important for practitioners to learn to perform than inferential statistics.

I hope you find *Using Data to Improve Student Learning in Elementary Schools,* as well as the rest of the series, to be helpful as you work through the processes of using data to improve learning for *all* students.

Victoria L. Bernhardt
Executive Director
Education for the Future
400 West First Street
Chico, CA  95929-0230
Tel: 530-898-4482
Fax: 530-898-4484
*http://eff.csuchico.edu*

# Introduction

Schools that gather, analyze, and use information about their school communities make better decisions, not only about what to change but also how to institutionalize systemic change. Schools that understand the needs of their primary customers—the students—are more successful in planning changes and remain more focused during implementation than those schools that simply gather, but make no sustained effort to analyze and use, data. Schools that *use* data understand the effectiveness of their reform efforts; those that do not can only assume that effectiveness.

Schools committed to improving student learning analyze data in order to plan for the future through understanding—

- ▼ the ways in which the school and the community have changed and are continuing to change

- ▼ the current and future needs of the students, parents, teachers, school, and community

- ▼ how well current processes meet these customers' needs

- ▼ the gaps between the results the school is getting and the results it wants

- ▼ the root causes for the gaps

- ▼ the types of education programs, expertise, and process adjustments that will be needed to alleviate the gaps and to meet the needs of all customers

- ▼ how well the new processes being implemented meet the needs of the students, parents, teachers, school, and community

## The Importance of Data

Businesses typically use data to determine customers' wants and needs. No matter what occupation we, or our students, aspire to, everyone can appreciate that fact. We can also appreciate the fact that businesses not properly analyzing and using data, more often than not, are not successful. Those of us who work in the business of education, however, may not be as familiar with the ways that *businesses* use *educational* data.

In many states, the prison systems look at the number of students not reading on grade level in grades two, three, or four to determine the number of prison cells to build ten years hence (*Lawmakers Move to Improve Literacy*, 2001). The fact that the prison system can use this prediction formula with great accuracy should make us all cringe, but the critical point is that if businesses can use educational data for predictions, so can educators. Not only can we predict, we can use the same data to *prevent* undesirable results from happening. Nothing would make educators happier than to hear that prison systems do not need as many cells because more students are being successful in school and, therefore, in life.

Schools in the United States have a long history of adopting innovations one after another as they are introduced. Very few schools take the time to understand the needs of the children being served. Few take the time to understand the impact current processes have on these children. Few take the time to determine the root causes of recurring problems, or to measure and analyze the impact of implementing new approaches. Fewer still use sound information to build and stick with a solid long-term plan that will improve learning for all students. Across our country, we have found that schools spend an average of about two years engaged in their school improvement efforts. The sad fact is that most schools really only implement their plans for the first six to twelve months. Is it any wonder that nothing seems to generate results for these schools?

We find a different story among the schools that measure and analyze the impact of implementing new approaches. These schools know if what they are doing is working, and if not, why not. These schools also stick with their efforts to create change long after most schools have switched to new efforts. These schools get results.

The use of data can make an enormous difference in school reform efforts by improving school processes and student learning. Data can help to—

▼ replace hunches and hypotheses with facts concerning what changes are needed

▼ facilitate a clear understanding of the gaps between where the school is and where the school wants to be

▼ identify the root causes of these gaps, so the school can solve the problem and not just treat the symptom

▼ understand the impact of processes on the student population

▼ assess needs to target services on important issues

▼ provide information to eliminate ineffective practices

▼ ensure the effective and efficient uses of dollars

▼ show if school goals and objectives are being accomplished

▼ ascertain if the school staffs are *walking the talk*

▼ promote understanding of the impact of efforts, processes, and progress

*If businesses can use educational data for predictions, so can educators. Not only can we predict, we can use the same data to "prevent" undesirable results from happening.*

▼ generate answers for the community related to: *What are we getting for our children by investing in the school's methods, programs, and processes?*

▼ continuously improve all aspects of the learning organization

▼ predict and prevent failures

▼ predict and ensure successes

## Data Barriers

Schools do not deliberately ignore data. Typically, schools say, "We have lots of data; we just do not know what *data* to use, or how or when to use them." When school personnel first get interested in *data* and want to do more with the data they have, they often hit the proverbial *brick wall*.

Schools do not have databases that allow for easy access and analysis of data. Brick walls can pop-up anywhere—

▼ The work culture in education usually does not focus on data in contrast to the work culture in business.

▼ Few people in schools and districts are adequately trained to gather and analyze data or to establish and maintain databases.

▼ Administrators and teachers do not see gathering and analyzing data as part of their jobs.

▼ District personnel have job definitions that often do not include, as a priority, helping individual schools with data.

▼ Gathering data is perceived to be a waste of time (after all, we are here every day—we know what the problems are!).

▼ Computer systems are outdated and inadequate; appropriate, user-friendly software is not available.

▼ Teachers have been trained to be subject-oriented, not data-oriented; process-oriented, rather than product-oriented.

▼ There is a lack of professional development for teachers to understand why data are important and how data can make a difference in their teaching.

▼ Some teachers see data as *another thing that takes away from teaching.*

▼ Data are not used systematically from the state to the regional and local levels, nor are they used particularly well.

▼ School personnel have had only negative experiences with data.

▼ There is a perception that data are collected for someone else's purposes.

- ▼ The legislature keeps changing the rules.

- ▼ Data have been used in negative ways in the past.

- ▼ There are not enough good examples of schools gathering, maintaining, and benefiting from the use of data.

While many schools gather data, barriers begin with attempts to analyze the data to help improve teaching and learning. Whatever it is that keeps us from assessing our progress and products adequately, we must learn to listen, to observe, and to gather data from all sources that will help us *know* how we are doing, where we are going, and how we can get there.

## The Purposes of this Book

This book has three purposes. The first is to provide a learning opportunity for readers. The analyses provided in these chapters are laboratories for learning—authentic tasks, if you will. The analyses are case studies, complete with study questions. The second, and main purpose is to show two sets of analyses, using a continuous school improvement planning model, that can be used to understand, explain, and continuously improve learning for students in elementary schools. The third purpose is to provide tools to do these analyses with your school or district. The analysis tools are found on the accompanying CD.

## The Structure of this Book

*Using Data to Improve Student Learning in Elementary Schools* begins with an overview of why data are important to continuous school improvement. Chapter 2 defines what data are important to have in comprehensive data analysis. It also discusses the intersections of four major data measures in terms of different levels of analyses that can be created using these measures. Chapter 3 describes how to get started and how data fit into a continuous school improvement planning model. Chapters 4 through 7 present an example school analysis using this continuous school improvement planning model, and show how the model assists in understanding what the school is doing that is working or not working for its students. The example used in Chapters 4 through 7 is a K-5 suburban school that is located in a state with criterion-referenced testing at grades three and four—testing different subjects at each grade level.

Chapter 4 focuses the example school's demographic data to answer the question, *Who are we?*, and to establish the context of the school.

Chapter 5 uses the example school's perceptions and process data to answer the question, *How do we do business?*, in terms of its work culture and organizational climate.

*Where are we now?* is the heart of Chapter 6. Ways to measure student learning are defined; analyses that can be made with different measures and their uses are discussed in this chapter. The example school's data assist us with understanding how to analyze state assessment results.

Chapter 7 discusses and shows gap and root cause analyses, answering the questions, *What are the gaps?* and *What are the root causes of the gaps?*

Chapter 8 synthesizes the analyses conducted in Chapters 4 through 7 and provides implications for the example school's continuous school improvement plan. A plan that grew out of this data analysis example is shown.

Chapter 9 looks at a different school through the continuous school improvement planning model. This K-6 urban school has been testing grades two through six on approximately nine subtests of the same nationally norm-referenced test for the past four years. The information presented in Chapter 9 enables us to compare the data analyses from the two example schools.

Questions to guide the study of the information presented in the chapters are included at the end of chapters 2 through 9 , followed by the author's analyses. These files are also found on the CD.

Chapter 10 provides a brief summary and discussion of the example schools' results and reflects on the differences in the analyses of the two schools. As the book concludes, typical process issues, such as *who does the analysis work, the role of the administrator of databases,* and *recommendations on how to get student learning increases,* are discussed.

The questionnaires, the *Continuous Improvement Continuums,* and related tools used by the two example schools are found on the CD, along with complete analyses, analysis templates, and questionnaire narratives. Whenever appears in the text, it means that file is on the CD. A list of CD files related to each chapter appears at the end of the chapter. A complete index of CD contents appears in the Appendix.

A comprehensive *Glossary of Terms* commonly used in data analysis and assessment, and other terms used in this book, is located just before the references and resources list.

## Summary

*Using Data to Improve Student Learning in Elementary Schools* illustrates the basic steps in conducting data analysis to inform continuous school improvement planning in elementary schools. Process implementation is provided, using two schools as examples. Readers will understand what data to gather, how to analyze the data, what the analyses look like, and how the analyses can lead to a school's continuous school improvement plan. Tools to help any school do this work are provided on the accompanying CD.

# What Data Are Important?

If the purpose of school is to ensure that all students learn, what data will help schools understand if they are effectively carrying out their purpose? What data analyses will help schools know if all students are learning?

## Chapter 2

Learning takes place neither in isolation, nor only at school. Multiple measures must be considered and used to understand the multifaceted world of learning from the perspective of everyone involved. Using more than one method of assessment allows students to demonstrate their full range of abilities, and collecting data on *multiple occasions* provides students several opportunities to demonstrate their various abilities. If staffs want to know if the school is achieving its purpose and how to continually improve all aspects of the school, multiple measures—gathered from varying points of view—must be used.

The major job of every school is student learning. Staff must think through the factors that impact student learning to determine other data requirements. We need to ask students what they like about the way they learn at school and how they learn best. School processes, such as programs and instructional strategies, need to be described in order for all staff to meet the learning styles that will optimize the learning of all students.

Because students neither learn only at school nor only through teachers, we need to know about the learning environment from the parent and community perspective. Schools may also need to know how employers are perceiving the abilities and skills of former students.

But will these data provide enough information to determine how well the school is meeting the needs of all students? Other factors over which we have little or no control, such as background or demographics, impact student learning. These data are crucial to our understanding of whom we serve, and whether or not our educational services are meeting the needs of every student.

Analyses of *demographics, perceptions, student learning,* and *school processes* provide a powerful picture that will help us understand the school's impact on student achievement. When used together, these measures give schools the information they need to improve teaching and learning and to get positive results.

In Figure 2.1, these four major categories of data are shown as overlapping circles. This figure illustrates the different types of information one can gain from individual measures and the enhanced levels of analyses that can be gained from the intersections of the measures.

## Figure 2.1

### Multiple Measures of Data

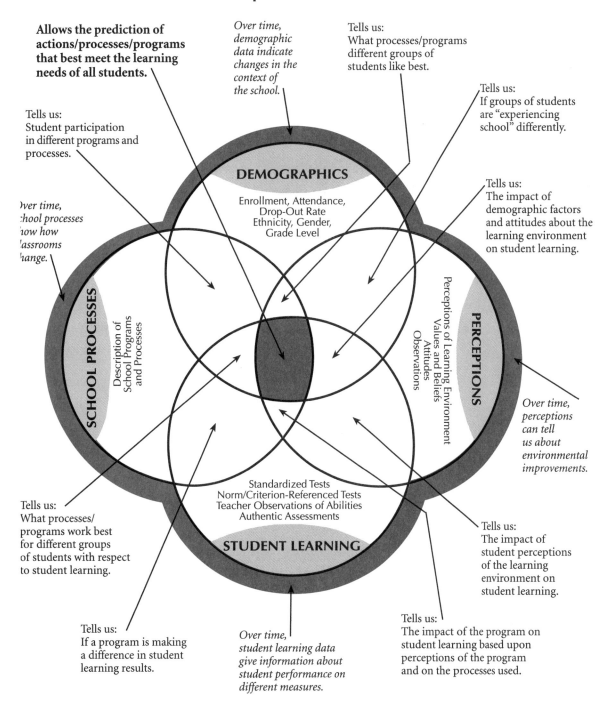

**Allows the prediction of actions/processes/programs that best meet the learning needs of all students.**

*Over time, demographic data indicate changes in the context of the school.*

Tells us:
What processes/programs different groups of students like best.

Tells us:
Student participation in different programs and processes.

Tells us:
If groups of students are "experiencing school" differently.

*Over time, school processes show how classrooms change.*

Tells us:
The impact of demographic factors and attitudes about the learning environment on student learning.

DEMOGRAPHICS

Enrollment, Attendance,
Drop-Out Rate
Ethnicity, Gender,
Grade Level

SCHOOL PROCESSES

Description of School Programs and Processes

Perceptions of Learning Environment
Values and Beliefs
Attitudes
Observations

PERCEPTIONS

*Over time, perceptions can tell us about environmental improvements.*

Standardized Tests
Norm/Criterion-Referenced Tests
Teacher Observations of Abilities
Authentic Assessments

STUDENT LEARNING

Tells us:
What processes/programs work best for different groups of students with respect to student learning.

Tells us:
If a program is making a difference in student learning results.

*Over time, student learning data give information about student performance on different measures.*

Tells us:
The impact of the program on student learning based upon perceptions of the program and on the processes used.

Tells us:
The impact of student perceptions of the learning environment on student learning.

One measure, by itself, gives useful information. Comprehensive measures, used together and over time, provide much richer information. Ultimately, schools need to be able to predict what they must do to meet the needs of *all* the students they have, or will have in the future. The information gleaned from the intersections of these four measures (demographics, perceptions, student learning, and school processes), helps us to define the questions we want to ask, and focuses us on what data are necessary in order to find the answers.

## Levels of Analysis

Different levels of analysis reveal answers to questions at varying depths of understanding. Each of the four measures, on its own, gives valuable descriptive information. However, more and better quality information can be found by digging deeper into the data through different levels of analysis in which one type of measure is analyzed and compared with other measures, over time.

Below are ten levels of analysis. Each level builds on the previous one to show how past data and intersections of measures provide more comprehensive information than a single measure of data taken one time. If you feel you are only at level one, hang in there; this book and your own work will help you get to level ten.

*Note:* Unless otherwise specified, *over time* refers to no less than three years. Definitions of terms appear in the Glossary at the back of the book.

### Level 1: Snapshots of Measures

Level one refers to the four major measures of data, shown in Figure 2.1, in their current state and independent of each other.

*Demographic* data provide descriptive information about the school community, such as enrollment, attendance, grade level, ethnicity, gender, and native language. Demographic data are very important for us to understand. They are the part of our educational system over which we have no control, but from which we can observe trends and glean information for purposes of prediction and planning. Demographic data assist us in understanding the results of all parts of our educational system through the disaggregation of other measures by demographic variables.

*Perceptions* data help us understand what students, parents, staff, and others think about the learning environment. Perceptions can be gathered in a variety of ways—through questionnaires, interviews, and observations. Perceptions are important since people act in congruence with what they believe, perceive, or think about different topics. It is important to know student, staff, and parent perceptions of the school so school personnel know what they can do to improve the system. Perceptions data can also tell us what is possible.

*Student Learning* describes the results of our educational system in terms of standardized test results, grade point averages, standards assessments, and authentic assessments. Schools use a variety of student learning measurements—usually separately—and sometimes without thinking about how these measurements are interrelated. Schools normally think of multiple measures as looking only at different measures of student learning, rather than including demographics, perceptions, and school processes.

*School Processes* define what teachers are doing to get the results they are getting. For example, how Reading is being taught at grade two, or Math at grade six. School processes include programs, instructional strategies, and classroom practices. This is the measure that seems to be the hardest for teachers to describe. Most often, teachers say they do what they do intuitively, and that they are too busy doing whatever they do to systematically document and reflect on their processes. To change the results schools are getting, teachers and school personnel must begin to document these processes and align them with the results they are getting in order to understand what to change to get different results, and to share their successes with others.

Looking at each of the four measures separately, we get snapshots of data in isolation from any other data at the school level. At this level we can answer questions such as—

- ▼ How many students are enrolled in the school this year? *(Demographics)*

- ▼ How satisfied are parents, students, and/or staff with the learning environment? *(Perceptions)*

- ▼ How did students at the school score on a test? *(Student Learning)*

- ▼ What programs are operating in the school this year? *(School Processes)*

## Level 2: Measures, Over Time

At the second level, we start digging deeper into each of the measures by looking over time to answer questions, such as, but not limited to—

- ▼ How has enrollment in the school changed over the past five years? *(Demographics)*

- ▼ How have student perceptions of the learning environment changed, over time? *(Perceptions)*

> *Different levels of analysis reveal answers to questions at varying depths of understanding.*

- Are there differences in student scores on standardized tests over the years? *(Student Learning)*
- What programs have operated in the school during the past five years? *(School Processes)*

## Level 3: Two or More Variables Within Measures

Looking at more than one type of data within each of the circles gives us a better view of the learning organization (e.g., one year's standardized test subscores compared with performance assessment measures). We can answer questions such as—

- What percentage of the students currently at the school are fluent speakers of languages other than English, and are there equal numbers of males and females? *(Demographics)*
- Are staff, student, and parent perceptions of the learning environment in agreement? *(Perceptions)*
- Are students' standardized test scores consistent with teacher-assigned grades and performance assessment rubrics? *(Student Learning)*
- What are the processes in the school's mathematics and science programs? *(School Processes)*

## Level 4: Two or More Variables Within One Type of Measure, Over Time

Level 4 takes similar measures as Level 3, across time (e.g., standardized test subscores and performance assessment measures compared over the past four years), and allows us to answer deeper questions such as—

- How has the enrollment of non-English-speaking kindergartners changed in the past three years? *(Demographics)*
- Are staff, students, and parents more or less satisfied with the learning environment now than they were in previous years? *(Perceptions)*
- Over the past three years, how do teacher-assigned grades and standardized test scores compare? *(Student Learning)*
- How have the processes used in the school's mathematics and science programs changed over time? *(School Processes)*

## Level 5: Intersection of Two Types of Measures

Level 5 begins the intersections across two circles (e.g., last year's standardized test results by ethnicity). Level 5 helps us to answer questions such as—

Demographics by Student Learning

▼ Do students who attend school every day perform better on the state assessment than students who miss more than five days per month? *(Demographics by Student Learning)*

▼ What strategies do third grade teachers use with students whose native languages are different from that of the teacher? *(Demographics by School Processes)*

Demographics by School Processes

▼ Is there a gender difference in students' perceptions of the learning environment? *(Perceptions by Demographics)*

▼ Do students with positive attitudes about school do better academically, as measured by the state assessment? *(Perceptions by Student Learning)*

Perceptions by Demographics

▼ Are there differences in how students enrolled in different programs perceive the learning environment? *(Perceptions by School Processes)*

▼ Do students who were enrolled in active hands-on content courses this year perform better on standardized achievement tests than those who took the content courses in a more traditional manner? *(Student Learning by School Processes)*

Perceptions by Student Learning

## Level 6: Intersection of Two Measures, Over Time

Looking at the intersection of two of the measures over time allows us to see trends as they develop (e.g., standardized achievement scores disaggregated by ethnicity over the past three years can help us see if the equality of scores, by ethnicity, is truly a trend or an initial fluctuation). This intersection also begins to show the relationship of the multiple measures and why it is so important to look at all the measures together.

Perceptions by School Processes

At Level 6 we are looking at the intersection of two of the circles over time. The questions we can answer at this level include, as examples—

▼ How have students of different ethnicities scored on standardized tests over the past three years? *(Demographics by Student Learning)*

Student Learning by School Processes

▼ Is there a difference in students' daily attendance for the different program offerings over time? *(Demographics by School Processes)*

▼ Have parent perceptions of the learning environment changed since the implementation of the new mathematics program? *(Perceptions by School Processes)*

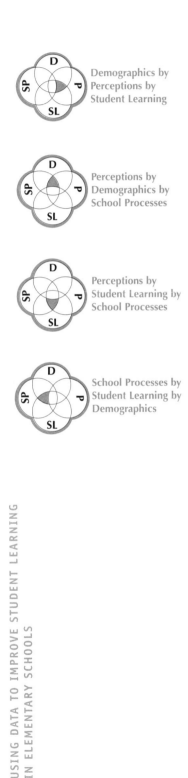

Demographics by
Perceptions by
Student Learning

Perceptions by
Demographics by
School Processes

Perceptions by
Student Learning by
School Processes

School Processes by
Student Learning by
Demographics

## Level 7: Intersection of Three Measures

As we intersect three of the measures at the school level (e.g., student learning measures disaggregated by ethnicity compared to student questionnaire responses disaggregated by ethnicity), the types of questions that we are able to answer include the following:

▼ Do students of different ethnicities perceive the learning environment differently, and are their scores on standardized achievement tests consistent with these perceptions? (*Demographics by Perceptions by Student Learning*)

▼ What instructional process(es) did the previously non-English-speaking students enjoy most in their all-English classrooms this year? (*Perceptions by Demographics by School Processes*)

▼ Is there a difference in students' reports of what they like most about the school by whether or not they participate in extracurricular activities? Do these students have higher grade point averages than students who do not participate in extracurricular activities? (*Perceptions by Student Learning by School Processes*)

▼ Which program is making the biggest difference with respect to student achievement for at-risk students this year, and is one group of students responding "better" to the processes? (*School Processes by Student Learning by Demographics*)

## Level 8: Intersection of Three Measures, Over Time

Looking at three measures over time allows us to see trends, to begin to understand the learning environment from the students' perspectives, and to know how to deliver instruction to get the desired results from and for *all* students.

Level 8 takes Level 7 intersections over time (e.g., standardized achievement scores disaggregated by ethnicity compared to student questionnaires disaggregated by ethnicity, for the past four years). Level 8 allows us to answer the following types of questions:

▼ What programs do all types of students like the most every year? (*Demographics by Perceptions by School Processes*)

▼ Have the processes used to teach English to English-learning students been consistent across grade levels so each student is able to build on her/his abilities? (*Demographics by Student Learning by School Processes*)

## Level 9: Intersection of All Four Measures

Our ultimate analysis is the intersection of all four measures at the school level (e.g., standardized achievement tests disaggregated by program, by gender, within grade level, compared to questionnaire results for students by program, by gender, within grade level). These intersections allow us to answer questions such as—

▼ Are there differences in achievement scores for 8th grade girls and boys who report that they like school, by the type of program and grade level in which they are enrolled? *(Demographics by Perceptions by School Processes by Student Learning)*

Demographics by
Perceptions by
School Processes by
Student Learning

## Level 10: Intersection of All Four Measures, Over Time

It is not until we intersect all four circles, at the school level and over time, that we are able to answer questions that will predict if the actions, processes, and programs that we are establishing will meet the needs of all students. With this intersection, we can answer the ultimate question:

▼ Based on whom we have as students, how they prefer to learn, and what programs they are in, are all students learning at the same rate? *(Student Learning by Demographics by Perceptions by School Processes)*

Do note that there might not always be a way to display these intersections in one comprehensive table or graph. Often, multiple graphs and/or tables are used together to observe intersection relationships.

It is important to look at each measure by itself to understand where the school is right now and over time. Intersecting the measures can give a broader look at the data and help everyone understand all facets of the school. Figure 2.2 summarizes two, three, and four-way intersections. On the CD are a *Data Discovery Activity* and two activities for creating questions from intersecting data, *Intersections Activity* and *Creating Intersections Activity.* Also on the CD are the *Data Analysis Presentation,* a *Microsoft PowerPoint* slideshow overview to use with your staffs in getting started analyzing your data, and three articles entitled *Multiple Measures* (Bernhardt, 1998), *Intersections: New Routes Open when One Type of Data Crosses Another* (Bernhardt, 2000), and *No Schools Left Behind* (Bernhardt, 2003).

Figure 2.2

## Summary of Data Intersections

| Intersections | Can tell us — |
|---|---|
| **Two-way Intersections** | |
| • Demographics by student learning | • If subgroups of students perform differently on student learning measures |
| • Demographics by perceptions | • If groups of students are experiencing school differently |
| • Demographics by school processes | • If all groups of students are represented in the different programs and processes offered by the school |
| • Student learning by school processes | • If different programs are achieving similar student learning results |
| • Student learning by perceptions | • If student perceptions of the learning environment have an impact on their learning results |
| • Perceptions by school processes | • If people are perceiving programs and processes differently |
| **Three-way Intersections** | |
| • Demographics by student learning by perceptions | • The impact demographic factors and attitudes about the learning environment have on student learning |
| • Demographics by student learning by school processes | • What processes or programs work best for different groups of students measured by student learning results |
| • Demographics by perceptions by school processes | • What programs or processes different students like best, or the impact different programs or processes have on student attitudes |
| • Student learning by school processes by perceptions | • The relationship between the processes students prefer and learning results |
| **Four-way Intersections** | |
| • Demographics by student learning by perceptions by school processes | • What processes or programs have the greatest impact on different groups of students' learning, according to student perceptions, and as measured by student learning results |

## Focusing the Data

Data analysis should not be about just gathering data. It is very easy to get *analysis paralysis* by spending time pulling data together and not spending time using the data. School-level data analyses should be about helping schools understand if they are achieving their purpose and meeting the needs of all students—and, if not, why not? A good way to avoid *analysis paralysis* is to consider using *key questions* and building your analyses around the answers to these questions.

The key questions used in this book are described in Chapter 3. The data we gather and analyze target the guiding principles of the school to achieve focused improvement. If this was not the case, the process could lead to nothing more than random acts of improvement, as shown in Figure 2.3.

> *Data analysis should not be about just gathering data. It is very easy to get "analysis paralysis" by spending time pulling data together and not spending time using the data.*

### Figure 2.3

### Focusing the Data

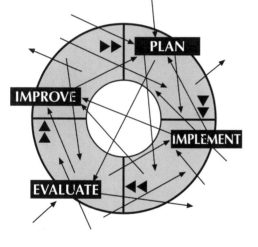

**Random Acts of Improvement**

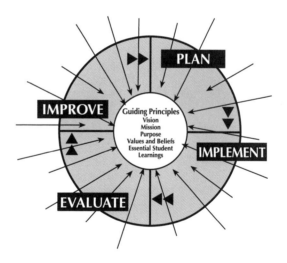

**Focused Improvement**

The benefits of a continuous improvement cycle could be missed altogether if the data analysis improvement process is not aimed at the school's guiding principles. A focused data analysis process will enhance the continuous improvement process and provide comprehensive information about how the school is doing in relationship to its guiding principles. The guiding principles are the vision, created from the mission/purpose of the school and built from the values and beliefs of the school community. Data analysis is focused when schools are clear on their purpose and on what they expect students to know and be able to do.

These analyses flow comfortably from questions that staff and administrators naturally ask to learn if the purpose is being met. The good news is that, by looking at trends of the intersected four measures, schools will have the same information required of program evaluations and needs analyses. These intersections can tell schools just about everything they would want to know, and the intersections are easy for everyone to understand.

## Study Questions for *What Data Are Important?* 💿

As mentioned previously, at the end of the chapters are study questions to help you think of your own data analysis and/or to analyze the example schools' results. Do take some time to consider these or other questions to get the maximum benefit from this publication.

Consider how you might intersect your school's data and what those intersections could tell you. Write in the spaces below at least one question you can answer about your school with these intersections, and what data you need to answer these questions. (Examples appear in the table to get you started.)

| Intersections | Questions | What data do you have or need to answer the questions? |
|---|---|---|
| **Demographics by Student Learning** | *Is there a relationship between attendance and standardized achievement results?* | *Number of days attended and state standardized test results for each student.* |
| **Demographics by School Processes** | *Is participation in the pre-school program representative of all students?* | *Pre-school enrollment by gender and ethnicity.* |

# Study Questions for *What Data Are Important?* *(Continued)*

| Intersections | Questions | What data do you have or need to answer the questions? |
|---|---|---|
| **Perceptions by Demographics** | *Are all students perceiving the learning environment in the same way?* | *Student questionnaire results disaggregated by gender, by ethnicity, and/or by grade level.* |
| **Perceptions by Student Learning** | *Are the students who are getting the best grades the happiest with the learning environment?* | *Student grades by student perceptions.* |
| **Perceptions by School Processes** | *Are there differences in how students perceive the learning environment, based on whom they have as teachers?* | *Student perceptions disaggregated by teacher.* |

USING DATA TO IMPROVE STUDENT LEARNING
IN ELEMENTARY SCHOOLS

| Intersections | Questions | What data do you have or need to answer the questions? |
|---|---|---|
| **Student Learning by School Processes** | *Is there a difference in student achievement results by program participation?* | *Student achievement test results by program.* |
| **Demographics by Perceptions by Student Learning** | *Are the differences in student learning results based on whom we have as students and how they perceive the learning environment?* | *Student achievement test results disaggregated by gender and ethnicity, compared to student questionnaire results disaggregated by gender and ethnicity.* |
| **Perceptions by Demographics by School Processes** | *Are the students most satisfied with school being taught differently from students not satisfied with school, and who are they?* | *Student questionnaires disaggregated by gender, ethnicity, grade level, and program participation.* |

| Intersections | Questions | What data do you have or need to answer the questions? |
|---|---|---|
| **Perceptions by Student Learning by School Processes** | *What are the differences in student achievement results because of attitudes related to whom students have as teachers?* | *Student achievement results disaggregated by teacher, compared to student questionnaire results disaggregated by teacher.* |
| **Demographics by Student Learning by School Processes** | *What are the differences in student learning results based on who the students are and how they are taught to read?* | *Student achievement results, disaggregated by gender and ethnicity, and sorted by what program they are in and whom they have as a teacher.* |
| **Student Learning by Demographics by Perceptions by School Processes** | *What are the differences in the results we are getting, based on whom we have as students and how they are being taught? How would they prefer to learn?* | *Student achievement results, disaggregated by gender, ethnicity, grade level, and program, compared to student questionnaire results, disaggregated by gender, ethnicity, grade level, and program.* |

## Summary

Schools cannot use student achievement measures alone for continuous school improvement. Why? Because the *context* is missing! Relying on only one measure can mislead schools into thinking they are analyzing student learning in a comprehensive fashion. Just looking at student learning measures alone could, in fact, keep teachers from progressing and truly meeting the needs of students, because they are not looking at the other elements that have a great impact on student learning and teaching.

If we want to get different results, we have to change the processes (e.g., instruction, system) that create the results. When we focus only on student learning measures, we see school personnel using their time figuring out how to look better on the student learning measures. We want school personnel to use their time to determine how to *do* better for *all* students. In order to do that, we must look at intersections of demographic, perceptual, student learning, and school process data, so we can understand the inter-relationships among these elements.

*Just looking at student learning measures alone could, in fact, keep teachers from progressing and truly meeting the needs of students, because they are not looking at the other elements that have a great impact on student learning and teaching.*

## On the CD Related to this Chapter

▼ *Multiple Measures of Data* Graphic (MMgraphc.pdf)
This is Figure 2.1 in a PDF (portable document file) for printing.

▼ *Summary of Data Intersections* (IntrscTbl.pdf)
This is Figure 2.2 in a PDF for your use with staff.

▼ *Data Discovery Activity* (ACTDiscv.pdf)
The purpose of this activity is to look closely at examples of data and to discover specific information and patterns of information, both individually and as a group.

▼ *Intersections Activity* (ACTIntrs.pdf)
The purpose of this activity is to motivate school improvement teams to think about the questions they can answer when they cross different data variables. It is also designed to help teams focus their data-gathering efforts so they are not collecting everything and anything.

▼ *Creating Intersections Activity* (ACTCreat.pdf)
This activity is similar to the *Intersections Activity.* The purpose is to have participants "grow" their intersections.

▼ *Data Analysis* Presentation (DASlides.ppt)
This *Microsoft PowerPoint* presentation is an overview to use with your staffs in getting started with data analysis.

▼ Articles
These read-only articles, by Victoria L. Bernhardt, will be useful in workshops or in getting started on data with staff.

◆ *Multiple Measures* (MMeasure.pdf)
This article summarizes why, and what, data are important to continuous school improvement.

◆ *Intersections: New Routes Open when One Type of Data Crosses Another* (Intersct.pdf)
This article, published in the *Journal of Staff Development* (Winter 2000), discusses how much richer your data analyses can be when you intersect multiple data variables.

◆ *No Schools Left Behind* (NoSchls.pdf)
This article, published in *Educational Leadership* (February 2003), summarizes how to improve learning for *all* students.

▼ Study Questions Related to *What Data are Important?* (Ch2Qs.pdf)
These study questions will help you better understand the information provided in Chapter 2. This file can be printed for use with staff as they think through the data questions they want to answer and the data they will need to gather to answer the questions.

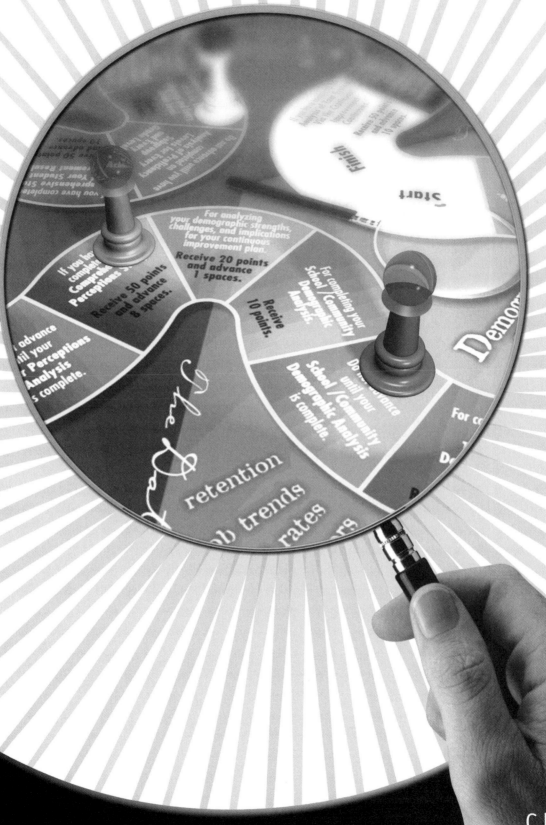

Chapter 3

*We want to gather and analyze data that will help us understand the system that produces the results we are getting. We also want to move our school improvement efforts from random acts of improvement to focused improvement that centers on our ultimate purpose—improving learning for all students.*

How does a school get started with comprehensive data analysis work? How do you and others at your school know if what you are currently doing for students is making a difference with respect to what you expect students to know and be able to do? How do you know which strategies ought to be the focus of your school improvement efforts?

If your school is like 95% of the schools in this country, my hunch is that your school improvement committee comes up with *achievable* school improvement goals each year, often focused on improving student attendance and/or parent involvement. The school improvement plan is sent to the district, which will allow staff to spend money on things they want to buy. Staff look at the state student assessment results, make statements about how these scores do not reflect what teachers are doing in their classrooms, attempt to explain the results to the school board and to the public, and then hope that the test will go away before students have to take it again next year. Your school might have special externally funded grants or programs that require the collection and analysis of data. Those who are providing the funds want progress described. Questionnaires are then sent out each year and are analyzed *for the funders*, not for those who implement the programs.

At the classroom level, some teachers have adopted rubrics and performance assessment measures. They know their students are learning, but performance assessment measures are not easy to talk about in terms of an entire class, let alone schoolwide, progress. It can be done, but it is difficult.

Unfortunately, the scenarios described above are all too familiar in schools across the United States. What is starting to change is a connection between the analysis of data and the school improvement plan to ensure that every student is learning. We want to see data about all parts of the school gathered and analyzed on a regular basis—not just when an external force requires it. We want members of the school community to understand how to use data to accurately inform their customers and other individuals of how the school is doing. Finally, we especially want schools to analyze data to understand which strategies are not working and what to do differently to get different results.

This chapter describes a process for analyzing data to plan for continuous schoolwide improvement. Data analysis in schools may be approached in many ways, and the effectiveness of school processes may be measured in many ways. The approach taken here is a systems approach: we want to gather and analyze data that will help us understand the *system that produces the results we are getting.* We also want to move our school improvement efforts from random acts of improvement to focused improvement that centers on our ultimate purpose—improving learning for *all* students.

## Analyzing Data Using a Continuous School Improvement Planning Model

Data analysis is very logical. We need to think about what we want to know and why, gather the data we have or need, and analyze the data to answer the questions that will lead to understanding not only the effectiveness of what we are doing, but also what we need to do differently to get different results.

One approach to data analysis is to analyze and use data for continuous school improvement planning. The *Multiple Measures of Data*, Figure 2.1 in Chapter 2, can be reorganized into a series of logical questions that can guide the analysis, as illustrated in the flowchart in Figure 3.1. If the data that are listed next to the questions in the boxes were gathered satisfactorily, one would be on the right track toward discovering how to continuously improve the school or district. Those questions, the data required, and discussion follow the flowchart.

## Continuous School Improvement Planning via The School Portfolio

Figure 3.1 shows the logical questions one could ask to plan for continuous school improvement, the data needed to answer the questions, and where that data would be housed in a school portfolio.[1] (See *The School Portfolio* [Bernhardt, 1999] and *The School Portfolio Toolkit* [Bernhardt, 2002] for complete information on creating a school portfolio.) On the CD is a *Microsoft PowerPoint* slideshow overview file, *The School Portfolio Presentation*, to use with your staffs in getting started on the school portfolio.

We need to generate answers through data for the questions that follow.

### Question 1: Who are we?

Continuous school improvement planning begins by asking a question that can be answered with demographic data: *Who are we?* Specifically—

▼ *Who are the students?*

▼ *Who is the staff?*

▼ *Who is the community?*

The answers to the first questions are important in understanding the school's and district's students, staff, and community, to determine future needs. These answers are critical for continuous school

---

[1]*Note:* The headings in the outside columns of the figure, e.g., *Information and Analysis* and *Student Achievement*, are categories of *The School Portfolio* (Bernhardt, 1999). If your school is documenting its data analysis in a school portfolio, these are the categories that typically house the data answering the related question.

Figure 3.1

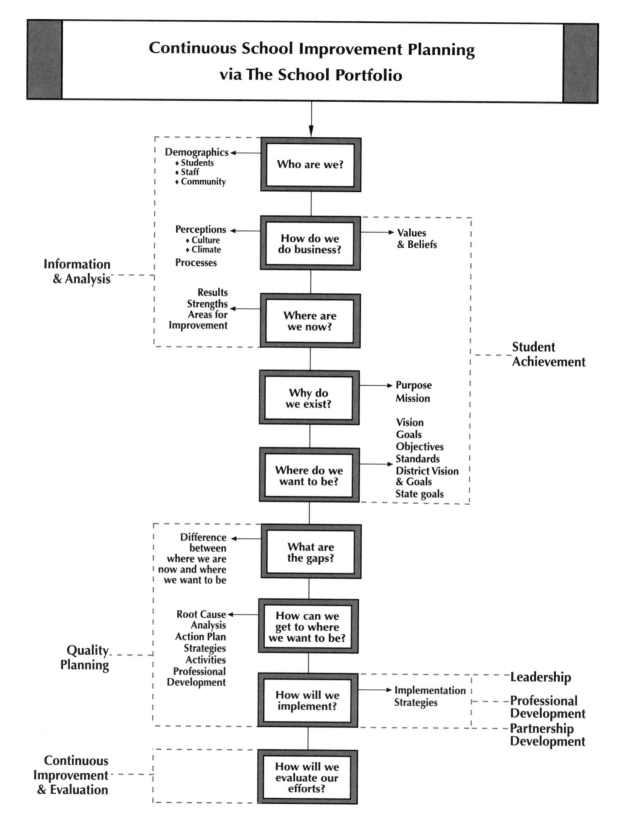

Continuous School Improvement Planning
via The School Portfolio

Demographics
◆ Students
◆ Staff
◆ Community

Who are we?

Perceptions
◆ Culture
◆ Climate
Processes

How do we
do business?

Values
& Beliefs

Information
& Analysis

Results
Strengths
Areas for
Improvement

Where are
we now?

Why do
we exist?

Purpose
Mission

Vision
Goals
Objectives
Standards
District Vision
& Goals
State goals

Where do we
want to be?

Student
Achievement

Difference
between
where we are
now and where
we want to be

What are
the gaps?

Root Cause
Analysis
Action Plan
Strategies
Activities
Professional
Development

How can we
get to where
we want to be?

Quality
Planning

How will we
implement?

Implementation
Strategies

Leadership

Professional
Development

Partnership
Development

Continuous
Improvement
& Evaluation

How will we
evaluate our
efforts?

USING DATA TO IMPROVE STUDENT LEARNING IN ELEMENTARY SCHOOLS

improvement planning, as they establish the *context* of the classroom, school, district, and community. It is important to understand how student and community populations have changed over time, as these changes are indicators of student characteristics to plan for in the future. Staff longevity within the system and plans for retirement might lead to establishing different types of school improvement plans, as would staff experiences, certification, and levels of education. Demographic changes can also help explain results. This question is further studied in Chapter 4.

## Question 2: How do we do business?

The second question, *How do we do business?*, is answered through data gathered to assess the school's culture, climate, and organizational processes. Perceptual data, school processes, and values and beliefs fall into this category. Staff values and beliefs, most often assessed through questionnaires and/or determined during visioning processes, can tell a staff what is possible to implement and if team building or specific professional development is necessary. Student and parent questionnaires can add different perspectives to the answers generated from staff data. An assessment on the *Education for the Future Continuous Improvement Continuums*[2] can provide an overview of where the staff believes the school is and where it can go, with respect to continuous school improvement. Chapter 5 reviews more on this question.

## Question 3: Where are we now?

The third data question, *Where are we now?*, requires a synthesis of student achievement, perceptual, demographic, and school process data to describe results and to uncover strengths and areas for improvement. We start by examining data for patterns and trends across the four multiple measures. Chapter 6 reviews the student achievement part of this question, including different types of student achievement assessments and terms associated with them.

## Question 4: Why do we exist?

Question number four can be answered by determining the purpose/mission of the school. Revisiting the results collected in

---

[2]*Note:* The *Education for the Future Continuous Improvement Continuums* (CICs) can be found in *The School Portfolio* (Bernhardt, 1999), *The School Portfolio Toolkit* (Bernhardt, 2002), and on the accompanying CD. The CICs are a type of assessment criteria rubric made up of seven key, interrelated, and overlapping components of systemic change, representing the theoretical flow of systemic school improvement. The *Continuums* take the theory and spirit of continuous school improvement, interweave educational research, and offer practical meaning to the components that must change simultaneously and systemically. A CIC analysis appears in Chapter 9.

questions one through three, one can determine how well the school is meeting its purpose. This question is answered in-depth in other resources, such as, *The School Portfolio* (Bernhardt, 1999), and *The School Portfolio Toolkit* (Bernhardt, 2002).

### Question 5: Where do we want to be?

A school defines its destination through its vision, goals, and standards. The school's destination falls under the umbrella of the district's vision, goals, and standards which, in turn, are aligned with the state vision, goals, and standards. One can determine how effective the vision is being implemented through the data used to answer questions one through four. This question is answered in-depth in other resources, such as, *The School Portfolio* (Bernhardt, 1999), and *The School Portfolio Toolkit* (Bernhardt, 2002).

### Question 6: What are the gaps?

Gaps are the differences between *Where are we now?* and *Where do we want to be?* Gaps are determined by synthesizing the differences in the results the school is getting with its current processes, and the results the school wants to be getting for its students. It is important to dig deep into each gap to uncover root causes, or the gap cannot be eliminated. Gaps and root causes are studied in Chapter 7.

### Question 7: How can we get to where we want to be?

The answer to *How can we get to where we want to be?* is key to unlocking how the vision will be implemented, or improved, and how gaps will be eliminated. An action plan, consisting of strategies, activities, people responsible, due dates, timelines, and resources, needs to be created to implement and achieve the vision and goals and to eliminate the root causes of the gaps. Chapter 8 shows how one can take the data analysis results and turn them into a continuous school improvement plan.

### Question 8: How will we implement?

This question is answered in the action plan. The action plan includes how the vision will be implemented, monitored, evaluated, and improved. Action plans need to clarify how decisions will be made, identify professional development required to learn new skills and gain new knowledge, and clarify the use of partners to achieve the vision. A school's leadership structure, professional development strategies, and partnership development plan are important components of the answer to this question. Chapter 8 discusses what a plan would look like when it includes action for implementing, monitoring, evaluating, and improving the action plan.

## Question 9: How will we evaluate our efforts?

*Continuous Improvement and Evaluation* are required to assess the alignment of all parts of the system to the vision and the results the learning organization is getting on an ongoing basis. All four data measures intersected to answer this question will assist with evaluating the continuously improving learning organization. Evaluation is a piece that needs to be built along the way, not only at the end, to know if what a school is doing is making a real difference. How the action plan will be evaluated is a part of the plan which can be pulled out, enhanced, and monitored. This piece is described in Chapter 8.

The chapters that follow show how two different schools answered these questions with data as they conducted their data analyses and built their continuous school improvement plans. Example one is shown in Chapters 4 through 8. Example two appears in Chapter 9. The two examples are separated in this manner for increased readability. Differences and similarities of the two examples are discussed in Chapter 10.

## Study Questions for *Getting Started* ✹

How will you get started with your school's continuous school improvement planning? What data do you have, or need to gather, to answer the questions discussed in this chapter? Fill in the blank cells in the table below to guide your work. Examples appear in the table for guidance.

| Questions | What data do you have or need to answer the questions? | What other data do you have or need to gather? |
|---|---|---|
| **Who are we?** | *Student enrollment by grade, by gender, by ethnicity, by free/reduced lunch status, for five years.*<br><br>*Number of teachers; number of years teaching by what grade level(s) and/or subject(s) they teach; which credentials teachers hold.* | *Information about predicted community changes.*<br><br>*Administrator information, such as number of years in current position, and number of years teaching.* |
| **How do we do business?** | *Perceptions: student, staff, parent questionnaires.*<br><br>*Education for the Future Continuous Improvement Continuums Assessment.* | |
| **Where are we now?** | *Student achievement results.*<br>*Process data.* | |

| Questions | What data do you have or need to answer the questions? | What other data do you have or need to gather? |
|---|---|---|
| **Why do we exist?** | *Mission statement.*<br>*Purpose of the school.* | |
| **Where do we want to be?** | *Vision.*<br>*Goals.* | |
| **What are the gaps? What are the root causes?** | *Number and percentage of students not proficient in each subject area.*<br>*Characteristics of the students not meeting mastery.*<br>*How these students scored.*<br>*What they know and do not know.*<br>*How they were taught.* | |

# Study Questions for *Getting Started* (Continued)

| Questions | What data do you have or need to answer the questions? | What other data do you have or need to gather? |
|---|---|---|
| **How can we get to where we want to be?** | *Interventions.*<br>*Professional Development.*<br>*Timeline.* | |
| **How will we implement?** | *Implementation strategies.*<br>*Leadership structure.*<br>*How we meet together to talk about the vision.* | |
| **How will we evaluate our efforts?** | *Rethinking our results data.*<br>*Monitoring and evaluating the plan.* | |

## Summary

Schools that are not gathering, analyzing, and using data in purposeful ways need to transform their thinking about data and start gathering, analyzing, and using data purposefully. Comprehensive data analyses focused on the continuous improvement of the entire learning organization will result in school improvement plans that will improve learning for all students.

Logical questions can be used to guide the gathering, analysis, and use of data. Recommended questions include:

▼ *Who are we?*

▼ *How do we do business?*

▼ *Where are we now?*

▼ *Why do we exist?*

▼ *Where do we want to be?*

▼ *What are the gaps?* and *What are the root causes?*

▼ *How can we get to where we want to be?*

▼ *How will we implement?*

▼ *How will we evaluate our efforts?*

*Comprehensive data analyses focused on the continuous improvement of the entire learning organization will result in school improvement plans that will improve learning for all students.*

## On the CD Related to this Chapter

▼ *Continuous School Improvement Planning via the School Portfolio* Graphic (CSIPlang.pdf)

This read-only graphic displays the questions that can be answered to create a continuous school improvement plan. The data that can answer the questions, and where the answers would appear in the school portfolio, also appear on the graphic. In the book, it is Figure 3.1.

▼ *Continuous School Improvement Planning via the School Portfolio* Description (CSIdscr.pdf)

This read-only file shows Figure 3.1, along with its description.

▼ *The School Portfolio Presentation* (SPSlides.ppt)

This *PowerPoint* Presentation is an overview to use with your staffs in getting started on the school portfolio.

▼ Study Questions Related to *Getting Started* (Ch3Qs.pdf)

These study questions will help you better understand the information provided in Chapter 3. This file can be printed for use with staffs as you begin continuous school improvement planning. Answering the questions will help staff determine the data needed to answer the questions discussed in this chapter.

# Analyzing the Data:
## *Who Are We?*

Chapter 4

> *Demographic data are required to answer the question, "Who are we?"*

Using the continuous school improvement planning model described in Chapter 3, our data analysis examples begin with setting the context of the school by answering the question, *Who are we?* Demographic data are required to answer this question. Demographic data enable us to:

▼ *explain* and *understand* the school's context and results

▼ *disaggregate* other types of data, such as perceptual, process, and student learning data, to ensure all subgroups of students are being served

▼ *predict* and *prepare* for the students we will have in the near future

We start with example one, Little River Elementary School, and then show Blue Bird Elementary School, as example two, in Chapter 9. Please note the study questions on page 61 to assist in studying the Little River data. Also note that space is provided in the margins on the data pages to write your impressions as you review the data. It is recommended that you jot down your thoughts about what you are seeing in the data as you read. These first thoughts are placeholders until additional data validate the thoughts. At the end of the chapter, I share what I saw in the data.

## Example One: Little River Elementary School
### *Who Are We?*

Little River Elementary School is a pre-kindergarten through grade five school located in the Midwest. According to the 2001 census, the city in which Little River is located has a population of around 80,000, up approximately 10,000 from the 1991 census *(http://www.census.gov)*. The census data also show that the average family income in 1991 was about $26,000, while in 2001, the average family income was approximately $31,219. The city is home to the main and largest of four university campuses, with 23,300 students. The university, the school district, and the university hospital are the major stable employers in this city. (Graphing templates are included on the CD.)

### Three Rivers Public School District

Little River Elementary is part of the Three Rivers Public School District, which currently serves 16,451 students in 28 schools: eighteen elementary (K-5), three middle (6-7), three junior high (8-9), three senior high (10-12), and a career center. Nine years ago, 14,022 students were served by the district. The percent increase in the student population mirrors the percent increase in the community population. This 2,429 student increase in overall district enrollment during the last ten years is charted in Figure 4.1.

Figure 4.1

## Three Rivers School District Student Enrollment
### 1993-94 to 2002-03

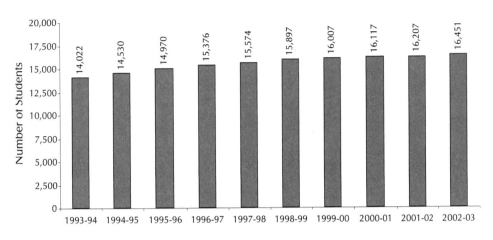

## The School

Little River Elementary opened in the 1958-59 school year with 216 students in grades pre-kindergarten through grade five. The 2002-03 marks its 44th year of continuous operation. Once located in a suburban area, Little River became a downtown school as the city grew out around it. The neighborhood around Little River has evolved from mostly Caucasian to one of the most ethnically diverse in the city.

## The Students

Little River Elementary School currently serves 472 students, down 109 students from four years earlier (Figure 4.2).

Figure 4.2

## Little River Elementary School Student Enrollment
### 1998-99 to 2002-03

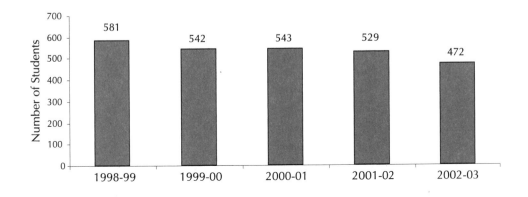

The current student population, as shown in Figure 4.3, consists of 235 African-Americans (49.8%), 218 Caucasians (46.2%), 8 Hispanics (1.7%), 8 Asians (1.7%), and 3 American Indians (.6%) .

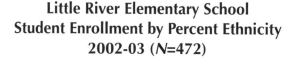

**Figure 4.3**

**Little River Elementary School
Student Enrollment by Percent Ethnicity
2002-03 (*N*=472)**

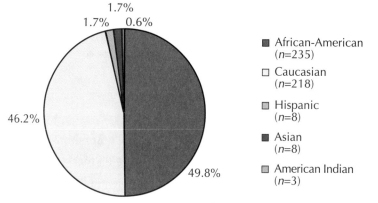

Over the past five years, the number of African-American students dipped from 39.9% (*n*=232) to 38.7% (*n*=210), increased to 45.1% (*n*=245), to 49.8% (*n*=235), while the percentage increased, in 2002-03. The number of Caucasian students decreased from 58.2% (*n*=338) to 46.2% (*n*=218) over the five years. The number of Hispanic students increased from 1% (*n*=6) to 2.6% (*n*=14), and decreased again to 1.7% (*n*=8) in the same time span. The numbers of American Indian and Asian students have remained small (less than 1%) and about the same (Figure 4.4).

## Figure 4.4

### Little River Elementary School
### Percentage of Students Enrolled by Ethnicity
### 1998-99 to 2002-03

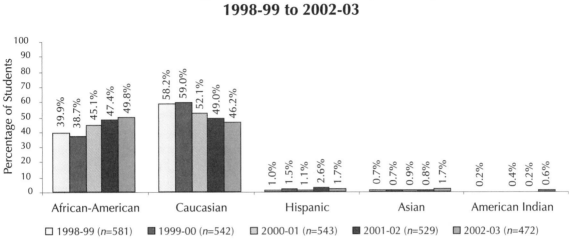

One can also see the fluctuating population of this school attendance area reflected in the school enrollment by grade level over the last four years (Figure 4.5). Looking at the same grade level over time is called *grade level analysis*. Reorganizing the data (Figure 4.6) to look at the groups of students progressing through the grades together over time is called a *cohort analysis*. If we were looking at the same students (as opposed to the groups of students), it would be called *matched cohorts. (Note: For the rest of the analyses in this book, we will not be including pre-kindergarten. Therefore, some of the total Little River numbers will be different.)*

## Figure 4.5

### Little River Elementary School
### Student Enrollment by Grade Level
### 1998-99 to 2002-03

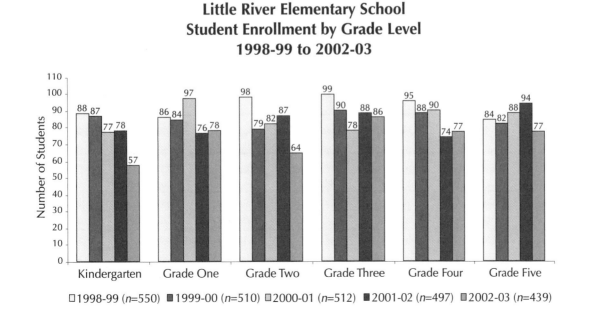

## Figure 4.6

### Little River Elementary School
### Student Cohorts by Grade Level
### 1998-99 to 2002-03

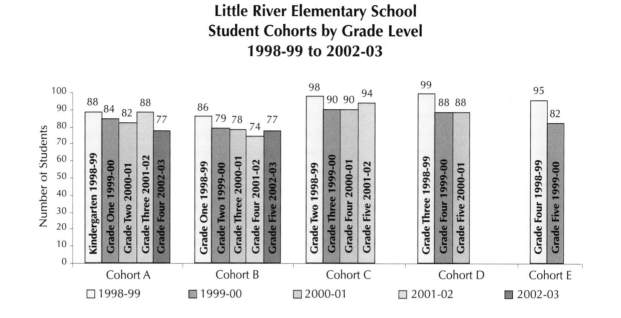

By analyzing grade level and gender, one can also see the fluctuations and differences in the numbers and percentages of males and females over time, within any grade level (Figure 4.7).

## Figure 4.7

### Little River Elementary School
### Numbers and Percentages of Students
### By Grade Level and Gender, 1998-99 to 2002-03

| Grade Level | Gender | 1998-99 (n=550) | | 1999-00 (n=510) | | 2000-01 (n=512) | | 2001-02 (n=497) | | 2002-03 (n=439) | |
|---|---|---|---|---|---|---|---|---|---|---|---|
| Kindergarten | Male | 45 | 51% | 51 | 59% | 37 | 48% | 40 | 51% | 33 | 58% |
| | Female | 43 | 49% | 36 | 41% | 40 | 52% | 38 | 49% | 24 | 42% |
| Grade One | Male | 38 | 44% | 46 | 55% | 58 | 60% | 33 | 43% | 36 | 46% |
| | Female | 48 | 56% | 38 | 45% | 39 | 40% | 43 | 57% | 42 | 54% |
| Grade Two | Male | 51 | 52% | 33 | 42% | 42 | 51% | 53 | 61% | 31 | 48% |
| | Female | 47 | 48% | 46 | 58% | 40 | 49% | 34 | 39% | 33 | 52% |
| Grade Three | Male | 44 | 44% | 43 | 48% | 33 | 42% | 43 | 49% | 50 | 58% |
| | Female | 55 | 56% | 47 | 52% | 45 | 58% | 45 | 51% | 36 | 42% |
| Grade Four | Male | 52 | 55% | 37 | 42% | 43 | 48% | 34 | 46% | 37 | 48% |
| | Female | 43 | 45% | 51 | 58% | 47 | 52% | 40 | 54% | 40 | 52% |
| Grade Five | Male | 45 | 54% | 41 | 50% | 37 | 42% | 48 | 51% | 40 | 52% |
| | Female | 39 | 46% | 41 | 50% | 51 | 58% | 46 | 49% | 37 | 48% |

## Attendance

Little River students have maintained an average of about 91% yearly attendance rate during the last five years. With 94% attending, students in 2002-03 had the highest rate for the past five years (Figure 4.8).

### Figure 4.8

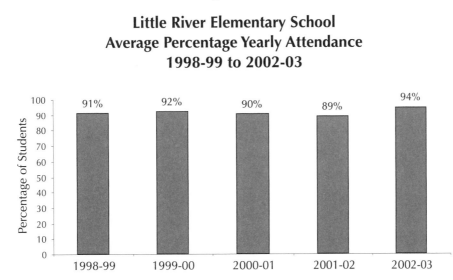

**Little River Elementary School
Average Percentage Yearly Attendance
1998-99 to 2002-03**

By grade level (Figure 4.9), one can see that, in general and over time, the slightly higher absentee rates were with the youngest students—kindergarten and grade one. Grade four had the lowest absentee rate all five years.

### Figure 4.9

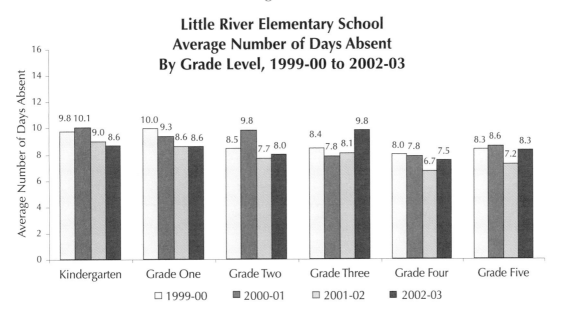

**Little River Elementary School
Average Number of Days Absent
By Grade Level, 1999-00 to 2002-03**

## Mobility

Little River's school mobility rate has been calculated to be less than 10% over each of the five years studied here. Figures 4.10 and 4.11 show the number of students who moved to or from the school zero, one, or two times between 1998-99 and 2002-03, first by school, and then by grade level. Approximately 90% were stable in 2002-03. The percentage of total students enrolled for that particular subgroup is in parenthesis under the number value on the bar graph.

### Figure 4.10

**Little River Elementary School
Student Mobility
1998-99 to 2002-03**

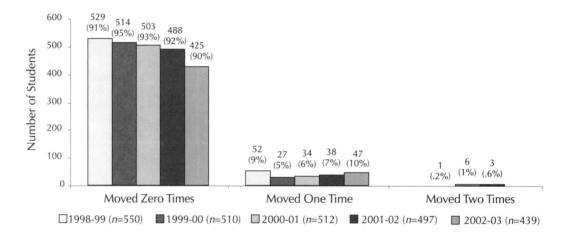

### Figure 4.11

**Little River Elementary School Student Mobility
By Grade Level, 1999-00 to 2002-03**

| Grade Level | Number of Moves | 1999-00 (n=510) | | 2000-01 (n=512) | | 2001-02 (n=497) | | 2002-03 (n=439) | |
|---|---|---|---|---|---|---|---|---|---|
| Kindergarten | 0 | 80 | 92% | 69 | 90% | 72 | 92% | 71 | 91% |
| | 1 | 7 | 8% | 7 | 9% | 5 | 6% | 6 | 8% |
| | 2 | | | 1 | 1% | 1 | 1% | 1 | 1% |
| Grade One | 0 | 80 | 95% | 90 | 93% | 72 | 95% | 71 | 93% |
| | 1 | 4 | 5% | 7 | 7% | 4 | 5% | 5 | 7% |
| Grade Two | 0 | 74 | 94% | 80 | 98% | 82 | 94% | 80 | 95% |
| | 1 | 4 | 5% | 2 | 2% | 5 | 6% | 4 | 5% |
| | 2 | 1 | 1% | | | | | | |
| Grade Three | 0 | 86 | 96% | 69 | 88% | 73 | 83% | 74 | 84% |
| | 1 | 4 | 4% | 8 | 10% | 13 | 15% | 12 | 14% |
| | 2 | | | 1 | 2% | 2 | 2% | 2 | 2% |
| Grade Four | 0 | 83 | 94% | 83 | 92% | 69 | 93% | 69 | 92% |
| | 1 | 5 | 6% | 6 | 7% | 5 | 7% | 5 | 7% |
| | 2 | | | 1 | 1% | | | 1 | 1% |
| Grade Five | 0 | 79 | 96% | 82 | 93% | 90 | 96% | 89 | 95% |
| | 1 | 3 | 4% | 3 | 3% | 4 | 4% | 5 | 5% |
| | 2 | | | 3 | 3% | | | | |

The number of English Learners (EL) by grade level has been small and has changed very little over time, as shown in Figure 4.12. As of 2002-03, there were five EL students—one in kindergarten and grades two and four; and two in grade five.

One of the reasons for the low numbers of English Learners is that not every school in this district has an EL program. Little River does not. EL students in this community are bussed to another school with an English Learner program.

Figure 4.12

**Little River Elementary School
English Learners by Grade Level
1998-99 to 2002-03**

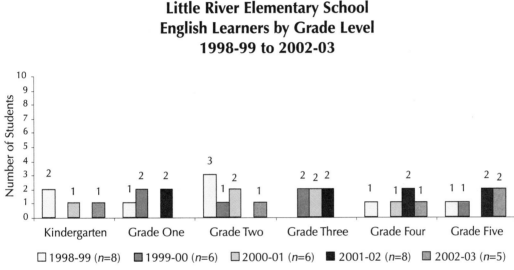

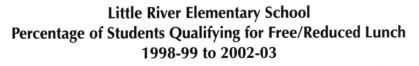

Over this same five-year period, the total number of students qualifying for free/reduced lunch has increased from 51% of the school population to 60%, an indicator of an increase in the number of families living in poverty (Figure 4.13).

Figure 4.13

**Little River Elementary School
Percentage of Students Qualifying for Free/Reduced Lunch
1998-99 to 2002-03**

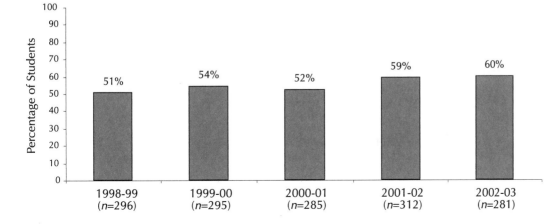

Figure 4.14 shows the percentages of students qualifying for free/reduced lunch have changed within grade levels over time—the actual numbers fluctuating more dramatically than the percentages.

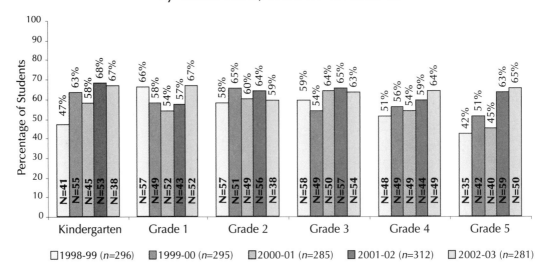

## Figure 4.14

### Little River Elementary School
### Percentage of Students Qualifying for Free/Reduced Lunch
### By Grade Level, 1998-99 to 2002-03

☐ 1998-99 (*n*=296)  ■ 1999-00 (*n*=295)  ☐ 2000-01 (*n*=285)  ■ 2001-02 (*n*=312)  ☐ 2002-03 (*n*=281)

Figure 4.15 follows the cohorts, or same groups of students over time, and their qualifications for free/reduced lunch.

## Figure 4.15

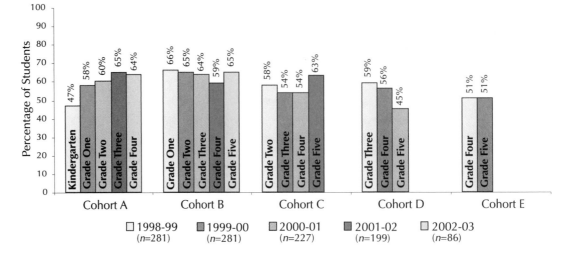

### Little River Elementary School
### Percentage of Student Cohorts Qualifying for Free/Reduced Lunch
### 1998-99 to 2002-03

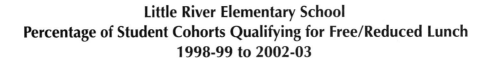

☐ 1998-99 (*n*=281)  ■ 1999-00 (*n*=281)  ☐ 2000-01 (*n*=227)  ■ 2001-02 (*n*=199)  ☐ 2002-03 (*n*=86)

By ethnicity, the number of African-American students qualifying for free/reduced lunch increased from 62% of the population (186) to 68% of the population (196) between 1998-99 and 2002-03. The number of Caucasian students qualifying for free/reduced lunch decreased between 1998-99 (N=111, 37%) and 2002-03 (N=84, 29%), while the average percentage stayed at around 35% (Figure 4.16).

**Figure 4.16**

**Little River Elementary School**
**Percentage of Students Qualifying for Free/Reduced Lunch**
**By Ethnicity, 1998-99 to 2002-03**

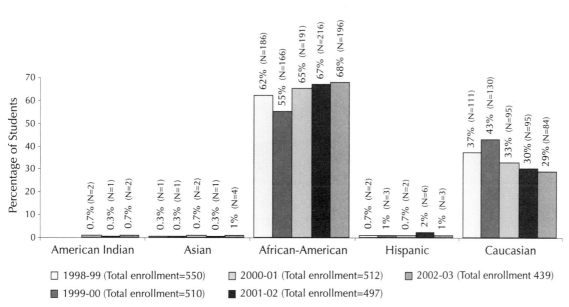

## Retentions

The number of Little River Elementary School students retained in a grade level has decreased in the past five years. In 1998-99, four students in the school were retained in a grade—one in kindergarten and three in grade one. No students at any grade level were retained in 1999-00. In 2000-01, seven students were retained—three in kindergarten, two in grade one, and one in grades two and three; in 2001-02, there were eight—four in kindergarten, two in grade one, and one each in grades two and five; and four in 2002-03—three in kindergarten and one in grade two. No students were retained in grade four during this five-year period, as shown in Figure 4.17. The graph also indicates that the number of students retained by grade level during this time period was highest at the kindergarten and first grade levels, and more in recent years than in the earlier years. The school's change in policy to *formally* monitor student progress in the early grades through a local reading assessment helps explain the decrease in retention numbers in the upper grades, according to Little River's principal.

Figure 4.17

**Little River Elementary School**
**Number of Students Retained by Grade Level**
**1998-99 to 2002-03**

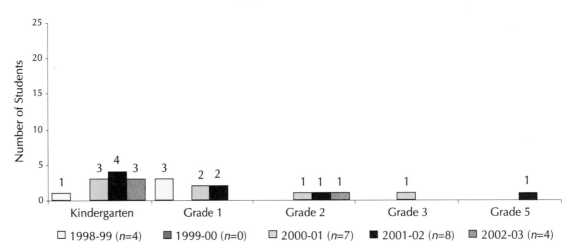

USING DATA TO IMPROVE STUDENT LEARNING IN ELEMENTARY SCHOOLS

Figure 4.18 digs a little deeper into this retention analysis and shows the number of retainees by grade level, gender, and ethnicity. One can see that more males (18) were retained than females (5) and more students were retained in 2000-01 and 2001-02 than in the other years. One can also see that the highest numbers of students retained by ethnicity over the five-year period were Caucasians, with twelve (one in 1998-99; four in 2000-01; six in 2001-02; and one in 2002-03), followed by African-Americans with nine (two in 1998-99, 2000-01, 2001-02; and three in 2002-03). Two Hispanic students were retained during this period (one in 1998-99, and one in 2000-01). No Asian or American Indian students were retained from 1998-99 through 2002-03.

## Figure 4.18

### Little River Elementary School
### Number of Students Retained
### By Grade Level, Gender, and Ethnicity, 1998-99 to 2002-03

| Grade Level | Gender | Ethnicity | 1998-99 n=4 | 1999-00 n=0 | 2000-01 n=7 | 2001-02 n=8 | 2002-03 n=4 |
|---|---|---|---|---|---|---|---|
| Kindergarten | Male | African-American | 1 | | | 2 | 2 |
| | | Caucasian | | | | 2 | 1 |
| | | Hispanic | | | 1 | | |
| | Female | Caucasian | | | 2 | | |
| Grade One | Male | African-American | 1 | | 1 | | |
| | | Caucasian | 1 | | 1 | 1 | |
| | | Hispanic | 1 | | | | |
| | Female | Caucasian | | | | 1 | |
| Grade Two | Male | African-American | | | 1 | | 1 |
| | | Caucasian | | | | 1 | |
| Grade Three | Female | Caucasian | | | 1 | | |
| Grade Five | Female | Caucasian | | | | 1 | |

## Discipline

Discipline is a big issue at Little River Elementary School. Teachers have been involved with a behavior modification program offered through the local university. Even with this program, the number of suspensions is currently almost double what it was in the previous year due to a new way discipline referrals are reported (according to the principal). In 2002-03, the average number of days suspended was 142, versus 46 days in 1998-99, 71 in 1999-00, 39 in 2000-01, and 85 days in 2001-02. Figure 4.19 shows the average number of days suspended between 1998-99 and 2002-03. Percentage of total population was not calculated because we do not know how many days an individual might have been suspended.

### Figure 4.19

### Little River Elementary School
### Average Number of Days Suspended
### 1998-99 to 2002-03

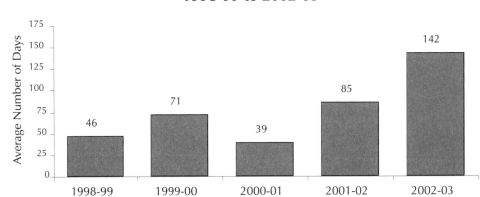

One can see in the graph below (Figure 4.20) that most of the students suspended in 2002-03 are male, African-American, and on Free/Reduced Lunch.

Figure 4.20

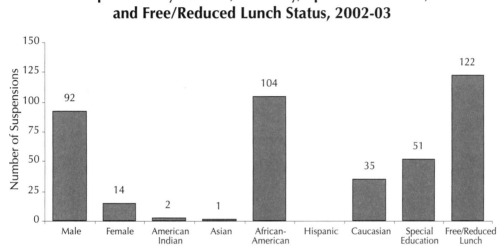

Figure 4.20

**Little River Elementary School
Suspensions by Gender, Ethnicity, Special Education,
and Free/Reduced Lunch Status, 2002-03**

Figure 4.21 shows the number of in-school and out-of-school suspensions, the majority of which were out-of-school suspensions. In-school and out-of-school suspensions increased in the past two years.

Figure 4.21

**Little River Elementary School
Suspensions 1998-99 to 2002-03**

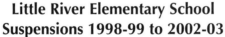

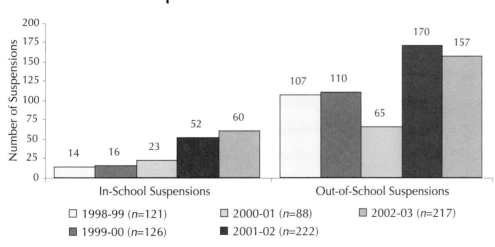

The majority of the suspensions have been for reasons "other" than assault or weapons, as shown in Figure 4.22.

Figure 4.22

**Little River Elementary School
Reason for Suspensions
1998-99 to 2002-03**

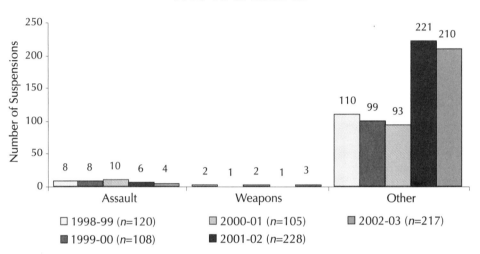

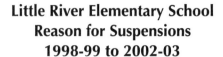

## Special Student Programs

### *Special Education*

Over the past four years, Little River has been serving an increasing number of students classified as needing special education. The majority of students receiving special education assistance were speech and language impaired and learning disabled, followed by behavior disorders and mental retardation. Over 100 students—almost one-fifth of the school enrollment—were classified as special education in 2000-01, as shown in Figure 4.23. Percentages could not be calculated because it is not known how many students had multiple disabilities within each category.

**Figure 4.23**

### Little River Elementary School
### Special Education Numbers by Learning Impairment
### 1999-00 to 2002-03

| Learning Impairment | 1999-00 | 2000-01 | 2001-02 | 2002-03 |
|---|---|---|---|---|
| Autism | | 1 | | 1 |
| Behavior disorders | 6 | 14 | 12 | 10 |
| Early childhood special education | 4 | 1 | 1 | 2 |
| Hearing impaired | 1 | 2 | 1 | 2 |
| Learning disabilities | 18 | 28 | 22 | 22 |
| Mental retardation | 8 | 13 | 11 | 11 |
| Multi-disabled | 3 | 6 | 3 | 2 |
| Speech and language impaired | 50 | 46 | 42 | 46 |
| **Total Number** | **90** | **111** | **92** | **96** |

Figure 4.24 shows the number of students by special education learning impairment, by grade level. Most impairments are fairly evenly distributed across grade levels.

## Figure 4.24

## Little River Elementary School Special Education
## By Grade Level, 1999-00 to 2002-03

| Learning Impairment | Grade Level | 1999-00 n=90 | 2000-01 n=111 | 2001-02 n=92 | 2002-03 n=96 |
|---|---|---|---|---|---|
| Autism | Grade One | | 1 | | 1 |
| Behavior disorders | Kindergarten | | 1 | | 1 |
| | Grade One | 2 | 3 | 1 | 1 |
| | Grade Two | | | 1 | 2 |
| | Grade Three | 1 | 4 | 1 | 2 |
| | Grade Four | 2 | 5 | 4 | 1 |
| | Grade Five | 1 | 1 | 5 | 3 |
| Early childhood special education | Kindergarten | 4 | 1 | 1 | 2 |
| Hearing impaired | Kindergarten | | | 1 | 1 |
| | Grade Two | 1 | | | 1 |
| | Grade Three | | 1 | | |
| | Grade Four | | 1 | | |
| Learning disabilities | Grade One | 1 | 4 | 1 | 1 |
| | Grade Two | 2 | 4 | 3 | 4 |
| | Grade Three | 5 | 6 | 7 | 5 |
| | Grade Four | 6 | 6 | 5 | 7 |
| | Grade Five | 4 | 8 | 6 | 5 |
| Mental retardation | Kindergarten | 1 | 2 | | |
| | Grade One | 2 | 1 | 3 | 1 |
| | Grade Two | 5 | 4 | 2 | 2 |
| | Grade Three | | 4 | 3 | 3 |
| | Grade Four | | 2 | 2 | 3 |
| | Grade Five | | | 1 | 2 |
| Multi-disabled | Kindergarten | 1 | 2 | | 1 |
| | Grade One | | 1 | | |
| | Grade Two | 2 | | | |
| | Grade Three | | 2 | | 1 |
| | Grade Four | | | 2 | |
| | Grade Five | | 1 | 1 | |
| Speech/Language impaired | Kindergarten | 5 | 4 | 10 | |
| | Grade One | 7 | 8 | 3 | 11 |
| | Grade Two | 7 | 8 | 7 | 8 |
| | Grade Three | 12 | 8 | 5 | 10 |
| | Grade Four | 9 | 11 | 6 | 8 |
| | Grade Five | 10 | 7 | 11 | 9 |

Figure 4.25 shows the spread of learning impairments by gender and ethnicity. One can see that almost twice as many boys than girls were identified as learning impaired over the years.

## Figure 4.25

### Little River Elementary School Special Education By Gender and Ethnicity, 1999-00 to 2002-03

| Learning Impairment | Gender | Ethnicity | 99-00 n=90 | 00-01 n=111 | 01-02 n=92 | 02-03 n=96 |
|---|---|---|---|---|---|---|
| Autism | Male | Caucasian | | 1 | | 1 |
| Behavior disorders | Male | African-American | 2 | 8 | 6 | 4 |
| | | Caucasian | 3 | 3 | 3 | 3 |
| | Female | African-American | 1 | 2 | 3 | 2 |
| | | Caucasian | | 1 | | 1 |
| Early childhood special education | Male | African-American | 1 | | | 2 |
| | | Hispanic | | | 1 | |
| | | Caucasian | 1 | | | |
| | Female | African-American | 2 | 1 | | |
| | | Caucasian | | | | |
| Hearing impaired | Male | Hispanic | 1 | 1 | | |
| | Female | African-American | | 1 | | |
| | | Caucasian | | | 1 | 2 |
| Learning disabilities | Male | African-American | 4 | 7 | 8 | 8 |
| | | Hispanic | 1 | 1 | 1 | |
| | | Caucasian | 5 | 8 | 5 | 6 |
| | Female | African-American | 5 | 6 | 5 | 4 |
| | | Caucasian | 3 | 6 | 3 | 4 |
| Mental retardation | Male | African-American | 3 | 5 | 5 | 3 |
| | | Caucasian | 3 | 4 | 2 | 3 |
| | Female | African-American | | 2 | 3 | 4 |
| | | Caucasian | 2 | 2 | 1 | 1 |
| Multi-disabled | Male | Caucasian | 1 | 3 | 1 | 1 |
| | Female | African-American | 1 | 1 | 1 | 1 |
| | | Caucasian | 1 | 2 | 1 | |
| Speech/Language impaired | Male | African-American | 16 | 12 | 14 | 13 |
| | | Caucasian | 15 | 14 | 15 | 14 |
| | Female | African-American | 9 | 9 | 7 | 12 |
| | | Caucasian | 10 | 11 | 6 | 7 |

Figure 4.26 shows the number of students in special education who qualify for free/reduced lunch. Considering the total number of students with learning impairments, one can see that the majority of these students also qualify for free/reduced lunch.

## Figure 4.26

### Little River Elementary School
### Free/Reduced Lunch Students
### By Special Education Status, 1999-00 to 2002-03

| Learning Impairment | 1999-00 $n=68$ | 2000-01 $n=82$ | 2001-02 $n=72$ | 2002-03 $n=84$ |
|---|---|---|---|---|
| Autism | | 1 | | 1 |
| Behavior disorders | 5 | 12 | 12 | 10 |
| Early childhood special education | 3 | 1 | | 4 |
| Hearing impaired | 1 | 2 | | 2 |
| Learning disabilities | 12 | 20 | 17 | 10 |
| Mental retardation | 8 | 11 | 11 | 10 |
| Multi-disabled | 2 | 3 | 1 | 3 |
| Speech and language impaired | 37 | 32 | 31 | 44 |

## The Staff

Little River Elementary School staff for 2002-03 is made up of:

26 Classroom Teachers

5 Title I Reading Recovery Specialists

1 Art Instructor

1 Physical Education Instructor

2 Permanent Substitute Teachers

3 Multicategorical Special Ed Specialists

2 Speech/Language Specialists

1 Early Childhood Speech Specialist

1 Title I Preschool Specialist

1 Title I Preschool Instructional Aide

1 Early Childhood Special Ed Specialist

1 Cross-category Special Ed Specialist

1 Mentor Teacher

1 Literacy Support Specialist

1 Vocal Music Instructor

1 School Psychologist

2 Counselors

1 Social Worker

3 Learning Disabilities Specialists

1 Nurse

6 Paraprofessionals

2 Media Clerks

3 Custodians

2 Cooks

2 Kitchen staff

1 Student Advocate

1 Classroom Aide

2 Secretaries

1 Home School Communicator

Twenty-six classroom teachers currently work at Little River, down from 28 in 2001-02, 31 in 2000-01, 30 in 1999-00, and 28 in 1998-99. All classroom teachers in 2002-03 are Caucasian, as is the female principal. There is one male teacher who teaches third grade. The average class size is 18 students. The number of classroom teachers is shown below, by grade level over time (Figure 4.27).

As can be seen by the makeup of the staff for 2002-03, many support personnel work at Little River. Since many of these specialists do not work with all of the students everyday, we focus our data on the classroom teachers.

**Figure 4.27**

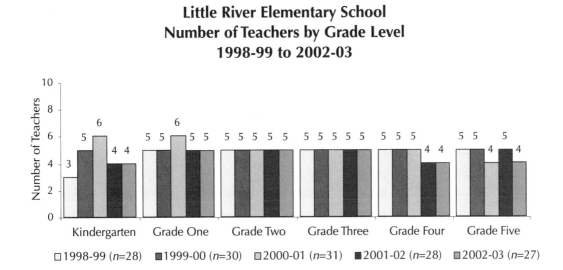

**Little River Elementary School
Number of Teachers by Grade Level
1998-99 to 2002-03**

Figure 4.28 shows the total number of years of teaching experience, by grade taught, for each of the classroom teachers at Little River Elementary for 2002-03. The principal has been the leader of this school for five years.

The scatter plot of data reveals that teachers with the least experience have a tendency to teach lower grades, while those with many years of experience teach the higher grades.

## Figure 4.28

### Little River Elementary School
### Teaching Experience by Grade Level and Teacher, 2002-03

| Grade Level<br>Overall Average 11.6 years | Teacher | Years of<br>Experience |
|---|---|---|
| Grade One<br>(Average=9.8 years) | One A | 6 |
| | One B | 3 |
| | One C | 7 |
| | One D | 23 |
| Grade Two<br>(Average=7.2 years) | Two A | 4 |
| | Two B | 1 |
| | Two C | 4 |
| | Two D | 12 |
| | Two E | 15 |
| Grade Three<br>(Average=4.3 years) | Three A | 2 |
| | Three B | 8 |
| | Three C | 3 |
| | Three D | 5 |
| | Three E | 4 |
| Grade Four<br>(Average=18.3 years) | Four A | 23 |
| | Four B | 13 |
| | Four C | 8 |
| | Four D | 29 |
| Grade Five<br>(Average=18.3 years) | Five A | 12 |
| | Five B | 28 |
| | Five C | 18 |
| | Five D | 15 |

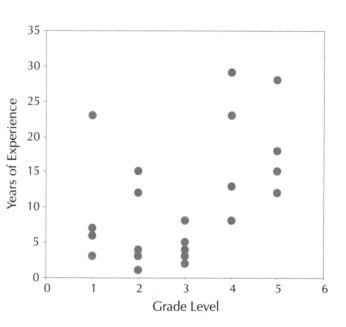

## Study Questions for *Who Are We?*

As you review Little River's data, use either the margins in the text, this page, or print this page from the CD to write down your early thinking. These notes, of course, are only hunches or placeholders until all the data are analyzed. It is important to jot down your thinking as you go through the data so you can see if additional data corroborate your "hunches."

| 1. What are the demographic *strengths* and *challenges* for Little River? | |
|---|---|
| *Strengths* | *Challenges* |
| | |

**2. What are some *implications* for the Little River school improvement plan?**

**3. Looking at the data presented, what other demographic data would you want to answer the question *Who are we?* for Little River Elementary School?**

## What I Saw in Example One:
### Little River Elementary School ⊙ <sub>CD-ROM</sub>

At the end of each chapter, I will add what I saw in the data, using the study questions as an outline. When applicable, I have referenced the figure that gave me my first impression of strengths and challenges.

| What are their demographic strengths? | What are their demographic challenges? |
|---|---|
| • Little River is in a university community, so there should be resources available. (Page 40)<br>• The school is not too large. (Figure 4.2)<br>• Student population has some ethnic diversity. (Figure 4.3)<br>• Attendance rates are pretty even across grade levels. (Figure 4.8)<br>• Few students are retained in grade levels. (Figure 4.17)<br>• Retentions have decreased over time. Early monitoring might be making the difference. (Figure 4.17)<br>• There are many support staff to help teachers. (Page 58)<br>• The school has a small teacher-to-student ratio. (Page 59)<br>• Class sizes are small. (Page 59)<br>• There are many experienced teachers in the school. (Figure 4.28) | • The fluctuations of enrollment within grade levels and across cohorts could be a challenge. (Figures 4.5 and 4.6)<br>• The fluctuations of enrollment by gender within grade levels could be a challenge. (Figure 4.7)<br>• Attendance could improve even more, especially at lower grades. (Figure 4.8)<br>• There is some mobility, which has to be frustrating to the teachers. (Figures 4.10 and 4.11)<br>• English Learners must go out of the community to go to school. Is this good? (Page 47)<br>• There is an increase in the percentage of free/reduced lunch students. (Figure 4.13)<br>• Over one-half of the families in the school qualify for free/reduced lunches. (Figures 4.13, 4.14, 4.15, and 4.16)<br>• More males than females are retained each year. (Figure 4.18)<br>• There have been increases in the number of days of suspensions, both in-school and out-of-school suspensions. (Figures 4.19 and 4.21)<br>• Most of the suspended students are African-American males qualifying for free/reduced lunch. (Figure 4.20)<br>• There are many Special Education students—especially males. How are special education students identified? Does every teacher know how to work with these students? (Figures 4.23, 4.24, 4.25, and 4.26)<br>• There is no ethnic or gender diversity in the teaching staff. (Page 59)<br>• Grade three, and three out of five grade two classrooms have teachers with little teaching experience. (Could this also have something to do with the grades having the highest absentee rate? Grade four has the most experienced teachers and the highest attendance rate with no retentions. Are these facts related?) (Figures 4.9 and 4.28) |

## What are some implications for their school improvement plan?

- Is there a plan or strategy in place to work with the students who are absent and their parents? Also, is there a plan to welcome new students and their parents to the school?
- Was anything special done to increase attendance in 2002-03?
- If mobility is within the district, there would be implications for a districtwide curriculum.
- The school should work with the school district to understand the impact of sending English Learners away from their neighborhood schools. How successful is this approach?
- Teachers might need professional development training in working with Special Education students, families living in poverty, cultural diversity, and discipline.
- Teachers need support with discipline issues.
- Does everyone know what the discipline issues are and when they happen?
- Was anything special done to decrease retentions?
- Perhaps some of the veteran teachers in the upper grades need to be spread out across all grade levels? Younger teachers, if left alone in the early grades, might need a better mentoring system.
- The racial and gender balance of teachers might better reflect the racial and gender balance of students.
- May want to follow these students into their next stages of development.

## Other desired data or information:

Little River Elementary School provided an excellent summary of who they are. Other data that would be helpful in understanding the context of the school might include:

- What is the impact of teachers' years of teaching experience and student absentee rates?
- What causes absenteeism? Are reasons for absences recorded?
- What are teacher absentee rates?
- How many English Learners go out of the community to learn, how many come back to this neighborhood school, is that transition difficult, and do they succeed when they return?
- We need to know more about the discipline issues. When do they occur, what are the issues, and how are they dealt with?
- How many students are suspended by grade level? Why are they suspended? How are suspensions determined?
- How are Special Education students designated? How many students have multiple disabilities and what are they? What percentage of students are in special education? Are students who are discipline problems designated as special education? Do students ever leave special education?
- More information on mobility is needed to really understand these numbers.
- What happens to these students later on? (e.g., drop-out, graduation, employment)
- How many students attend pre-school? How many of the students who are behavior problems, suspended, or retained, attended pre-school?
- What about the success rate for those students who were retained? Do they catch-up?
- What happens to the students when they leave Little River School for middle school, junior high, and high school?
- What educational background do the teachers have? Are they all credentialed, certificated and/or licensed?
- Why so many support staff?
- What about the parents?

## Summary

Some of the first data required for continuous school improvement planning are demographic data. With demographic data, we are answering the basic question, *Who are we?* The answers to the question, *Who are we?*, set the context for the school, have huge implications for the direction the continuous school improvement plan will take, and can help explain how the school gets the results it is getting. Our example school, Little River Elementary, showed how a demographic analysis could look. The accompanying CD has tools to help your school create a comprehensive demographic profile.

### Typical Demographic Data to Gather to Answer the Question, *Who Are We?*

*Community*
- ▼ Location and history
- ▼ Economic base, population trends, and community resources (*www.census.gov* is a great resource for getting information about the community, as is your local chamber of commerce)
- ▼ Community involvement
- ▼ Business partnerships

*School District*
- ▼ Description and history
- ▼ Number of schools, administrators, students and teachers over time, and by grade level

*School*
- ▼ Description and history, attendance area, location
- ▼ Type of school, e.g., magnet, alternative, charter, private, private management
- ▼ Number of administrators, students and teachers over time, and by grade level
- ▼ Number of students electing to come to the school from out of the attendance area
- ▼ Grants and awards received
- ▼ Title 1/Schoolwide
- ▼ Safety/crime data
- ▼ *State designation as a dangerous school
- ▼ Uniqueness and strengths
- ▼ Class sizes
- ▼ After-school programs/summer school
- ▼ Extracurricular activities
- ▼ Advisors for extracurricular activities
  - ◆ Are they teachers on staff who receive extra pay?
  - ◆ Are they teachers in district, but at other schools, who receive extra pay?
  - ◆ Are they non-teachers paid to be advisors?
- ▼ Tutoring/peer mentoring
- ▼ Community support-services coordinated
- ▼ Counseling opportunities

- ▼ *Facilities: equipped for networked computers and handicapped
- ▼ Facilities: age, capacity, maintenance
- ▼ Availability of necessities and other supplies

*Students Over Time, and by Grade Level*
- ▼ Living situation/family structure/family size
- ▼ Preschool/Head Start/Even Start
- ▼ Preschool attendance
- ▼ *Number of students
- ▼ Gender of students
- ▼ *Race/ethnicity numbers and percentages
- ▼ Free/reduced lunch numbers and percentages
- ▼ *Language fluency by language
- ▼ *Migrant/immigrants by country, home languages
- ▼ *Homeless
- ▼ *Special Education by disability, gender, ethnicity, language fluency, free/reduced lunch
- ▼ *Attendance/tardies
- ▼ Mobility (where students go/come from)
- ▼ Retention rates by gender, ethnicity, language fluency, free/reduced lunch
- ▼ *Dropout rates by gender, ethnicity, free/reduced lunch, migrant, special education (where students go/what they do)
- ▼ Number of students leaving school overall by gender, ethnicity, language fluency, free/reduced lunch
- ▼ Extracurricular activity participation/clubs/service learning by gender, ethnicity, language fluency, free/reduced lunch
- ▼ Number of participants in programs, such as AP, IB, Honors, Upward Bound, Gear-up, college-prep, vocational
- ▼ Number of home schoolers associated with school, along with how they are associated with the school
- ▼ Number of students electing to come to the school from out-of-the-attendance area
- ▼ Number of bus riders and distances they ride
- ▼ Student employment
- ▼ *Discipline indicators (e.g., suspensions, referrals, types of incidences, number of students carrying weapons on school property)
- ▼ *Number of drugs on school property (offered, sold, or given illegal drugs)
- ▼ *Graduation rates by gender, ethnicity, language proficiency, free/reduced lunch, migrant, and special education (where students go/what they do)
- ▼ Number of high school students concurrently enrolled in college courses
- ▼ Number of students meeting college course entrance requirements by gender, ethnicity, language fluency, free/reduced lunch
- ▼ Number of middle students concurrently enrolled in high school courses
- ▼ Number of scholarships by gender, ethnicity, language proficiency, free/reduced lunch
- ▼ Number of students completing GEDs
- ▼ Adult education programs
- ▼ Number and percentage of students going on to college, post-graduate training, and/or employment
- ▼ Grade-point average in college
- ▼ Number of graduates ending up in college remedial classes

*Staff Over Time*

▼ *Number of teachers, administrators, instructional specialists, support staff by roles

▼ *Years of experience, by grade level and/or role, in this school/in teaching

▼ Ethnicity, gender, languages spoken

▼ Retirement projections

▼ *Types of certifications/licenses/teacher qualifications/percentage of time teaching in certified area(s)

▼ Grades/subjects teachers are teaching

▼ Degrees

▼ *Educational training of paraprofessionals

▼ Teacher-student ratios by grade level

▼ Teacher turnover rates

▼ Attendance rates

▼ Teacher involvement in extracurricular activities, program participation

▼ *Number of teachers receiving high-quality professional development

▼ *Percent of teachers qualified to use technology for instruction

▼ National Board for Professional Teaching Standards (NBPTS) teachers

*Parents*

▼ Educational levels, home language, employment, socioeconomic status

▼ Involvement with their child's learning

▼ Involvement in school activities

▼ Incarceration

*Required for *No Child Left Behind* (includes the numbers required to understand the disaggregated numbers required by NCLB).

## On the CD Related to This Chapter

▼ Study Questions Related to *Who are we?* (Ch4Qs.pdf)

These study questions will help you better understand the information provided in Chapter 4. This file can be printed for use with staffs as you begin setting the context of your school by answering the question, *Who are we?*

▼ Demographic Graphing Templates (ElemDemog.xls)

All of the *Microsoft Excel* files that were used to create the demographic graphs in the Little River example (Chapter 4) appear on the CD. Use these templates by putting your data in the data table and changing the title/labels to reflect your data. Your graphs will build automatically. This file also explains how to use the templates.

▼ Demographic Data Table Templates (ElemDemog.doc)

All of the *Microsoft Word* files that were used to create the demographic data tables in the Little River example (Chapter 4) appear on the CD. Use these templates by putting your data in the data table and changing the title/labels to reflect your data.

▼ *School Data Profile Template* (ElemProfil.doc)

This *Microsoft Word* file provides a template for creating your own school data profile like the one for example one: *Little River Elementary School,* using the graphing and table templates provided.

▼ Profile templates for gathering and organizing data, prior to graphing, that can be adjusted to add data elements you feel are important to fully complete the profile. If you just need to graph your data, use the graphing templates.

◆ *School Profile* (ProfilSc.doc)

The *School Profile* is a template for gathering and organizing data about your school, prior to graphing. Please adjust the profile to add data elements you feel are important for describing the context of your school. This information is then graphed and written into a narrative form. If creating a school portfolio, the data graphs and narrative would appear in *Information and Analysis.* (If you already have your data organized and just need to graph it, you might want to skip this step and use the graphing templates, described above.)

◆ *Community Profile* (ProfilCo.doc)

The *Community Profile* is a template for gathering and organizing data about your community, prior to graphing. Please adjust the profile to add data elements you feel are important for describing the context of your community. It is important to describe how the community has changed over time, and how it is expected to change in the near future. This information is then graphed and written into a narrative form. If creating a school portfolio, the data graphs and narrative would appear in *Information and Analysis.* (If you already have your data organized and just need to graph it, you might want to skip this step and use the graphing templates, described on the previous page.)

◆ *Administrator Profile* (ProfilAd.doc)

The *Administrator Profile* is a template for gathering and organizing data about your school administrators, prior to graphing. Please adjust the profile to fully describe your administrators. This information is then graphed and written into a narrative form. If creating a school portfolio, the data graphs and narrative would appear in the *Information and Analysis* and *Leadership* sections. (If you already have your data organized and just need to graph it, you might want to skip this step and use the graphing templates, described on the previous page.)

◆ *Teacher Profile* (ProfilTe.doc)

The *Teacher Profile* is a template for gathering and organizing data about your school's teachers, prior to graphing. Please adjust the profile to fully describe your teachers. The synthesis of this information is then graphed and written into a narrative form. If creating a school portfolio, the data graphs and narrative would appear in *Information and Analysis*. (If you already have your data organized and just need to graph it, you might want to skip this step and use the graphing templates, described on the previous page.)

◆ *Staff (other than teacher) Profile* (ProfilSt.doc)

The *Staff (Other than Teacher) Profile* is a template for gathering and organizing data about school staff who are not teachers, prior to graphing. Please adjust the profile to fully describe your non-teaching staff. The synthesis of this information is then graphed and written into a narrative form. If creating a school portfolio, the data graphs and narrative would appear in *Information and Analysis*. (If you already have your data organized and just need to graph it, you might want to skip this step and use the graphing templates, described on the previous page.)

▼ *History Gram Activity* (ACTHstry.pdf)

A team-building activity that will "write" the history of the school, which could help everyone see what staff has experienced since coming to the school, and how many school improvement initiatives have been started over the years. It is helpful for understanding what it will take to keep this current school improvement effort going.

▼ *Questions to Guide the Analysis of Demographic Data* (QsDemogr.doc)

This *Microsoft Word* file provides a guide for interpreting your demographic data. Adjust the questions to better reflect the discussion you would like to have with your staff about the gathered demographic data.

▼ *What I Saw in Example One* (Ch4Saw.pdf)

*What I Saw in Example One* is a file, organized by the demographic study questions, that summarizes what I saw in the demographic data provided by Little River Elementary School.

▼ *Demographic Data to Gather to Create the Context of the School* (DemoData.pdf)

This file defines the types of demographic data that are important to gather to build the context of the school and describe *Who are we?*

# Analyzing the Data:
## *How Do We Do Business?*

Chapter 5

The second question in our continuous school improvement planning model, described in Chapter 3, is *How do we do business?* How a school does business can be ascertained through studying student, staff, and parent questionnaire results, and through assessing with tools that can tell how staffs work together and with the larger school community. The answers to this question can inform a school staff of what is possible as they plan for the future, and what it will take to systemically change how they work together.

Since humans cannot *act* any differently from what they value, believe, or perceive, and because we want all staff to *act* in the same way, as the vision directs, it seems wise to understand what staff are perceiving about the learning environment and what they believe will improve student learning. These results can provide information about needs for professional development, team building, and motivation. Parent and student questionnaire results can point to needs that must also be considered in the continuous school improvement plan.

The example schools in this book used the *Education for the Future* (EFF) student, staff, and parent questionnaires to assess how they do business. Both schools also used the *EFF Continuous Improvement Continuums* (CICs). The CICs are powerful tools for assessing the health of a school system. Little River's CIC report is found only on the CD (to save space), while Blue Bird Elementary School's report is in Chapter 9.

We start on *How do we do business?* example one with Little River Elementary School, and then show Blue Bird Elementary School's example two in Chapter 9. Please note the study questions on page 88 to assist in studying the Little River data. Also note that there is space in the margins on the data pages to write your impressions as you review the data. At the end of the chapter, I share what I saw in the data. For reviewing your own data, you might want to use a comparison table to look across student, staff, and parent questionnaire results. Such a table is on the CD entitled, *QTable.doc.* You are welcome to use this as well as the study questions.

## Example One: Little River Elementary School

### *How Do We Do Business?*

To get a better understanding of the learning environment at Little River Elementary School and to measure change, staff administered student, staff, and parent questionnaires three years in a row. Summaries of those results follow. *Note:* The complete narrative of these results is located on the CD, along with the tools used to assess perceptions, including questionnaires, and the *School IQ,* which includes the templates to administer the questionnaires online, and to analyze and graph results. For more information about designing questionnaires, see Appendix A, *Data Analysis for Comprehensive Schoolwide Improvement* (Bernhardt, 1998).

### Student Questionnaire Results

Students in grades three through five at Little River Elementary School responded to an *Education for the Future* questionnaire designed to measure how they feel about their learning environment in May 2001 (*N*=349), May 2002 (*N*=203), and May 2003 (*N*=157). Students were asked to respond to items using a five-point scale: 1 = strongly disagree; 2 = disagree; 3 = neutral; 4 = agree; and, 5 = strongly agree.

Average responses to each item on the questionnaire were graphed by the totals for the three years and the disaggregated totals by gender, grade level, and ethnicity. A summary for each disaggregation follows.

The icons, in the figures that follow, show the average responses to each item by disaggregation indicated in the legend. The lines join the icons to help the reader know the distribution results for each disaggregation. The lines have no other meaning.

### Student Responses for Three Years

Overall, the average responses to the questions in the student questionnaire were in agreement all three years, as shown in Figure 5.1. May 2001 responses generally were in highest agreement. The responses dropped approximately .25 points across most responses in May 2002. The 2002 questionnaire administration saw all but a couple of responses going up from May 2002, none exceeding the May 2001 responses.

For all three years, students were in strongest agreement, scoring between 4.75 and 5.0 on the five-point scale, to the following statements:

▼ My family wants me to do well in school

▼ My family believes I can do well in school

Students were in next strongest agreement all three years, scoring above 4.5 on the scale, to the statement: *My teacher believes I can learn.*

The items which elicited a response that fell above 4.5 (strong agreement) on the scale from one or more year included, from highest to lowest:

▼ I have support for learning at home (May 2001)

▼ Very good work is expected at my school (May 2001)

▼ My teacher is a good teacher (May 2001, May 2003)

▼ My principal cares about me (May 2001, May 2003)

▼ My teacher thinks I will be successful (May 2001)

▼ I know what I am supposed to be learning in my classes (May 2001)

▼ My teacher cares about me (May 2001)

### Student Responses by Gender

When the data were disaggregated by gender, the three years of graphs revealed that the disaggregated responses were very similar and clustered around the overall average.

Figure 5.1

## Little River Elementary School Student Responses By Year
### Grades 3 through 5
### May 2001, May 2002, and May 2003

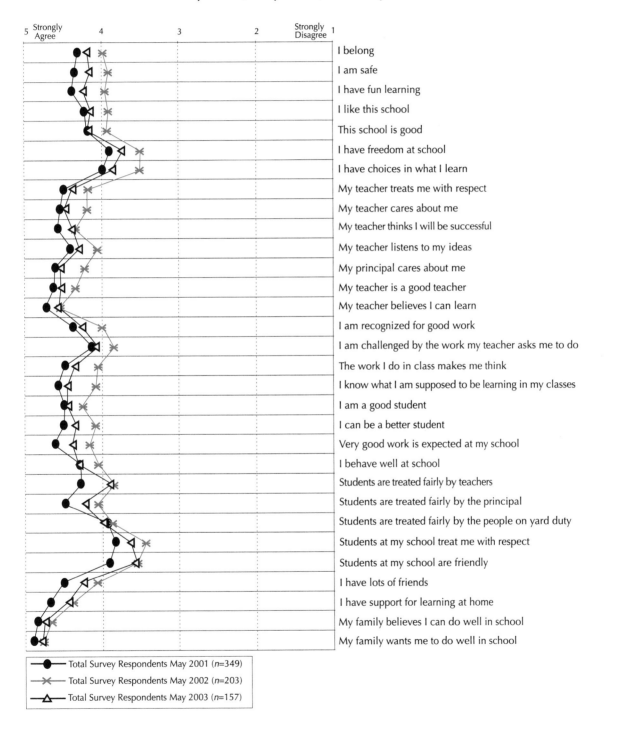

*Student Responses by Grade Level*

The questionnaire results were also disaggregated by grade level. In 2003, there were 58 third graders (67% of third graders); 35 fourth graders (45% of fourth graders); and 49 fifth graders (64% of fifth graders) responding. (*Note:* Grade-level numbers do not add up to the total number of respondents because some students did not identify themselves by this demographic.) The differences in responses to the items by grade level were greatest during the second year, although not appreciably different. May 2003 student responses by grade level are shown in Figure 5.2.

The graph revealed few differences disaggregated by grade level. While third-grade students generally responded in stronger agreement than other subgroups to most items on the questionnaire, fifth-grade students responded least positively. Fifth-graders' averages were noticeably lower on the items:

▼ Students are treated fairly by teachers

▼ My teacher listens to my ideas

No significant distinguishing pattern emerged when looking at the data by these subgroups.

# Figure 5.2

## Little River Elementary School Student Responses by Grade Level
## Grades 3 through 5, May 2003

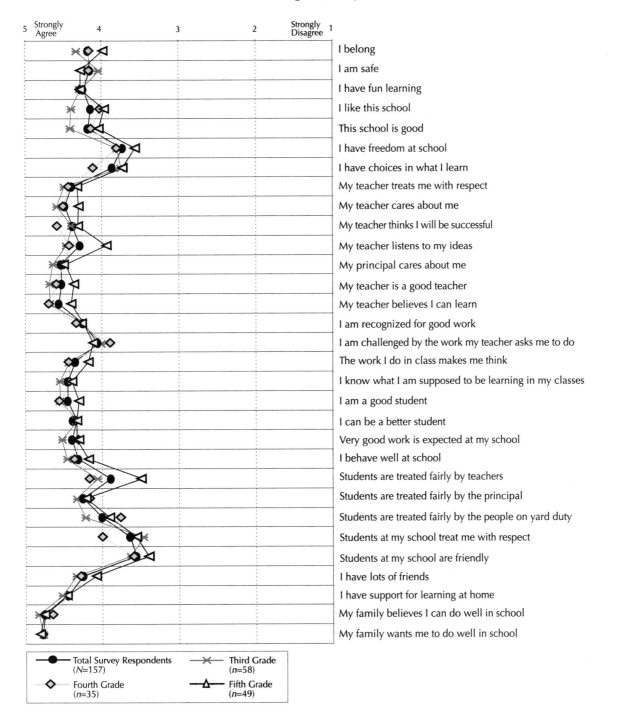

*Student Responses by Ethnicity*

Student questionnaire data were also disaggregated by ethnicity. In 2003, 55 African-Americans (35% of the responding population); 53 Caucasians (34%); 21 American Indians (13%); 6 Asians (3%); and 30 Others (19%) responded. (*Note:* Ethnicity numbers add up to more than the total number of respondents because some students identified themselves by more than one ethnicity.)

In general, Figure 5.3 shows few differences in responses by ethnicity, except for two items. American Indian students responded in disagreement (below 3.0 on the five-point scale), while all other subgroups were in agreement, to two statements on the questionnaire:

▼ Students at my school treat me with respect

▼ Students at my school are friendly

Overall, Asian respondents were more positive than other subgroups.

## Figure 5.3

### Little River Elementary School Student Responses by Ethnicity
### Grades 3 through 5, May 2003

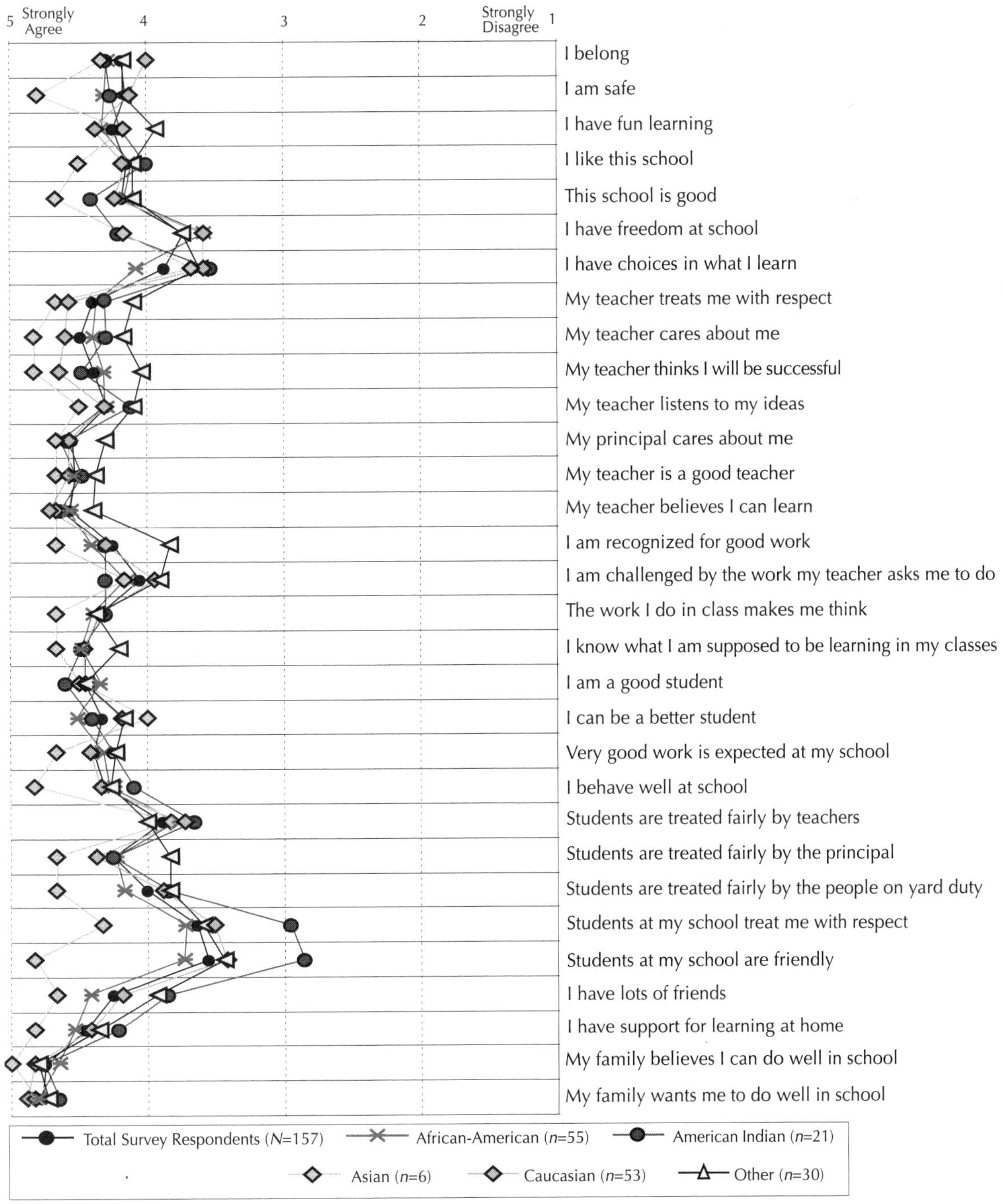

*Student Open-ended Responses*

In May 2001 and May 2003, Little River Elementary School students were asked to respond to three open-ended questions: *What do you like about your school?, What do you wish was different at your school?,* and *What do you wish we would have asked you about your school?* The complete list of responses, grouped into like categories, are on the CD with the complete narrative of student questionnaire results. Below are the top ten written-in responses for the first two questions. (*Note:* When analyzing open-ended results, one must keep in mind the number of responses that were written in. Open-ended responses often help us understand the multiple choice responses, although caution must be exercised around small numbers of respondents saying any one thing.) *How to Analyze Open-ended Responses* is also on the CD, along with *Questions to Guide the Analyses of Perceptions Data.*

---

**1.  What do you like about your school?**

| May 2001 (N=349) | May 2003 (N=157) |
|---|---|
| • The teachers (89) | • The teacher (54) |
| • Recess (39) | • Students are nice (27) |
| • I like learning new things (23) | • Recess and playground/free time (17) |
| • I have fun at school (22) | • We have computers (12) |
| • P.E. (21) | • I like the principal (9) |
| • My friends (19) | • P.E. (9) |
| • The playground (16) | • Math (9) |
| • Lunch/the food (15) | • School is fun (6) |
| • The principal (12) | • It's a great school (6) |
| • Using computers (12) | • It is a good place to learn stuff (6) |
| | • I like art because it's fun (6) |

**2.  What do you wish was different at your school?**

| May 2001 (N=349) | May 2003 (N=157) |
|---|---|
| • Better food (22) | • Nicer/more respectful kids (33) |
| • No fighting and a better behavioral program (18) | • A new playground (10) |
| • Better/more playground equipment (18) | • Longer recess (9) |
| • Longer recess (11) | • We could chase, play tag, kickball, football, or whatever we want, and didn't always have to be so safe (9) |
| • Treated better by teachers (10) | • Better lunches (5) |
| • We need air conditioning (8) | • Better teachers (4) |
| • Bigger classrooms (8) | • No homework/more challenging classes (4) |
| • More computers (6) | • No detention and no recovery rooms (4) |
| • Cleaner bathrooms (6) | • Teachers and principal would pay more attention to bullies and the way they treat people at school (3) |
| • Let us choose what we want to learn (5) | • I wish that we could eat earlier (2) |

## Staff Questionnaire Results

Little River Elementary School staff responded to a questionnaire designed to measure their perceptions of the school environment in May 2001 (*N*=61), May 2002 (*N*=25), and May 2003 (*N*=37). Members of the staff were asked to respond to items using a five-point scale: 1 = strongly disagree; 2 = disagree; 3 = neutral; 4 = agree; 5 = strongly agree.

Average responses to each item on the questionnaire were graphed by year. The results for the three years are summarized below.

### Staff Responses for Three Years

Results graphed by year, shown in Figures 5.4 and 5.5 (two-page questionnaire), revealed some differences.

In strongest agreement all three years (scoring above 4.5 on the five-point scale), were the following statements from highest to lowest average:

- ▼ I believe student achievement can increase through effective parent involvement
- ▼ I believe student achievement can increase through providing a threat-free environment
- ▼ I believe every student can learn
- ▼ I think it is important to communicate often with parents
- ▼ I believe student achievement can increase through close personal relationships between students and teachers
- ▼ I feel that learning can be fun
- ▼ I believe student achievement can increase through the use of varied technologies

Continuing in strong agreement (above 4.5), staff agreed with the statements:

- ▼ I believe student achievement can increase through the use of computers (May 2001, May 2002)
- ▼ I believe student achievement can increase through "hands-on" learning (May 2001, May 2003)
- ▼ I love seeing the results of my work with students (May 2002, May 2003)
- ▼ I believe quality work is expected of me (May 2003)
- ▼ I think it is important to communicate often with parents (May 2001)

# Figure 5.4

## Little River Elementary School Staff Responses
## By Year, May 2001, May 2002, and May 2003

| 5 Strongly Agree | 4 | 3 | 2 Strongly Disagree | 1 | |
|---|---|---|---|---|---|
| | | | | | I feel like I belong at this school |
| | | | | | I feel that the staff cares about me |
| | | | | | I feel that learning can be fun |
| | | | | | I feel that learning is fun at this school |
| | | | | | I feel recognized for good work |
| | | | | | I feel intrinsically rewarded for doing my job well |
| | | | | | I work with people who treat me with respect |
| | | | | | I work with people who listen if I have ideas about doing things better |
| | | | | | My administrator treats me with respect |
| | | | | | My administrator is an effective instructional leader |
| | | | | | My administrator facilitates communication effectively |
| | | | | | My administrator supports me in my work with students |
| | | | | | My administrator supports shared decision making |
| | | | | | My administrator allows me to be an effective instructional leader |
| | | | | | My administrator is effective in helping us reach our vision |
| | | | | | I have the opportunity to develop my skills |
| | | | | | I have the opportunity to think for myself, not just carry out instructions |
| | | | | | I love working at this school |
| | | | | | I love seeing the results of my work with students |
| | | | | | I work effectively with special education students |
| | | | | | I work effectively with English Learners |
| | | | | | I work effectively with an ethnically/racially diverse population of students |
| | | | | | I work effectively with heterogeneously grouped classes |
| | | | | | I work effectively with low-achieving students |
| | | | | | I believe every student can learn |
| | | | | | I BELIEVE STUDENT ACHIEVEMENT CAN INCREASE THROUGH: "hands-on learning" |
| | | | | | effective professional development related to our vision |
| | | | | | integrating instruction across the curriculum |
| | | | | | thematic instruction |

—●— Total Survey Respondents May 2001 (*n*=61)

—✕— Total Survey Respondents May 2002 (*n*=25)

—△— Total Survey Respondents May 2003 (*n*=37)

Figure 5.5

## Little River Elementary School Staff Responses
## By Year, May 2001, May 2002, and May 2003

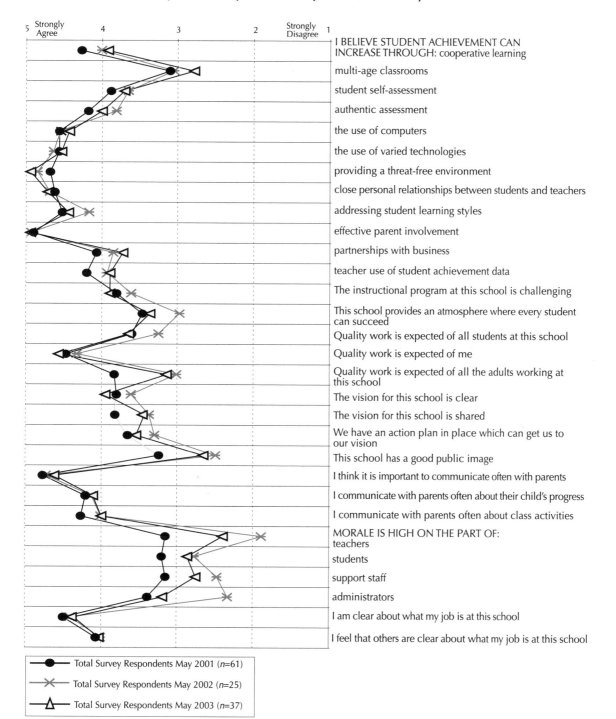

▼ I believe student achievement can increase through integrating instruction across the curriculum (May 2001)

▼ I believe student achievement can increase through addressing student learning styles (May 2001)

May 2001 respondents were in agreement with all items on the questionnaire. The statements which elicited a response that fell below neutral (3.0 on the scale), in disagreement, from both May 2002 and May 2003, were:

▼ Morale is high on the part of students

▼ This school has a good public image

▼ Morale is high on the part of support staff

▼ Morale is high on the part of teachers

May 2002 respondents also disagreed or were neutral with respect to the following items:

▼ This school provides an atmosphere where every student can succeed

▼ I work effectively with English Learners

▼ Morale is high on the part of administrators

May 2003 respondents disagreed with the statement: *I believe student achievement can increase through multi-age classrooms.* May 2001 and 2003 respondents were neutral in their response to the item: *I work effectively with English Learners.*

### *Items for Teachers and Instructional Assistants Only*

In addition to items completed by all staff, the questionnaire contained a set of five statements for teachers and instructional assistants only. The results are summarized below.

As shown in Figure 5.6, respondents were in agreement with all items on the questionnaire, with the exception of the May 2002 instructional staff, whose average response fell below neutral (at 2.73 on the scale), in disagreement, with one item on the questionnaire: *Teachers in this school communicate with each other to make student learning consistent across grades.*

# Figure 5.6

## Little River Elementary School Staff
## Items for Teachers and Instructional Assistants by Year
## May 2001, May 2002, and May 2003

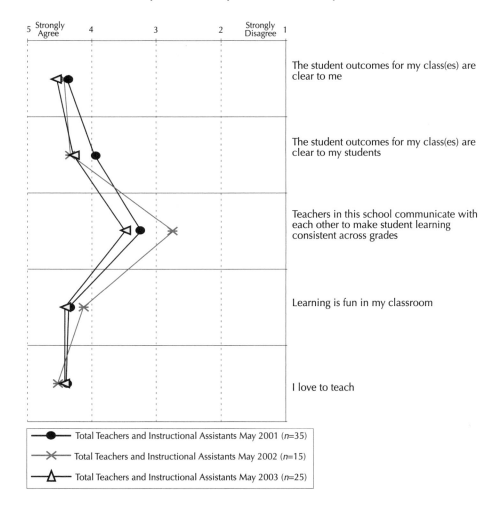

The student outcomes for my class(es) are clear to me

The student outcomes for my class(es) are clear to my students

Teachers in this school communicate with each other to make student learning consistent across grades

Learning is fun in my classroom

I love to teach

● Total Teachers and Instructional Assistants May 2001 (*n*=35)

✕ Total Teachers and Instructional Assistants May 2002 (*n*=15)

△ Total Teachers and Instructional Assistants May 2003 (*n*=25)

*Staff Open-ended Responses*

Little River Elementary School staff completed two open-ended questions in 2002 and 2003: *What are the strengths of this school?* and *What needs to be improved?* Additional comments were also requested. The complete list of responses, grouped into like categories, appear in the narrative on the CD with the complete narrative of staff questionnaire results. The top ten responses to these two questions appear below.

---

### 1. What are the strengths of this school?

| May 2002 (N=25) | May 2003 (N=37) |
|---|---|
| ◆ Excellent teachers (7) | ◆ Dedicated administrators, teachers, and staff (16) |
| ◆ Innovative teaching practices with computers (7) | ◆ Sense of community among the staff (7) |
| ◆ Hardworking office staff (6) | ◆ The technology (7) |
| ◆ The principal is wonderful (5) | ◆ Good relationship/collaboration between grade-level teachers (5) |
| ◆ Great custodial staff (2) | ◆ Administration motivated and open to new ideas (5) |
| ◆ Diverse population (2) | ◆ Great support staff (5) |
| ◆ Increasing literacy through literacy support teachers | ◆ Diverse population (3) |
| ◆ Most students are glad to be here | ◆ Our new set of teachers (the last few years) are willing to try new things and listen to others' ideas (2) |
| ◆ The facility is well-kept | ◆ A core group of parents that work very hard (2) |
| ◆ We have great parent support | ◆ Lots of resources |

### 2. What needs to be improved?

| May 2002 (N=25) | May 2003 (N=37) |
|---|---|
| ◆ Consistency and appropriateness dealing with problem students (11) | ◆ Discipline among all staff members needs to be more consistent and stricter (27) |
| ◆ Administration needs teamwork and equality of workload (6) | ◆ Communication between administration and teachers on student behavior problems (6) |
| ◆ We need better instructional support from our administrators and to hear when we are not doing well (6) | ◆ Improved teacher morale (6) |
| ◆ We need to have the staff on a more supportive team effort, such as ways to improve behaviors (5) | ◆ More supervision on the playground and more structure for certain students at recess time (6) |
| ◆ Teacher morale (4) | ◆ Too much time spent in meetings and not enough time for classroom planning (3) |
| ◆ More parent involvement (4) | ◆ More parent involvement (3) |
| ◆ Building-wide expectations, administrative focus, staff cohesiveness (3) | ◆ Mediocre teachers continue to return to work beside the many excellent teachers |
| ◆ State test scores | ◆ More emphasis on formal training in social behavior would greatly benefit this student population |
| ◆ Working outside our grade levels needs to be improved | ◆ More teachers who are willing to assume extra duties |
| ◆ Student/teacher ratio | ◆ We need the *because it's the way we've always done it* mentality erased from the building |

## Parent Questionnaire Responses

Parents of students attending Little River Elementary School completed a questionnaire designed to measure their perceptions of the school environment in May 2001 (*N*=98), and again in May 2003 (*N*=119). Parents were asked to respond to items using a five-point scale: 1 = strongly disagree; 2 = disagree; 3 = neutral; 4 = agree; and, 5 = strongly agree.

Average responses to each item on the questionnaire were graphed by year and are shown below. Average responses by children's grade levels, ethnicity, number of children in the household, and number of children in the school display no differences by these disaggregations, and are shown in the narrative on the CD.

### *Parent Responses for Two Years*

Average responses graphed by year, shown in Figure 5.7, were very similar. While parents responding in May 2003 generally responded in stronger agreement than those responding in 2001, respondents were in agreement with all statements on the questionnaire.

Responses were in strongest agreement both years (scoring between 4.5 and 4.75 on the five-point scale), with the following statements:

- ▼ I support my child's learning at home
- ▼ I feel good about myself as a parent
- ▼ I feel welcome at my child's school

May 2003 parents responded in strong agreement (between 4.5 and 4.75) to the statements:

- ▼ I know what my child's teacher expects of my child
- ▼ I am informed about my child's progress
- ▼ I respect the school's principal
- ▼ I respect the school's teachers

Scoring just above neutral (at or above 3.0 and below 3.5), parents were in low agreement both years with the statement: *The students show respect for other students.* May 2001 parents also responded just above neutral to: *There is adequate playground supervision during school.*

Average responses disaggregated by children's grade level, ethnicity, number of children in the household, and number of children in the school did not show any differences by subgroups.

Figure 5.7

## Little River Elementary School Parent Responses by Year
## May 2001 and May 2003

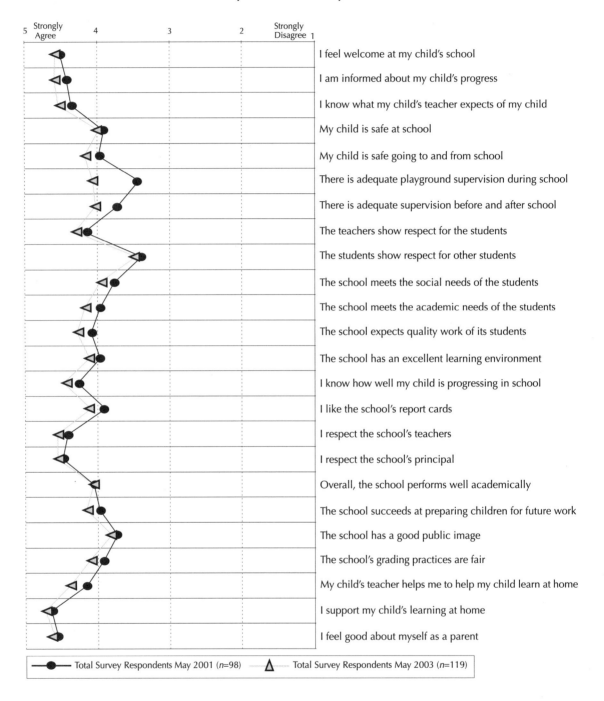

*Parent Open-ended Responses*

In May 2003, parents of students attending Little River Elementary School were asked to complete three open-ended questions: *What are the strengths of your child's school?*, *What needs to be strengthened at your child's school?*, and *What would make the school better?* The complete list of responses, grouped into like categories, is on the CD with the complete narrative of parent questionnaire results. 💿 The top ten written-in responses appear below.

---

### 1. What are the strengths of your child's school?

- The great teachers and staff (43)
- The administration (10)
- Teaching and reinforcing positive behavior (5)
- It is a small school (4)
- Parent/teacher communication (3)
- Teachers are a resource for parents having trouble with kids (3)
- The use of computer technology (3)
- Strong discipline (3)
- Music (2)
- Library resources (2)

### 2. What needs to be strengthened at your child's school?

- A better system of discipline/punishment (16)
- Computer access/more software/exposure (6)
- Increased parent/community involvement (4)
- A more structured curriculum and more basic skill instruction (3)
- Continue stressing respect to those students that may not get the message at home (2)
- Supervision/supervisors during lunch (2)
- Better/more playground supervision (2)
- Better bus drivers (2)
- Communication from the school (2)
- The administration needs to communicate better with teachers

### 3. What would make the school better?

- Improve discipline (7)
- Smaller class size (7)
- Address maintenance/facility issues (7)
- Use positive reinforcement in the classroom (3)
- More qualified bus drivers (3)
- Air conditioning (3)
- More homework (3)
- Longer lunch and recess periods (3)
- Better meal plans/food (3)
- More support for teachers in dealing with disruptive students (2)
- Students who are advanced should get the same attention as those who are behind (2)

## Study Questions for *How Do We Do Business?*

As you review Little River's perceptual data, use either the margins in the text, this page, or print this page from the CD to write down your early thinking. These notes, of course, are only hunches or placeholders until all the data are analyzed.

| 1. What are the perceptual *strengths* and *challenges* for Little River? | |
|---|---|
| Strengths | Challenges |
| | |

**2. What are some *implications* for the Little River school improvement plan?**

**3. Looking at the data presented, what other perceptual data would you want to answer the question *How do we do business?* for Little River Elementary School?**

## What I Saw in Example One:
## Little River Elementary School

Using the study questions as an outline, what I saw in the data for Chapter 5 appears below. When applicable, I have referenced the figure that gave me my first impression of strengths and challenges.

| What are their perceptual strengths? | What are their perceptual challenges? |
|---|---|
| *Student Questionnaires* | *Student Questionnaires* |
| ◆ The school surveyed students three years in a row. (Page 71) | ◆ Little River did not seem to get all the students in grades three through five over the three years to answer the questionnaires. (Figure 5.1) |
| ◆ All student responses were in agreement or strong agreement all three years. (Figure 5.1) | ◆ Students in grades three through five represent one-half of the school. Perhaps, perceptions of kindergarten through grade two could be gathered as well. (Figure 5.1) |
| ◆ Students were in strong agreement with most items all three years—strongest in 2001, followed by 2003, and then 2002. (Figure 5.1) | ◆ Students were in strongest agreement with the items in 2001 and have not regained that level of agreement. (Figure 5.1) |
| ◆ While averages dropped across the board in the second year, they increased in year three (although the fluctuations of the total number of respondents must be taken into consideration. (Figure 5.1) | ◆ Fifth-grade students' responses varied the most from the other grade levels, with respect to the item, *Students are treated fairly by teachers* and *My teacher listens to my ideas.* (Figure 5.2) |
| ◆ Students were passionate about their families wanting them to do well in school, believing they can do well in school, and supporting their learning at home. (Figure 5.1) | ◆ Students who identified themselves as American Indians disagreed with two items: *Students at my school treat me with respect* and *Students at my school are friendly.* (Figure 5.3) (There might be a problem with the way students identified themselves since the demographic data do not show there are 21 American Indian students at the school.) |
| ◆ Students strongly agreed each year that their teacher believes they can learn. (Figure 5.1) | |
| ◆ There were no differences in responses by genders. (Page 72) | ◆ Students often commented in the open-ended responses about other students needing to be nicer and to behave better. (Page 78) |
| ◆ There were few differences in responses by grade level. Fifth grade was the lowest in 2002-03, which one would expect. (Most student questionnaire results show that the older the students get, the less agreement they show with the learning organization questions.) (Figure 5.2) | ◆ Students would like to have more say in some matters (especially choices in what they learn. (Figures 5.2 and 5.3, and page 78) |
| ◆ Asian students seem to be very happy with this school. (Pages 76 and 77) | |
| ◆ All but two items for one ethnicity were in agreement with the items on the questionnaire. (Figure 5.3) | |
| ◆ Open-ended responses showed that students like the teachers most of all, both years. (Page 78) | |

## What I Saw in Example One:
## Little River Elementary School (Continued)

| What are their perceptual strengths? | What are their perceptual challenges? |
|---|---|
| *Staff Questionnaires* | *Staff Questionnaires* |
| ◆ Teachers appear to have gotten into teaching for the right reasons. Their responses were in strong agreement with the items, *I love seeing the results of my work with students, I believe every student can learn,* and *I love to teach.* (Figures 5.5 and 5.6) <br><br> ◆ Teachers believe that student achievement can increase through close personal relationships between students and teachers, through providing a threat-free environment, and through the use of varied technologies. Teachers also believe that learning can be fun, that learning is fun in their classrooms, and that student outcomes are clear. (Figures 5.4, 5.5, and 5.6) <br><br> ◆ Over the three years, teachers improved their communication with each other to make student learning consistent across grade levels, according to teacher perceptions. (Figure 5.6) <br><br> ◆ In writing responses to the open-ended questions, staff indicated that the staff is the greatest strength of the school. (Page 84 and CD narrative) | ◆ Not all staff members' responses were gathered in 2002 and 2003. The inconsistency with numbers could cause misrepresentations. (Figures 5.4 and 5.5) <br><br> ◆ Staff perceives morale to be low for teachers, students, and administrators, and that the school does not have a good public image. (Figure 5.5) <br><br> ◆ Staff were neutral or disagreed with the statement, *Student achievement can increase through multi-age classrooms.* (Figure 5.5) <br><br> ◆ Staff probably need to go back and revisit the vision and action plan. (Figure 5.5) <br><br> ◆ Staff who have been teaching seven to ten years are in less agreement than other teachers to the question, *I work effectively with Special Education students.* (CD narrative) <br><br> ◆ In the open-ended questionnaire results, staff talked about discipline needing to be consistent. Student behavior issues are found throughout the comments. (Page 84 and CD narrative) <br><br> ◆ The principal might need some help with supporting a stronger discipline program and follow-through with the students and staff. (Page 84 and CD narrative) |
| *Parent Questionnaires* | *Parent Questionnaires* |
| ◆ Parent responses on the questionnaire were in agreement or strong agreement with all the items. (Figure 5.7) <br><br> ◆ Parents were in strongest agreement to feeling good about themselves as parents, supporting their child's learning at home, and feeling welcome at the school. (Figure 5.7) <br><br> ◆ Parents feel that they know what is expected of their children and that they are informed about progress. (Figure 5.7) <br><br> ◆ Parents respect the school's principal and teachers. (Figure 5.7) <br><br> ◆ Playground supervision during school appears to have improved over time. (Figure 5.7) <br><br> ◆ No real differences appeared between parents' responses for students of different grade levels, by ethnicity, or by number of children in the household. (CD narrative) <br><br> ◆ Parents think the teachers and principal are great. (Figure 5.7 and open-ended responses) | ◆ The relatively lower agreement with the items related to student behavior, student respect for other students, and open-ended responses indicate parent concern for discipline and supervision of the discipline issues. (Figure 5.7 and page 87) |

## What are some implications for their school improvement plan?

- When administering the questionnaires, the school needs to try to get more respondents. Student and staff are captive audiences; therefore, we should see 100% response rates from both groups. Parent questionnaires administered during parent-teacher conferences can yield a much higher response rate. Consistently administering the questionnaire will help with understanding perceptions data over time. There is a questionnaire (found on the CD) for very young students that would get them used to providing feedback to staff.
- Students were passionate each year about their families wanting them to do well in school, believing they can do well in school, and supporting their learning at home. This is leverage that the teachers must use.
- Students strongly agreed that their teacher believes they can learn, and that they like their teachers. Parents respect the principal and the teachers. These are leverage points for bringing up other averages.
- Is something going on in grade five that needs a look?
- Staff questionnaire results imply that the staff needs a strong dose of inspiration to get them going again. They appear to feel like a group of teachers who have been doing the right things for students over time but are not getting the results. It appears they need to be refreshed and to bring the new teachers with them. They need to use the leverage of getting into teaching for the right reasons to assist with this. They also need to review the results after conducting and analyzing questionnaires.
- Communication of teachers across grade levels needs to improve.
- Staff should consider ways to improve the climate and morale—perhaps social activities, celebration events, or staff meetings for "fun."
- Staff does not believe the school has a good public image. Possibly more interaction with the community would help.
- Staff should revisit the mission, vision, and plan for the school. This can be an inspirational process that will make all the difference for this staff.
- Staff and parents want more parent involvement. Staff needs to understand effective strategies to improve parent involvement by thinking *out of the box* and eliciting input from parents.
- Perhaps training for supervisors of the playground, the lunchroom, and before and after school is needed.
- I would want to know more about the discipline issues. When do they occur and with which students?
- Has the staff truly implemented the Behavior Modification Program? The program was described as a solution to the school's biggest issue, but was neither mentioned as a strength nor as a need for improvement by teachers in the questionnaire open-ended section. Students want a different discipline program. The issue of behavior seems even bigger in the most current year than in previous years. In other words, it is not getting better.
- Something has to be done about the discipline issue. Perhaps staff can develop, by consensus, a schoolwide discipline plan with total staff engagement.
- The principal might need some help with a stronger discipline program and follow-through with the students.
- Little River staff needs to schedule time to assess on the *Continuous Improvement Continuums* and determine next steps, preferably twice a year.
- Maybe EL training would help teachers so English Learners do not have to be sent to other schools.

## Other desired data or information

Little River Elementary School had three years of questionnaire data displaying its annual progress. A recommendation for other data that would be helpful in understanding how Little River does business would be to keep assessing over time on the questionnaires and to use the *Education for the Future Continuous Improvement Continuums* every six months to see and inspire progress. A review of the results will ensure that progress can be made.

Little River might need to follow-up on the fifth-grade students to understand if there are relationship issues between students and teachers.

## Summary

The second question, *How do we do business?*, tells us about perceptions of the learning environment from student, staff, and parent perspectives. Multiple-choice questionnaires can give us a quick snapshot of different groups' perspectives. Open-ended responses, used with the multiple choice responses, help paint the picture of the school. Understanding how we do business can help a school know what is possible, what is appropriate, and what is needed in the continuous school improvement plan.

The *Education for the Future Continuous Improvement Continuums* are also a valuable assessment tool for understanding the system. A *Continuum* assessment is shown in the Blue Bird Elementary School, Example Two, narrative in Chapter 9, and is further explained on the CD.

## On the CD Related to this Chapter

▼ *Continuous Improvement Continuums* Graphic (CICs.pdf)
This read-only file contains the seven *School Portfolio Continuous Improvement Continuums*. These can be printed as is or enlarged for posting individual staff opinions during staff assessments.

▼ *Continuous Improvement Continuums* for Districts (CICsDstrct.pdf)
This read-only file contains the seven *School Portfolio Continuous Improvement Continuums* for assessing the district level. These can be printed as is and enlarged for posting individual staff opinions during staff assessments.

▼ *Little River Elementary School Baseline CIC Results* (LRBase.pdf)
This read-only file is the summary of Little River's baseline assessment on the *School Portfolio Continuous Improvement Continuums*.

▼ *Continuous Improvement Continuum* Tools
These files are tools for assessing on the CICs and for writing the CIC report.

♦ *Continuous Improvement Continuums Self-Assessment Activity* (ACTCIC.pdf)
Assessing on the *Continuous Improvement Continuums* will help staffs see where their systems are right now with respect to continuous improvement and ultimately will show they are making progress over time. The discussion has major implications for the *Continuous School Improvement (CSI) Plan*.

♦ *Coming to Consensus* (Consenss.pdf)
This read-only file provides strategies for coming to consensus.

◆ *Continuous Improvement Continuums Report Example* (ExReprt1.pdf)

This read-only file shows a real school's assessment on the *School Portfolio Continuous Improvement Continuums,* as an example.

◆ *Continuous Improvement Continuums Report Example for Follow-up Years* (ExReprt2.pdf)

This read-only file shows a real school's assessment on the *School Portfolio Continuous Improvement Continuums* over time, as an example.

◆ *Continuous Improvement Continuums Baseline Report Template* (ReptTemp.doc)

This *Microsoft Word* file provides a template for writing your school's report of its assessment on the *School Portfolio Continuous Improvement Continuums.*

◆ *Continuous Improvement Continuums Graphing Templates* (CICGraph.xls)

This *Microsoft Excel* file is a template for graphing your assessments on the seven *School Portfolio Continuous Improvement Continuums.*

▼ Study Questions Related to *How Do we Do Business?* (Ch5Qs.pdf)

These study questions will help you better understand the information provided in Chapter 5. This file can be printed for use with staffs as you answer the question, *How do we do business?,* through analyzing Little River's perceptual data.

▼ *What I Saw in Example One* (Ch5Saw.pdf)

*What I Saw in Example One* is a file, organized by the perceptual study questions, that summarizes what I saw in the perceptual data provided by Little River Elementary School.

▼ *Analysis of Questionnaire Data Table* (QTable.doc)

This *Microsoft Word* file is a tabular guide for interpreting your student, staff, and parent questionnaires, independently and interdependently. It will help you see the summary of your results and write the narrative.

▼ Full Narratives of Questionnaire Results Used in Example One:
   ◆ *Little River Student Questionnaire Results* (StuNarr1.pdf)
   ◆ *Little River Staff Questionnaire Results* (StfNarr1.pdf)
   ◆ *Little River Parent Questionnaire Results* (ParNarr1.pdf)

▼ *Education for the Future* Perception Questionnaires Used in Example One:
   ◆ *Student Questionnaire* (LRStudnt.pdf)
   ◆ *Staff Questionnaire* (LRStaff.pdf)
   ◆ *Parent Questionnaire* (LRParent.pdf)

▼ *School IQ: School Improvement Questionnaire Solutions* is a powerful tool for analyzing *Education for the Future* questionnaires. *School IQ* reduces an otherwise technical and complicated process to one that can be navigated with pushbutton ease. There are different versions of *IQ* for each of the eleven standard *Education for the Future* questionnaires. *School IQ* includes online questionnaire templates, all eleven questionnaires in PDF format, the analysis tool, the *School IQ,* and graphing templates.

♦ Other Popular *Education for the Future* Questionnaires:
(Online templates and graphs are located with the *School IQ*)

　✳ *Student (Kindergarten to Grade 3) Questionnaire* (StQKto3.pdf)

　✳ *Student Questionnaire* (StQ1to6.pdf)

　✳ *Student (Grades 6 to 12) Questionnaire* (StQ6to12.pdf)

　✳ *Student (High School) Questionnaire* (StQHS.pdf)

　✳ *Staff Questionnaire* (StaffQ.pdf)

　✳ *Administrator Questionnaire* (Admin.pdf)

　✳ *Teacher Predictions of Student Responses (Grades 1 to 6) Questionnaire* (TchPr1.pdf)

　✳ *Teacher Predictions of Student Responses (Grades 6 to 8) Questionnaire* (TchPr2.pdf)

　✳ *Parent Questionnaire* (ParntK12.pdf)

　✳ *High School Parent Questionnaire* (ParntHS.pdf)

　✳ *Alumni Questionnaire* (Alumni.pdf)

▼ *How to Analyze Open-ended Responses* (OEanalz.pdf)
This read-only file discusses how to analyze responses to the open-ended questions on questionnaires.

▼ *Questions to Guide the Analysis of Perceptions Data* (PerceptQ.doc)
This *Microsoft Word* file is a tabular guide for interpreting your perceptions data. You can change the questions if you like or use the file to write in the responses. It will help you write the narrative for your results.

# Analyzing the Data:
## *Where Are We Now?*

*So, what are the results of current processes? Where are we now? How do we determine results?* Most often, the way schools determine their results is through student learning measures only. With this continuous school improvement planning process, we want to take into consideration much more than just student learning results. The results shown in Chapters 4 and 5 also need to be taken into consideration. As you explore student learning results, it is good to begin by learning where your school is with your state-required assessments.

*Why do we measure student learning?*
We measure student learning to know—

▼ if students have particular skills and knowledge

▼ if students have attained a level of proficiency/competence/mastery

▼ if instructional strategies are making a difference for all students

▼ the effectiveness of instructional strategies and curricula

▼ how to improve instructional strategies

▼ how to classify students into instructional groups

▼ that students are ready to graduate or proceed to the next level of instruction

▼ if school processes are making the intended progress

Unfortunately, student learning results are not always used in these ways. Most of the time it is because school personnel struggle with the way student learning is measured and the analyses to display the results. The purpose of this chapter is to show different ways of measuring, analyzing, and reporting student learning results.

We start with discussions of different ways to measure student learning in elementary schools, then example one, Little River Elementary School is shown, followed by Blue Bird Elementary School, as example two, in Chapter 9. Please note the study questions on page 129 to assist in interpreting the data. Also note that there is space in the margins on the data pages to write your impressions as you review the data. At the end of the chapter, I have shared what I saw in the data.

## How Can Elementary Schools Measure Student Learning?

Elementary schools use a variety of means to assess student learning. Most schools are members of districts and states that use standardized tests across or at some grade levels. Other common means of assessing student learning are more classroom-based, such as performance assessments, portfolio assessments, teacher-given grades, and teacher observations. Different means of assessing student learning are defined below, followed by the analyses of the example school, Little River, created with its criterion-referenced state assessment.

### Standardized Tests

Standardized tests are assessments that have uniformity in content, administration, and scoring. They can be used for comparing results across students, classrooms, schools, school districts, and states. Norm-referenced, criterion-referenced, and diagnostic tests are the most commonly used standardized tests. Arguments *for* and *against* standardized testing appear in Figure 6.1.

Figure 6.1

## Arguments For and Against Standardized Testing

### Arguments For Standardized Testing

- Standardized testing can be designed to measure performance, thinking, problem solving, and communication skills.
- The process students use to solve a problem can be tested, rather than just the result.
- Standardized tests can be developed to match state standards.
- Standardized tests can help drive the curriculum standards that are supposed to be taught.
- Ways need to be developed to determine if students have the skills to succeed in society; standardized tests can ensure all students, across a country or state, have essential skills.
- Employers and the public need to know if students are able to apply skills and knowledge to everyday life; standardized testing can help with that assurance.
- Standardized testing may be helping to raise the bar of expectations for students in public schools—especially the lowest performing schools.
- Many schools, districts, and states have seen achievement levels rise in recent years which they attribute to higher expectations of students because of tests.
- Standardized tests provide data that show which skills students are lacking, giving educators the information necessary to tailor classes and instructional strategies to student needs.
- Standardized tests can tell how the school or student is doing in comparison to a norming group, which is supposed to represent the typical students in the country.
- With most standardized tests, one can follow the same students over time.

### Arguments Against Standardized Testing

- Standardized testing often narrows student learning to what is tested; what is tested is usually only a sample of what students should know.
- Standardized tests typically focus on what is easy to measure, not the critical thinking skills students need to develop.
- Standardized tests do not always match the state standards.
- To make standardized tests align to the state standards requires expertise and can be costly.
- The quality of standardized tests is a concern.
- Standardized tests are better at measuring rote learning than evaluating thinking skills.
- Too much instructional time is used to prepare students for multiple-choice tests, to the detriment of other uses of instructional time.
- Standardized tests could be culturally biased, drawing primarily upon the experiences of one socio-economic group.
- Decisions are sometimes made about a student's promotion from grade to grade or graduation based solely on one multiple-choice test.
- It is not fair to hold students accountable on one test when the schools might not be providing students with quality teachers, curricula, and time to master concepts.
- Students are not always provided with time to master what is expected on the standardized tests.
- There is a concern with standardized tests over getting the right answers.
- Standardized tests sometimes measure only what students know, not what they understand.
- Standardized testing is expensive.
- Testing is costly in teaching time and student time.

## Norm-referenced Tests

Norm-referenced tests are also standardized tests. Norm-referenced test scores create meaning through comparing the test performance of a school, group, or individual with the performance of a norming group. A norming group is a representative group of students whose results on a norm-referenced test help create the scoring scales with which others compare their performance. Norming groups' results are professed to look like the normal curve, shown in Figure 6.2 below.

### Figure 6.2

### The Normal Curve and Scores

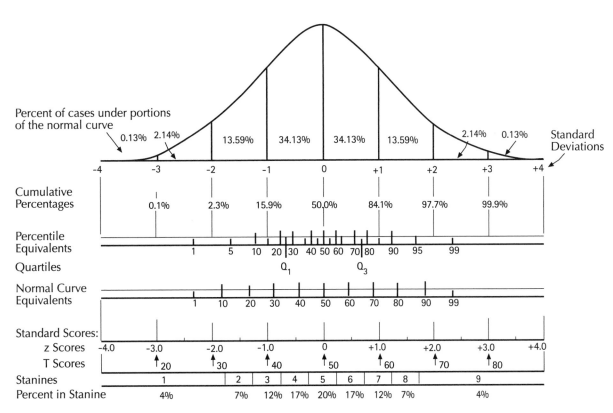

*The national percentile rank is one of the most used scales; it is also misused the most.*

*Normal curve equivalent scores are excellent for looking at scores over time.*

The normal curve is a distribution of scores or other measures that in graphic form has a distinctive bell-shaped appearance. In a normal distribution, the measures are distributed symmetrically about the mean, or average score. Most results are near the mean and decrease in frequency the farther one departs from the mean. Stated another way—the theory of the normal curve basically says that when test publishers give a test to a representative sample of students, most students score around the mean with very few students scoring very high or very low. Using this theory, test publishers are able to create scales that are useful for schools to compare their scores with the norming group.

*National Percentile Ranks.* The two most commonly used and useful normed scales, or score types, are national percentile ranks and normal curve equivalents. The national percentile rank (NPR), also known as the national percentile equivalent, ranges from 1 to 99, with a midscore of 50. The NPR is one of the most used scales; it is also misused the most. The misuse of this scale stems from the fact that it is an unequal interval scale, which *prohibits* adding, subtracting, multiplying, and dividing the scores. *One should not look at gains, losses, or averages with percentile ranks.* Median scores, or the middle scores, are the most appropriate means of describing a whole school's typical performance.

*Normal Curve Equivalent Scores.* Normal curve equivalent (NCE) scores were created by test developers to alleviate the problem of unequal interval scales. This equal interval scale has a mean of 50, and range of 1 to 99, just like the NPR. A standard deviation of 21.06 forces the intervals to be equal, spreading the scores away from the mean. NCEs have the same meaning across students, subtests, grade levels, classrooms, schools, and school districts. Fifty (50) is what one would expect for an average year's growth. You can look at how close your scores are to expected performance, averages, gains, losses, highest, and lowest scores. NCEs are excellent for looking at scores over time.

*Grade-level Equivalent Scores.* Another score type used with norm-referenced tests is grade-level equivalent. Grade-level equivalent scores result in an interesting scale that shows the grade and month of the school year for which a given score is the actual or estimated average. Its meaning is that the student obtained the same score that one would expect average $x^{th}$ grade students in their x<sup>th</sup> month to score if they took the $x^{th}$ grade test. Based on a ten-month school year, scores would be noted as 3.1 for third grade, first month, or 5.10 for fifth grade, tenth month. For example, if a third grader scored a 5.8 on a subtest, that does not mean that she/he should be doing fifth grade, eighth-month work. It only means that the student obtained the same score that one would expect average fifth grade students to score if they took the same third-grade test during the eighth month of grade five. Grade-level equivalent scores are okay for a snapshot in time, but they should not be averaged or taken literally.

*Standard Scores.* Standard scores, or scaled scores, refer to scores that have been *transformed* for reasons of convenience, comparability, and ease of interpretation. Ranges vary depending upon the test, and sometimes even the subtest. The best uses of standard scores are averages calculated over time allowing for the study of change. These scores are good to use for calculations because of their equal intervals and their easy conversions to other score types. The downsides are that, with the various ranges, it is difficult to look across subtests, grade levels, and years. It is often hard for the layperson to create meaning from these scores. The normal curve is needed to interpret the results with respect to other scores and people.

*Anticipated Achievement/Cognitive Abilities Scores.* Occasionally, norm-referenced tests provide indicators of ability, such as anticipated achievement scores, cognitive abilities, or cognitive skills indexes. The anticipated achievement score is an estimate of the average score for students of a similar age, grade, and academic aptitude. It can be computed in grade-level equivalents, normal curve equivalents, standard scores, and national percentiles. The higher the student scores on sequences, analogies, memory, and verbal reasoning tests, the higher the student is expected to score on standardized tests.

A cognitive abilities or cognitive skills index is also created from the same four tests mentioned above, and assesses the student's academic aptitude. The range of this scale is 58 to 141, with a mean of 100. Two-thirds of the scores will fall between 84 and 118. Anticipated Achievement/Cognitive Abilities scores can tell teachers if they are teaching to students' potential.

> *Grade-level equivalent scores are okay for a snapshot in time, but they should not be averaged or taken literally.*

> *The best uses of standard scores are averages calculated over time allowing for the study of change.*

> *Anticipated Achievement/ Cognitive Abilities scores can tell teachers if they are teaching to the students' potential.*

> *Criterion-referenced assessments tell us how well students are performing on specific criteria, goals, or standards.*

> *Diagnostic tests can help teachers know the nature of students' difficulties, but not the cause of the difficulty.*

### Criterion-referenced Tests

Criterion-referenced tests compare an individual's performance to a specific learning objective or performance standard and not to the performance of other test takers. Criterion-referenced assessments tell us how well students are performing on specific criteria, goals, or standards. For school level analyses, criterion-referenced tests are usually scored in terms of the number or percentage of students meeting the standard or criterion, or the number or percentage of students falling in typical descriptive categories, such as *far below basic, below basic, basic, proficient,* and *advanced.* Criterion-referenced tests can be standardized or not, and they can also have norming groups.

### Diagnostic Tests

Diagnostic tests, usually standardized and normed, are given before instruction begins to help the instructor(s) understand student learning needs. Diagnostic tests can help teachers know the nature of students' difficulties, but not the cause of the difficulty. Many different score types are used with diagnostic tests.

These tests, score types, and other frequently used terms are defined in Figure 6.3, along with a description of most effective uses and cautions for use.

Figure 6.3

## Standardized Test Score Terms,
## Their Most Effective Uses, and Cautions for Their Uses

| Score | Definition | Most Effective Uses | Cautions |
|---|---|---|---|
| *Anticipated Achievement Scores* | A student's anticipated achievement score is an estimate of the average score for students of similar ages, grade levels, and academic aptitude. It is an estimate of what we would expect the student to score on an achievement test. | Anticipated achievement scores can be used to see if a student is scoring "above" or "below" an expected score, indicating whether or not she/he is being challenged enough, or if her/his needs are being met. | It is easy to think of these scores as "IQ" scores. They are just achievement indicators on a standardized test. |
| *Cognitive Abilities or Skills Index* | The cognitive skills index is an age-dependent normalized standard score based on a student's performance on a cognitive skills test with a mean of 100 and standard deviation of 16. The score indicates a student's overall cognitive ability or academic aptitude relative to students of similar age, without regard to grade level. | Cognitive skills index scores can be used to see if a student is scoring "above" or "below" an expected score, indicating whether or not she/he is being challenged enough, or if her/his needs are being met. | It is easy to think of these scores as "IQ" scores. They are just achievement indicators on a standardized test. |
| *Criterion-referenced Tests* | Tests that judge how well a test-taker does on an explicit objective relative to a predetermined performance level. There is no comparison to any other test-takers. | Tell us how well students are performing on specific criteria, goals, or standards. | CRTs test only what was taught, or planned to be taught. CRTs can not give a broad estimate of knowledge. |
| *Deciles* | Deciles divide a distribution into ten equal parts: 1–10; 11–20; 21–30; 31–40; 41–50; 51–60; 61–70; 71–80; 81–90; 91–99. Just about any scale can be used to show deciles. | Deciles allow schools to show how all students scored throughout the distribution. One would expect a school's distribution to resemble a normal curve.<br><br>Watching the distribution move to the right, over time, could imply that all students in the distribution are making progress. | One must dig deeper to understand if all students and all groups of students are moving forward. |
| *Diagnostic Tests* | Diagnostic tests, usually standardized and normed, are given before instruction begins to help the instructor(s) understand student learning needs. Many different score types are used with diagnostic tests. | Help teachers know the nature of students' difficulties, but not the cause of the difficulty. | Make sure the diagnostic test is measuring what you want it to measure and that it can be compared to formative and summative assessments used. |

Figure 6.3 (Continued)

## Standardized Test Score Terms,
## Their Most Effective Uses, and Cautions for Their Uses

| Score | Definition | Most Effective Uses | Cautions |
|---|---|---|---|
| **Grade-level Equivalents** | Grade-level equivalents indicate the grade and month of the school year for which a given score is the actual or estimated average. Based on a ten-month school year, scores would be noted as 3.1 for third grade, first month, or 5.10 for fifth grade, tenth month. | Grade-level equivalents are most effectively used as a snapshot in time. Scores are comparable across subtests. | These scores should not be taken literally. If a third grader scored a 5.8 on a subtest, that does not mean that she/he should be doing fifth grade, eighth-month work. It only means that the student obtained the same score that one would expect average fifth-grade students in their eighth month of school to score if they took the third-grade test. |
| **Latent-trait Scale** | A latent-trait scale is a scaled score obtained through one of several mathematical approaches collectively known as Latent-Trait Procedures or Item Response Theory. The particular numerical values used in the scale are arbitrary, but higher scores indicate more knowledgeable students or more difficult items. | Latent-trait scales have equal intervals allowing comparisons over time. | These are scores set up by testing professionals. Lay people typically have difficulty understanding their meaning. |
| **NCE (National or Local)** | Normal Curve Equivalent (NCE) scores are standard scores with a mean of 50, a standard deviation of 21.06, and a range of 1 to 99. The term National would indicate that the norming group was national; local usually implies a state or district norming group. | NCEs have equal intervals so they can be used to study gains over time. The scores have the same meaning across subtests, grade levels, and years. A 50 is what one would expect in an average year's growth. | This score, just like all scores related to norm-referenced tests, cannot be taken literally. The score simply shows relative performance of a student group or of students to a norming group. |
| **Percent Passing** | Percent passing is a calculated score implying the percentage of the student group meeting and exceeding some number, usually a cut score, proficiency/mastery level, or a standard. | With standards-based accountability, it is beneficial to know the percentage of the population meeting and exceeding a standard and to compare a year's percentages with the previous year(s) to understand progress being made. | This is a very simple statistic, and its interpretation should be simple as well. Total numbers ($n=$) of students included in the percentage must always be noted with the percentage to assist with the understanding. |

Figure 6.3 (Continued)

## Standardized Test Score Terms,
## Their Most Effective Uses, and Cautions for Their Uses

| Score | Definition | Most Effective Uses | Cautions |
|---|---|---|---|
| *Percentile / Percentile Rank (PR) (National or Local)* | Percentile ranks indicate the percentage of students in a norm group (e.g., national or local) whose scores fall below a given score. The range is from 1 to 99. 50th percentile ranking would mean that 50 percent of the scores in the norming group fall below a specific score.<br><br>The term National would indicate that the norming group was national; local usually implies a state or district norming group. | One-year comparison to the norming group. Schools can see the relative standing of a student or group in the same grade to the norm group who took the test at a comparable time. | Percentile rank is not a score to use over time to look for gains because of unequal intervals, unless the calculations are made with equal interval scores and then converted to percentile ranks.<br><br>One cannot calculate averages using NPR because of the unequal intervals. Medians are the most appropriate statistic to use. |
| *Quartiles* | There are three quartiles—Q1, Q2, Q3 — that divide a distribution into four equal groups:<br>Q1=25th percentile<br>Q2=50th percentile (Median)<br>Q3=75th percentile | Quartiles allow schools to see the distribution of scores for any grade level, for instance. Over time, schools trying to increase student achievement would want to monitor the distribution to ensure that all students are making progress. | With quartiles, one cannot tell if the scores are at the top of a quartile or the bottom. There could be "real" changes taking place within a quartile that would not be evident. |
| *Raw Scores* | Raw scores are the number of questions answered correctly on a test or subtest.<br>A raw score is simply calculated by adding the number of questions answered correctly. The raw score is a person's observed score. | The raw score provides information about the number of questions answered correctly. To get a perspective on performance, raw scores must be used with the average score for the group and/or the total number of questions. Alone, it has no meaning. | Raw scores do not provide information related to other students taking the test or to other subtests. One needs to keep perspective by knowing the total number possible.<br><br>Raw scores should never be used to make comparisons between performances on different tests unless other information about the characteristics of the tests are known and identical. |
| *RIT Scale Scores* | RIT scores, named for George Rasch who developed the theory of this type of measurement, are scaled scores that come from a series of tests created by the Northwest Evaluation Association (NWEA). The tests, which draw from an item bank, are aligned with local curriculum and state/local standards. | RIT scores provide ongoing measurement of curriculum standards and a way for students to see progress in their knowledge. The scores can also be shown as percentiles to know performance related to other students of similar ages and/or grades. You will most probably see gains each time a measurement is taken with a group of students. | RIT scores are great as long as the test was carefully designed to measure standards. |

**Figure 6.3** (Continued)

**Standardized Test Score Terms,
Their Most Effective Uses, and Cautions for Their Uses**

| Score | Definition | Most Effective Uses | Cautions |
|---|---|---|---|
| **Scaled Scores** | A scaled score is a mathematical transformation of a raw score. | The best uses of scaled scores are averages and averages calculated over time allowing for the study of change. These scores are good to use for calculations because of equal intervals. The scores can be applied across subtests on most tests. Scaled scores facilitate conversions to other score types. | Ranges vary, depending upon the test. Watch for the minimum and maximum values. It is sometimes hard for laypeople to create meaning from these scores. The normal curve is needed to interpret the results with respect to other scores and people. |
| **Standard Scores** | Standard score is a general term referring to scores that have been "transformed" for reasons of convenience, comparability, ease of interpretation, etc. z-scores and T-scores are standard scores. | The best uses of standard scores are averages and averages calculated over time, allowing for the study of change. These scores are good to use for calculations because of equal intervals. The scores can be applied across subtests on most tests. Scaled scores facilitate conversions to other score types. | Ranges vary, depending upon the test. Watch for the minimum and maximum values. It is sometimes hard for laypeople to create meaning from these scores. The normal curve is needed to interpret results with respect to other scores and people. |
| **Standards-based Assessments** | Standards-based assessments measure students' progress toward mastering local, state, and/or national content standards. | The way standards-based assessments are analyzed depends upon the scales used. The most effective uses are in revealing the percentage of students achieving a standard. | One has to adhere to the cautions of whatever test or score type used. It is important to know how far from mastering the standard the students were when they did not meet the standard. |
| **Stanines** | Stanines are a nine-point standard score scale. Stanines divide the normal curve into nine equal points: 1 to 9. | Stanines, like quartiles, allow schools to see the distribution of scores for any grade level, for instance. Over time, schools trying to increase student achievement would want to monitor the distribution to ensure that all student scores are improving. | Often, the first three stanines are interpreted as "below average," the next three as "average," and the top three as "above average." This can be misleading. As with quartiles, one cannot tell if the scores are at the top of a stanine or the bottom. There could be "real" changes taking place within a stanine that would not be evident. |

Figure 6.3 (Continued)

**Standardized Test Score Terms,
Their Most Effective Uses, and Cautions for Their Uses**

| Score | Definition | Most Effective Uses | Cautions |
|---|---|---|---|
| *T-scores* | A T-score is a standard score with a mean of 50 and a standard deviation of 10. T-scores are obtained by the following formula:<br>$T = 10z + 50$ | The most effective uses of T-scores are averages and averages calculated over time.<br>T-scores are good to use for calculations because of their equal intervals.<br>T-scores can be applied across subtests on most tests because of the forced mean and standard deviation. | T-scores are rarely used because of the lack of understanding on the part of most test users. |
| *z-scores* | A z-score is a standard score with a mean of zero and a standard deviation of one. z-scores are obtained by the following formula:<br>"z = raw score (x):− mean standard deviation (sd)" | z-scores can tell one how many standard deviations a score is away from the mean.<br>z-scores are most useful, perhaps, as the first step in computing other types of standard scores. | z-scores are rarely used by the lay public because of the difficulty in understanding the score. |

## Performance Assessments

The term *performance assessment* refers to assessments that measure skills, knowledge, and ability directly—such as through *performance*. In other words, if you want students to learn to write, you assess their ability on a writing activity. One must find a way to score these results and make sense for individual students and groups of students. Some of the arguments for and against performance assessments are listed in Figure 6.4. (See *References* for sources.)

## Figure 6.4

## Arguments For and Against Performance Assessments

| **Arguments For Performance Assessments** |
|---|

- Performance assessments can be designed to measure performance, thinking, problem solving, and communication skills.
- Performance assessments can be used to measure the process students use to solve problems.
- Performance assessments can be developed to match state standards.
- Many schools, districts, and states have seen achievement levels rise in recent years, which they attribute to higher expectations of students and what they can do, attributed to the use of performance assessments.
- Performance assessments provide data that show what students are lacking, giving educators the information necessary to tailor classes and instructional strategies to student needs.
- Students can learn during a performance task.
- Some teachers believe that when students participate in developing a rubric for evaluating their performance, they come to appreciate high-quality work.
- Performance assessments provide opportunities for students to reflect on their own work.
- Performance assessments can allow students to work until standards are met—to ensure quality work from all students.
- Performance assessments can help the teacher improve instructional strategies.
- Performance assessments allow students to perform in the learning style that suits them best.

| **Arguments Against Performance Assessments** |
|---|

- Designing good performance assessments that accurately measure performance, thinking, problem solving, and communication skills is difficult.
- Some performance tasks require long periods of time to complete, such as graduation or end-of-course exhibitions.
- To be effective, skills and performances being assessed should be taught in the same way they are measured.
- The quality of performance assessments is a concern.
- It is not fair to hold students accountable on one test when the schools might not be providing students with quality teachers, curricula, and time to master concepts.
- Scoring criteria requires analyzing performance into its components, such as breaking out the craft of writing into developmental elements.
- Many scoring criteria are no different from giving grades or norm-referenced scoring.
- Good scoring criteria could take a long time to develop.
- It is very difficult to design performance assessments that can be compared across grade levels in other than descriptive terms.

## Grades

Teachers use number or letter grades to judge the quality of a student's performance on a task, unit, or during a period of time. Grades are most often given as A, B, C, D, F, with pluses and minuses given by some teachers for the first four to distinguish among students. Grades mean different things to different teachers. Needless to say, grades can be subjective. "It appears that teachers consider grading to be a private activity, thus 'guarding practices with the same passion with which one might guard an unedited diary' (Kain, 1996, p. 569)" (O'Connor, 2000, p. 11). Some of the arguments for and against teacher grading are shown in Figure 6.5.

CD-ROM

Figure 6.5

## Arguments For and Against Teacher Grading

---

**Arguments For Teacher Grading**

- Grades can be designed to reflect performance, thinking, problem solving, and communication skills.
- Teachers can grade the process students use to solve a problem, rather than just the result.
- Grades can communicate to students, parents, and administrators the student's level of performance.
- Grading can allow teachers to be very flexible in their approaches to assessing student performance.
- Grades can match teaching.
- Grades can be given for team work and not just individual work.
- Grades can be effective if students are aware of expectations.
- Grades can cover multiple standards.
- Certain teacher-developed tests can be graded quickly.
- Most people believe they know what grades mean.

**Arguments Against Teacher Grading**

- It is difficult to convert activities, such as performance, thinking, and problem solving, into numbers or letters and have them hold true for all students in a class.
- Grading can be very subjective.
- Grading can be distorted by effort, extra credit, attendance, behavior, etc.
- To be beneficial, students must trust the grader and the grading process, have time to practice and complete an assessment, and have choices in how they are assessed—all of which make it time-consuming for teachers to do this type of assessment well.
- To be beneficial, grading assessments must be meaningful and promote learning.
- Grades must include a variety of assessment techniques to get to all areas of student understanding and performance.
- Often parents, students, and teachers focus on grades and not on learning.
- Grading is not reflective of instructional strategies.
- Grades are not always motivators; in fact, they can demoralize students on the low end, and on the high end.
- Grades tell little about student strengths and areas for improvement.
- Grading can mean many different things within a grade level, across grade levels by teacher, subject area, and school.
- Some teachers' highest priorities with grading are to use techniques where the grades can be calculated quickly.
- Grading is not always compatible with all instructional strategies.
- Grades often are given for more than achievement.
- Grading is not essential for learning.

## Analyzing the Results, Descriptively

Descriptive statistics (i.e., mean, median, percent correct) can give schools very powerful information. It is imperative that the appropriate analyses be used for the specific score type. Figure 6.6 summarizes terms of analyses, their definitions, their most effective uses, and cautions for their uses in analyzing student achievement scores descriptively. Descriptive statistics are used in the examples in this chapter largely because they can show a school how its students are doing, and because anyone can do the calculations.

Descriptive statistics summarize the basic characteristics of a particular distribution, without making any inferences about population parameters. Graphing the information can also be considered descriptive.

## Figure 6.6

### Terms Related to Analyzing Student Achievement Results, Descriptively, Their Most Effective Uses, and Cautions for Their Uses

| Term | Definition | Most Effective Uses | Cautions |
|------|-----------|---------------------|----------|
| *Disaggregate* | Disaggregation is breaking a total score into groups for purposes of seeing how subgroups performed. One disaggregates data to make sure all subgroups of students are learning. | Disaggregating student achievement scores by gender, ethnicity, backgrounds, etc., can show how different subgroups performed. | Disaggregations are for helping schools understand how to meet the needs of all students, not to say, "This group always does worse than the other group and always will." We must exercise caution in reporting disaggregations with small Ns. |
| *Gain* | Gain scores are the change or difference between two administrations of the same test. Gain scores are calculated by subtracting the previous score from the most recent score. One can have negative gains, which are actually losses. | One calculates gains to understand improvements in learning for groups of students and for individual students. | Gain scores should not be calculated using unequal interval scores, such as percentiles. The quality of gain score results is dependent upon the quality of the assessment instrument; the less reliable the assessment tool, the less meaningful the results. One needs to make sure the comparisons are appropriate, e.g., same groups of students over time. |
| *Maximum* | A maximum is the highest score achieved, or the highest possible score on a test. | Maximum possible scores and highest received scores are important for understanding the relative performance of any group or individual, especially when using scaled or standard scores. | A maximum can tell either the highest score possible or the highest score received by a test-taker. One needs to understand which maximum is being used in the analysis. It is best to use both. |
| *Mean* | A mean is the average score in a set of scores. One calculates the mean, or average, by summing all the scores and dividing by the total number of scores. | A mean can be calculated to provide an overall average for the group, and/or student, taking a specific test. One can use any equal interval score to get a mean. | Means should not be used with unequal interval scores, such as percentile ranks. Means are more sensitive to extreme results when the size of the group is small. |
| *Median* | A median is the score that splits a distribution in half: 50 percent of the scores fall above and 50 percent of the scores fall below the median. If the number of scores is odd, the median is the middle score. If the number of scores is even, one must add the two middle scores and divide by two to calculate the median. | Medians are the way to get a midpoint for scores with unequal intervals, such as percentile ranks. The median splits all scores into two equal parts. Medians are not sensitive to outliers, like means are. | Medians are relative. Medians are most effectively interpreted when reported with the possible and actual maximum and minimum. |
| *Minimum* | A minimum is the lowest score achieved, or the lowest possible score on the test. | Minimum possible scores and lowest received scores are important for understanding the relative performance of any group or individual. | A minimum tells either the lowest score possible or the lowest score received by a test-taker. One needs to understand which minimum is being used. It is best to use both. |

Figure 6.6 (Continued)

## Terms Related to Analyzing Student Achievement Results, Descriptively, Their Most Effective Uses, and Cautions for Their Uses

| Term | Definition | Most Effective Uses | Cautions |
|---|---|---|---|
| *Mode* | The mode is the score that occurs most frequently in a scoring distribution. | The mode basically tells which score or scores appear most often. | There may be more than one mode. The mode ignores other scores. |
| *Percent Correct* | Percent correct is a calculated score implying the percentage of students meeting and exceeding some number, usually a cut score, or a standard. | This calculated score can quickly tell educators how well the students are doing with respect to a specific set of items. It can also tell educators how many students need additional work to become proficient. | Percent correct is a calculated statistic, based on the number of items given. |
| *Percent Proficient* *Percent Passing* *Percent Mastery* | Percent proficient, passing, or mastery represent the percentage of students who passed a particular test at a "proficient," "passing," or "mastery" level, as defined by the test creators or the test interpreters. | With standards-based accountability, it is beneficial to know the percentage of the population meeting and exceeding the standard and to compare a year's percentage with the previous year(s) to understand progress being made. | This is a very simple statistic, and its interpretation should be simple as well. Total numbers (N=) of students included in the percentage must always be noted with the percentage to assist in understanding the results. Ninety percent passing means something very different for 10 or 100 test-takers. |
| *Range* | Range is a measure of the spread between the lowest and the highest scores in a distribution. Calculate the range of scores by subtracting the lowest score from the highest score. Range is often described as end points also, such as the range of percentile ranks is 1 and 99. | Ranges tell us the width of the distribution of scores. Educators working on continuous improvement will want to watch the range, of actual scores, decrease over time. | If there are no outliers present, the range can give a misleading impression of dispersion. |
| *Raw Scores* | Raw scores refer to the number of questions answered correctly on a test or subtest. A raw score is simply calculated by adding the number of questions answered correctly. The raw score is a person's observed score. | The raw score provides information only about the number of questions answered correctly. To get a perspective on performance, raw scores must be used with the average score for the group and the total number of questions. Alone, raw scores have little meaning. | Raw scores do not provide information related to other students taking the test or to other subtests or scores. One needs to keep perspective by knowing the total number possible. Raw scores should never be used to make comparisons between performances on different tests unless other information about the characteristics of the tests are known and identical. |

Figure 6.6 (Continued)

## Terms Related to Analyzing Student Achievement Results, Descriptively, Their Most Effective Uses, and Cautions for Their Uses

| Term | Definition | Most Effective Uses | Cautions |
|---|---|---|---|
| *Relationships* | Relationships refer to looking at two or more sets of analyses to understand what they mean to each other without using any statistical techniques. | Descriptive statistics lend themselves to looking at the relationships of different analyses to each other; for instance, student learning results disaggregated by ethnicity, compared to student questionnaire results disaggregated by ethnicity. | This type of analysis is general and the results should be considered general as well. This is not a "correlation." |
| *Rubric* | A rubric is a scoring tool that rates performance according to clearly stated levels of criteria. The scales can be numeric or descriptive, or both | Rubrics are used to give teachers, parents, and students an idea of where they started, where they want to be with respect to growth, and where they are right now. | Students need to know what the rubrics contain or, even better, help with the development of the rubrics. |
| *Standard Deviation* | The standard deviation is a measure of variability in a set of scores. The standard deviation indicates how far away scores are from the mean. The standard deviation is the square root of the variance. Unlike the variance, the standard deviation is stated in the original units of the variable. Approximately 68 percent of the scores in a normal distribution lie between plus one and minus one standard deviation of the mean. The more scores cluster around the mean, the smaller the variance. | Tells us about the variability of scores. Standard deviations indicate how spread-out the scores are without looking at the entire distribution. A low standard deviation would indicate that the scores of a group are close together. A high standard deviation would imply that the range of scores is wide. | Often this is a confusing statistic for laypeople to understand. There are more descriptive ways to describe and show the variability of student scores, such as with a decile graph. Standard deviations only make sense with scores that are distributed normally. |
| *Triangulation* | Triangulation is a term used for combining three or more measures to get a more complete picture of student achievement. | If students are to be retained based on standards proficiency, educators must have more than one way of knowing if the students are proficient or not. Some students perform well on standardized measures and not on other measures, while others do not do well with standardized measures. Triangulation allows students to display what they know on three different measures. | It is sometimes very complicated to combine different measures to understand proficiency. When proficiency standards change, triangulation calculations will need to be revised. Therefore, all the calculations must be documented so they can be recalculated when necessary. |

## Analyzing the Results, Inferentially

Many school administrators and teachers have taken statistics courses that taught them that it is important to have control groups, experimental designs, and to test for significant differences. These terms fall in the category of *inferential statistics*. Inferential statistics are concerned with measuring a sample from a population, and then making estimates, or inferences, about the population from which the sample was taken. Inferential statistics help generalize the results of data analysis, when one is not using the entire population in the analysis.

The main purpose of this book is to model analyses that school personnel can perform *without* the assistance of statisticians. Descriptive analyses provide helpful and useful information and can be understood by a majority of people. When using the entire school population in your analyses, there is no need to generalize to a larger population—you have the whole population. There is no need for inferential statistics.

Inferential statistical methods, such as analyses of variance, correlations, and regression analyses are complex and require someone who knows statistics to meet the conditions of the analyses. Since there are times when a statistician is available to perform inferential statistics, some of the terms the statistician might use with tests include those listed in Figure 6.7.

*A Note About "Scientifically-based Research."* With the passage of the *No Child Left Behind* (NCLB) *Act of 2001*, which reauthorized the *Elementary and Secondary Education Act of 1965*, school districts and schools are required to gather, analyze, and use data to ensure adequate yearly progress or continuous school improvement. While increased accountability is just one part of NCLB, all schools must gather data and overcome the barriers to analyzing and using the data.

The term *scientifically-based research* (Title IX, General Provisions, Part A, Section 9101, Definitions) means (A) research that involves the application of rigorous, systematic, and objective procedures to obtain reliable and valid knowledge relevant to education activities and programs; and (B) includes research that:

▼ employs systematic, empirical methods that draw on observation or experiment

▼ involves rigorous data analyses that are adequate to test the stated hypotheses and justify the general conclusions drawn

▼ relies on measurements or observational methods that provide reliable and valid data across evaluators and observers, across multiple measurements and observations, and across studies by the same or different investigators

▼ is evaluated using experimental or quasi-experimental designs in which individuals, entities, programs, or activities are assigned to different conditions and with appropriate controls to evaluate the effects of the condition of interest, with a preference for random-assignment experiments, or other designs to the extent that condition controls

▼ ensures that experimental studies are presented in sufficient detail and clarity to allow for replication or, at a minimum, offer the opportunity to build systematically on their findings

▼ has been accepted by a peer-reviewed journal or approved by a panel of independent experts through a comparably rigorous, objective and scientific review

While NCLB calls for scientific and experimental procedures, in reality, they are not always possible or ethical. Case studies are powerful designs as well.

Figure 6.7

## Terms Related to Analyzing Student Achievement Results, Inferentially, Their Most Effective Uses, and Cautions for Their Uses

| Term | Definition | Most Effective Uses | Cautions |
|---|---|---|---|
| *Analysis of Variance (ANOVA)* | Analysis of variance is a general term applied to the study of differences in the application of approaches, as opposed to the relationship of different levels of approaches to the result. With ANOVAs, we are testing the differences of the means of at least two different distributions. | ANOVAs can be used to determine if there is a difference in student achievement scores between one school and another, keeping all other variables equal. It cannot tell you what the differences are, per se, but one can compute confidence intervals to estimate these differences. | Very seldom are the conditions available to study differences in education in this manner. Too many complex variables get in the way, and ethics may be involved. There are well-defined procedures for conducting ANOVAs to which we must adhere. |
| *Correlation Analyses* | Correlation is a statistical analysis that helps one understand the relationship of scores in one distribution to scores in another distribution. Correlations show magnitude and direction. Magnitude indicates the degree of the relationship. Correlation coefficients have a range of -1.0 to +1.0. A correlation of around zero would indicate little relationship. Correlations of .8 and higher, or -.8 and lower would indicate a strong relationship. When the high scores in one distribution are also high in the comparing distribution, the direction is positive. When the high scores in one distribution are related to the low scores in the other distribution, the result is a negative correlational direction. | Correlations can be used to understand the relationship of different variables to each other, e.g., attendance and performance on a standardized test .40 to .70 are considered moderate correlations. Above .70 is considered to be high correlations. | It is wise to plot the scores to understand if the relationship is linear or not. One could misinterpret results if the scores are not linear. Pearson correlation coefficient requires linear relationships. Also, a few outliers could skew the results and oppositely skewed distributions can limit how high a Pearson coefficient can be. Also, one must remember that correlation does not suggest causation. |
| *Regression Analyses* | Regression analysis results in an equation that describes the nature of the relationship between variables. Simple regression predicts an object's value on a response variable when given its value on one predictor variable. Multiple regression predicts an object's value on a response variable when given its value on each of several predictor variables. Correlation tells you strength and direction of relationship. Regression goes one step further and allows you to predict. | A regression equation can be used to predict student achievement results, for example. Regression can determine if there is a relationship between two or more variables (such as attendance and student background) and the nature of those relation-ships. This analysis helps us predict and prevent student failure, and predict and ensure student successes. | One needs to truly understand the statistical assumptions that need to be in place in order to perform a regression analysis. This is not an analysis to perform through trial and error. |

Figure 6.7 (Continued)

## Terms Related to Analyzing Student Achievement Results, Inferentially, Their Most Effective Uses, and Cautions for Their Uses

| Term | Definition | Most Effective Uses | Cautions |
|---|---|---|---|
| *Control Groups* | During an experiment, the control group is studied the same as the experimental group, except that it does not receive the treatment of interest. | Control groups serve as a baseline in making comparisons with treatment groups. Control groups are necessary when the general effectiveness of a treatment is unknown. | It may not be ethical to hold back from students some method of learning that we believe would be useful. |
| *Experimental Design* | The detailed planning of an experiment, made beforehand, to ensure that the data collected are appropriate and obtained in a way that will lead to an objective analysis, with valid inferences. | Experimental designs can maximize the amount of information gained, given the amount of effort expended. | Sometimes it takes statistical expertise to establish an experimental design properly. |
| *Tests of Significance* | Procedures that use samples to test claims about population parameters. | Can estimate a population parameter, with a certain amount of confidence, from a sample. | Often lay people do not know what *statistically significant* really means. |

The Little River Elementary School example that follows shows a sampling of descriptive analyses they performed using their state criterion-referenced test. (Chapter 9 shows a sampling of descriptive analyses performed by Blue Bird Elementary School using its state norm-referenced test.)

## Example One: Little River Elementary School
### *How Are We Doing Compared to the District?*

Little River Elementary School and Three Rivers Public Schools use the State Assessment Program (SAP) criterion-referenced test as their main basis for assessing student performance. Most of the test is given in grades three, four, eight, and ten.

The SAP test results in Figure 6.8 show the percentages of Little River students scoring at the five reported levels of achievement—*Step 1, Progressing, Nearing Proficient, Proficient,* and *Advanced*—the way the data are reported to the school, compared to the district. Since Little River houses only grades three and four, related to these tests, results are shown for grades three and four only for 2000-01 through 2002-03. Communication Arts (Language Arts) and Science subtests are given at grade three. Mathematics and Social Studies subtests are given at grade four. (*Note:* The grade four Social Studies testing began in 2001-02.) While the total numbers of students taking the test varied for the three years shown, the majority of students fall into the *Nearing Proficient* and *Progressing* categories each year. One can see that in all subtests, except Science, grade three 2000-01, the percentages of Little River students in the *Proficient* and *Advanced* categories, the two categories indicating proficiency, were lower than the district's percentages. Notice also that grade four 2000-01 percentages are better if you include *Nearing Proficient.* (The templates used to build the analyses in this section appear on the CD for use with your criterion-referenced scores.)

Figure 6.8

## Little River Elementary School
## Compared to Three Rivers Public School District
## SAP Achievement Level Percentages, 2000-01 to 2002-03

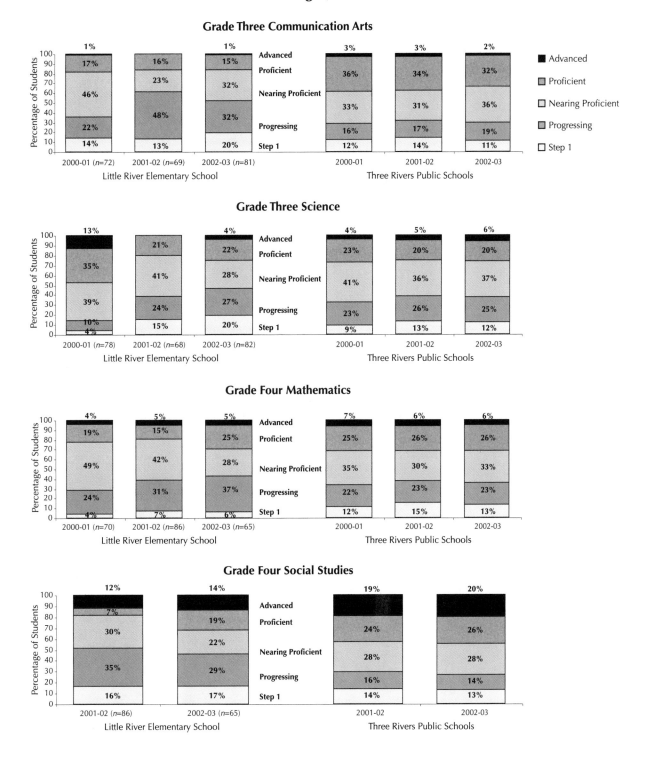

## How Are We Doing for ALL Our Students?

SAP numbers and percentages at the five achievement levels, disaggregated by gender and ethnicity, are shown in Figures 6.9 through 6.12.

In grade three Communication Arts (Figure 6.9), only one Caucasian female in 2000-01 and one Caucasian male in 2002-03 scored in the *Advanced* category. Only one African-American female, five Caucasian females, and six Caucasian males scored in the *Proficient* category in 2002-03.

On the other end, over one-third of the African-American females scored in *Step 1,* one-third were *Progressing,* and one-quarter were *Nearing Proficient* in 2002-03. Half of the Caucasian females were *Nearing Proficient,* with almost one-quarter scoring in *Step 1* and *Proficient.* Over half of the African-American males in 2002-03 were *Progressing,* while 21.1% scored in Step 1 and 21.1% *Nearing Proficient.*

Caucasian males had a basically even break with approximately one-third scoring *Proficient,* over a third *Nearing Proficient,* and less than one-third scoring in *Step 1* and *Progressing,* collectively.

## Figure 6.9

## Number and Percentage of Little River Elementary School Students Scoring in SAP Achievement Levels by Gender and Ethnicity Grade Three Communication Arts, 2000-01 to 2002-03

| Gender and Ethnicity | | Year | Step 1 | | Progressing | | Nearing Proficient | | Proficient | | Advanced | | Totals |
|---|---|---|---|---|---|---|---|---|---|---|---|---|---|
| | | | Number | Percent | Number | Percent | Number | Percent | Number | Percent | Number | Percent | |
| Females | Asian | 2001-02 | | | | | | | 1 | 100% | | | 1 |
| | African-American | 2000-01 | 4 | 25% | 7 | 43.8% | 5 | 31.3% | | | | | 16 |
| | | 2001-02 | 3 | 15% | 13 | 65% | 3 | 15% | 1 | 5% | | | 20 |
| | | 2002-03 | 9 | 37.5% | 8 | 33.3% | 6 | 25% | 1 | 4.2% | | | 24 |
| | Caucasian | 2000-01 | 3 | 14.3% | 4 | 19% | 7 | 33.3% | 6 | 28.6% | 1 | 4.8% | 21 |
| | | 2001-02 | 2 | 8.7% | 7 | 30.4% | 7 | 30.4% | 7 | 30.4% | | | 23 |
| | | 2002-03 | 1 | 5.6% | 3 | 16.7% | 9 | 50% | 5 | 27.8% | | | 18 |
| Males | American Indian | 2001-02 | | | | | 1 | 100% | | | | | 1 |
| | Asian | 2002-03 | | | 1 | 100% | | | | | | | 1 |
| | African-American | 2000-01 | 1 | 10% | 5 | 50% | 3 | 30% | 1 | 10% | | | 10 |
| | | 2001-02 | 3 | 27.3% | 7 | 63.6% | 1 | 9.1% | | | | | 11 |
| | | 2002-03 | 4 | 21.1% | 11 | 57.9% | 3 | 21.1% | | | | | 19 |
| | Hispanic | 2000-01 | | | | | 1 | 100% | | | | | 1 |
| | | 2001-02 | | | | | 2 | 100% | | | | | 2 |
| | Caucasian | 2000-01 | 2 | 8.3% | | | 17 | 70.8% | 5 | 20.8% | | | 24 |
| | | 2001-02 | 1 | 9.1% | 6 | 54.5% | 2 | 18.2% | 2 | 18.2% | | | 11 |
| | | 2002-03 | 2 | 10.5% | 3 | 15.8% | 7 | 36.8% | 6 | 31.6% | 1 | 5.3% | 19 |

USING DATA TO IMPROVE STUDENT LEARNING IN ELEMENTARY SCHOOLS

In 2002-03, grade three Science (Figure 6.10), only one Caucasian female and two Caucasian males scored in the *Advanced* category, while close to one-half of these same sub-populations scored in the *Proficient* category.

Either a quarter or one-third of the sub-populations (females only, but males were in-between) scored in the *Nearing Proficient* category in 2002-03. Over half of the African-American males were *Progressing* and over a third of African-American females scored in *Step 1* and *Progressing.*

## Figure 6.10

### Number and Percentage of Little River Elementary School Students Scoring in SAP Achievement Levels by Gender and Ethnicity Grade Three Science, 2000-01 to 2002-03

| Gender and Ethnicity | | Year | Step 1 | | Progressing | | Nearing Proficient | | Proficient | | Advanced | | Totals |
|---|---|---|---|---|---|---|---|---|---|---|---|---|---|
| | | | Number | Percent | Number | Percent | Number | Percent | Number | Percent | Number | Percent | |
| Females | Asian | 2001-02 | | | | | | | 1 | 100% | | | 1 |
| | African-American | 2000-01 | 2 | 11.8% | 2 | 11.8% | 8 | 47.1% | 4 | 23.5% | 1 | 5.9% | 17 |
| | | 2001-02 | 8 | 40% | 7 | 35% | 5 | 25% | | | | | 20 |
| | | 2002-03 | 9 | 37.5% | 9 | 37.5% | 6 | 25% | | | | | 24 |
| | Caucasian | 2000-01 | 1 | 3.8% | 2 | 7.7% | 13 | 50% | 7 | 26.9% | 3 | 11.5% | 26 |
| | | 2001-02 | 2 | 8.7% | 3 | 13% | 13 | 56.5% | 5 | 21.7% | | | 23 |
| | | 2002-03 | 3 | 16.7% | | | 6 | 33.3% | 8 | 44.4% | 1 | 5.6% | 18 |
| Males | American Indian | 2001-02 | | | | | | | 1 | 100% | | | 1 |
| | Asian | 2002-03 | | | 1 | 100% | | | | | | | 1 |
| | African-American | 2000-01 | | | 2 | 18.2% | 5 | 45.5% | 3 | 27.3% | 1 | 9.1% | 11 |
| | | 2001-02 | | | 4 | 44.4% | 5 | 55.6% | | | | | 9 |
| | | 2002-03 | 2 | 10% | 11 | 55% | 6 | 30% | 1 | 5% | | | 20 |
| | Hispanic | 2000-01 | | | | | | | 1 | 100% | | | 1 |
| | | 2001-02 | | | | | | | 2 | 100% | | | 2 |
| | Caucasian | 2000-01 | | | 2 | 8.7% | 4 | 17.4% | 12 | 52.2% | 5 | 21.7% | 23 |
| | | 2001-02 | | | 2 | 16.7% | 5 | 41.7% | 5 | 41.7% | | | 12 |
| | | 2002-03 | 2 | 10.5% | 1 | 5.3% | 5 | 26.3% | 9 | 47.4% | 2 | 10.5% | 19 |

Grade four Mathematics subscores (Figure 6.11) show that the only students (3) scoring in the *Advanced* category in 2002-03 were Caucasians—one was a female, two were males. No other ethnic group scored in the *Advanced* category for the last three years.

No African-American male or female scored in the *Proficient* category in 2002-03, although they each had one in this category in previous years. Eighty percent of African-American males scored in the *Progressing* category in 2002-03.

Percentage-wise, Caucasian females and males showed increases in the *Proficient* category in the last year. Caucasian males appear to be losing ground in the *Step 1* and *Progressing* categories.

## Figure 6.11

### Number and Percentage of Little River Elementary School Students Scoring in SAP Achievement Levels by Gender and Ethnicity Grade Four Mathematics, 2000-01 to 2002-03

| Gender and Ethnicity | | Year | Step 1 | | Progressing | | Nearing Proficient | | Proficient | | Advanced | | Totals |
|---|---|---|---|---|---|---|---|---|---|---|---|---|---|
| | | | Number | Percent | Number | Percent | Number | Percent | Number | Percent | Number | Percent | |
| Females | African-American | 2000-01 | | | 9 | 47.4% | 8 | 42.1% | 2 | 10.5% | | | 19 |
| | | 2001-02 | 3 | 13.6% | 2 | 54.5% | 6 | 27.3% | 1 | 4.5% | | | 12 |
| | | 2002-03 | 2 | 15.5% | 5 | 38.5% | 6 | 46.2% | | | | | 13 |
| | Hispanic | 2002-03 | | | | | 1 | 50% | 1 | 50% | | | 2 |
| | Caucasian | 2000-01 | 1 | 5% | | | 11 | 55% | 6 | 30% | 2 | 10% | 20 |
| | | 2001-02 | 1 | 4.3% | 7 | 30.4% | 9 | 39.1% | 5 | 21.7% | 1 | 4.3% | 23 |
| | | 2002-03 | | | 4 | 21.1% | 6 | 31.6% | 8 | 42.1% | 1 | 5.3% | 19 |
| Males | American Indian | 2002-03 | | | | | | | 1 | 100% | | | 1 |
| | African-American | 2000-01 | 2 | 15.4% | 5 | 38.5% | 5 | 38.5% | 1 | 7.7% | | | 13 |
| | | 2001-02 | 2 | 11.1% | 7 | 38.9% | 8 | 44.4% | 1 | 5.6% | | | 18 |
| | | 2002-03 | 1 | 6.7% | 12 | 80% | 2 | 13.3% | | | | | 15 |
| | Hispanic | 2001-02 | | | | | 2 | 100% | | | | | 2 |
| | | 2002-03 | | | | | 1 | 50% | 1 | 50% | | | 2 |
| | Caucasian | 2000-01 | | | 3 | 16.7% | 10 | 55.6% | 4 | 22.2% | 1 | 5.6% | 18 |
| | | 2001-02 | | | 1 | 4.8% | 11 | 52.4% | 6 | 28.6% | 3 | 14.3% | 21 |
| | | 2002-03 | 1 | 7.7% | 3 | 23.1% | 2 | 15.4% | 5 | 38.5% | 2 | 15.4% | 13 |

In 2002-03, grade four Social Studies (Figure 6.12), four Caucasian females and four Caucasian males were the only ones who scored in the *Advanced* category of the grade four Social Studies subtest. One African-American female, one Hispanic male, six Caucasian females, and three Caucasian males scored as *Proficient*, as did the lone American Indian male.

The percentage of African-American males in *Nearing Proficient* decreased from 33.3% in 2001-02 to 13.3% in 2002-03. The percentage in *Progressing* rose from 33.3% to 53.3% during this same time period. The percentage of African-Americans in *Step 1* is high. The percentage of Caucasian females in *Progressing* decreased from 43.5% in 2001-02 to 15.8% in 2002-03—percentages in the *Proficient* category increased from 8.7% to 31.6%, and in *Advanced* from 13% to 21.1%.

## Figure 6.12

### Number and Percentage of Little River Elementary School Students Scoring in SAP Achievement Levels by Gender and Ethnicity Grade Four Social Studies, 2001-02 to 2002-03

| Gender and Ethnicity | | Year | Step 1 | | Progressing | | Nearing Proficient | | Proficient | | Advanced | | Totals |
|---|---|---|---|---|---|---|---|---|---|---|---|---|---|
| | | | Number | Percent | Number | Percent | Number | Percent | Number | Percent | Number | Percent | |
| Females | African-American | 2001-02 | 7 | 31.8% | 8 | 36.4% | 6 | 27.3% | | | 1 | 4.5% | 22 |
| | | 2002-03 | 5 | 38.5% | 5 | 38.5% | 2 | 15.4% | 1 | 7.7% | | | 13 |
| | Hispanic | 2002-03 | | | | | 1 | 50% | | | 1 | 50% | 2 |
| | Caucasian | 2001-02 | 2 | 8.7% | 10 | 43.5% | 6 | 26.1% | 2 | 8.7% | 3 | 13% | 23 |
| | | 2002-03 | | | 3 | 15.8% | 6 | 31.6% | 6 | 31.6% | 4 | 21.1% | 19 |
| Males | American Indian | 2002-03 | | | | | | | 1 | 100% | | | 1 |
| | African-American | 2001-02 | 5 | 27.8% | 6 | 33.3% | 6 | 33.3% | 1 | 5.6% | | | 18 |
| | | 2002-03 | 5 | 33.3% | 8 | 53.3% | 2 | 13.3% | | | | | 15 |
| | Hispanic | 2001-02 | | | 1 | 50% | | | | | 1 | 50% | 2 |
| | | 2002-03 | | | | | 1 | 50% | 1 | 50% | | | 2 |
| | Caucasian | 2001-02 | | | 5 | 23.8% | 8 | 38.1% | 3 | 14.3% | 5 | 23.8% | 21 |
| | | 2002-03 | 1 | 7.7% | 3 | 23.1% | 2 | 15.4% | 3 | 23.1% | 4 | 30.8% | 13 |

Figure 6.13 shows the number and percentage of free/reduced lunch students scoring in the five SAP Achievement Levels. One can see the percentages of free/reduced lunch students falling in the *Step 1* category increased in every subtest over time. Only one third-grade student qualifying for free/reduced lunch scored at the *Advanced* level in 2002-03 in Math, and none in Communication Arts. No third-grade student qualified for free/reduced lunch at the *Advanced* level in Science, while two fourth-grade students did qualify in Social Studies. The greatest percentage of students in the *Advanced* category were *not* free/reduced.

Figure 6.13

## Number and Percentage of Little River Elementary School Students Scoring in SAP Achievement Levels by Free/Reduced Lunch Status 2000-01 to 2002-03

### Grade Three Communication Arts

| Lunch Status | Year | Step 1 | | Progressing | | Nearing Proficient | | Proficient | | Advanced | | Totals |
|---|---|---|---|---|---|---|---|---|---|---|---|---|
| | | Number | Percent | Number | Percent | Number | Percent | Number | Percent | Number | Percent | |
| Free/Reduced | 2000-01 | 6 | 15% | 13 | 32% | 16 | 39% | 5 | 12% | 1 | 2% | 41 |
| | 2001-02 | 7 | 16% | 25 | 57% | 10 | 23% | 2 | 5% | | | 44 |
| | 2002-03 | 14 | 27% | 23 | 44% | 11 | 21% | 4 | 8% | | | 52 |
| Not Free/Reduced | 2000-01 | 4 | 13% | 3 | 10% | 17 | 55% | 7 | 23% | | | 31 |
| | 2001-02 | 2 | 8% | 8 | 32% | 6 | 24% | 9 | 36% | | | 25 |
| | 2002-03 | 2 | 7% | 3 | 10% | 15 | 52% | 8 | 28% | 1 | 3% | 29 |

### Grade Three Science

| Lunch Status | Year | Step 1 | | Progressing | | Nearing Proficient | | Proficient | | Advanced | | Totals |
|---|---|---|---|---|---|---|---|---|---|---|---|---|
| | | Number | Percent | Number | Percent | Number | Percent | Number | Percent | Number | Percent | |
| Free/Reduced | 2000-01 | 2 | 5% | 5 | 12% | 19 | 46% | 13 | 32% | 2 | 5% | 41 |
| | 2001-02 | 8 | 19% | 12 | 29% | 18 | 43% | 4 | 10% | | | 42 |
| | 2002-03 | 15 | 28% | 20 | 38% | 13 | 25% | 5 | 9% | | | 53 |
| Not Free/Reduced | 2000-01 | 1 | 3% | 3 | 8% | 11 | 30% | 14 | 38% | 8 | 22% | 37 |
| | 2001-02 | 2 | 8% | 4 | 15% | 10 | 38% | 10 | 38% | | | 26 |
| | 2002-03 | 1 | 3% | 2 | 7% | 10 | 34% | 13 | 45% | 3 | 10% | 29 |

### Grade Four Mathematics

| Lunch Status | Year | Step 1 | | Progressing | | Nearing Proficient | | Proficient | | Advanced | | Totals |
|---|---|---|---|---|---|---|---|---|---|---|---|---|
| | | Number | Percent | Number | Percent | Number | Percent | Number | Percent | Number | Percent | |
| Free/Reduced | 2000-01 | 2 | 6% | 15 | 42% | 16 | 44% | 3 | 8% | | | 36 |
| | 2001-02 | 3 | 7% | 17 | 37% | 23 | 50% | 3 | 7% | | | 46 |
| | 2002-03 | 4 | 11% | 19 | 50% | 10 | 26% | 4 | 11% | 1 | 3% | 38 |
| Not Free/Reduced | 2000-01 | 1 | 3% | 2 | 6% | 18 | 53% | 10 | 29% | 3 | 9% | 34 |
| | 2001-02 | 3 | 8% | 10 | 25% | 13 | 33% | 10 | 25% | 4 | 10% | 40 |
| | 2002-03 | | | 5 | 19% | 8 | 30% | 12 | 44% | 2 | 7% | 27 |

### Grade Four Social Studies

| Lunch Status | Year | Step 1 | | Progressing | | Nearing Proficient | | Proficient | | Advanced | | Totals |
|---|---|---|---|---|---|---|---|---|---|---|---|---|
| | | Number | Percent | Number | Percent | Number | Percent | Number | Percent | Number | Percent | |
| Free/Reduced | 2001-02 | 12 | 26% | 19 | 41% | 12 | 26% | 3 | 7% | | | 46 |
| | 2002-03 | 11 | 29% | 15 | 39% | 5 | 13% | 5 | 13% | 2 | 5% | 38 |
| Not Free/Reduced | 2001-02 | 2 | 5% | 11 | 28% | 14 | 35% | 3 | 8% | 10 | 25% | 40 |
| | 2002-03 | | | 4 | 15% | 9 | 33% | 7 | 26% | 7 | 26% | 27 |

Three Rivers School District also administers a cognitive abilities test of general abilities test (COGAT). The COGAT can be considered a predictor of student achievement results on the SAP or other measures of achievement. COGAT is given to a student once, either in second grade or fourth grade. On a scale converted to make the district average equal 100, Little River second graders scored in the low nineties on COGAT in 2002-03. Disaggregating the second and fourth-grade COGAT by ethnicity, and then by free/reduced lunch, one can see that the Little River students scored below the district half the time and slightly higher than the district the other half of the time. Figure 6.14 indicates that Little River Caucasians and paid lunch students would be predicted to score higher than the district's average and the Little River average on the SAP.

## Figure 6.14

### Little River Elementary School COGAT Compared to Three Rivers Public School District 2002-03

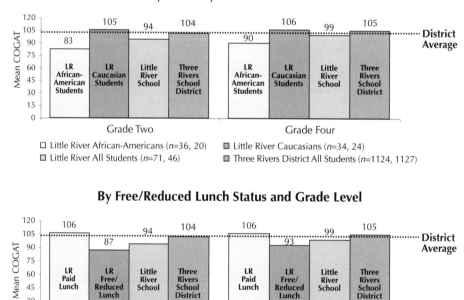

## Study Questions for *Where Are We Now?*

As you review Little River's data, use either the margins in the text, this page, or print this page from the CD to write down your early thinking. These notes, of course, are only hunches or placeholders until all the data are analyzed.

| | |
|---|---|
| **1. What are the student learning *strengths* and *challenges* for Little River?** | |
| *Strengths* | *Challenges* |
| | |

**2. What are some *implications* for the Little River school improvement plan?**

**3. Looking at the data presented, what other student learning data would you want to answer the question *Where are we now?* for Little River Elementary School?**

## What I Saw in Example One:
### Little River Elementary School 💿

Using the study questions as an outline, what I saw in the data for Chapter 6 appears below. When applicable, I have referenced the figure that gave me my first impression of strengths and challenges.

| What are their student learning strengths? | What are their student learning challenges? |
|---|---|
| • With respect to SAP score numbers, there are fewer students in *Step 1, Progressing,* and *Nearing Proficient* in grade four Math and Social Studies in 2002-03 than in 2001-02. Fewer students were *Nearing Proficiency* in grade three Science in 2002-03 than in 2000-01. More students are at the *Proficient* level in Communication Arts, Mathematics, Science, and Social Studies in 2002-03, than in 2001-02. At least one student performed at the *Advanced* level in each subtest in 2002-03. (Figures 6.8, 6.9, 6.10, 6.11, and 6.12)<br><br>• The percentage of students scoring at *Proficient* and *Advanced* Social Studies levels increased in 2002-03, over the previous year. (Figures 6.8 and 6.12)<br><br>• The percentage of Little River students scoring in the *Proficient* and *Advanced* categories in Science was greater than the district percentages. (Figure 6.8)<br><br>• Little River's paid lunch students outscored the overall school and district students on the COGAT. (Figure 6.14) | • With respect to SAP scores, there are more students in *Step 1* in 2002-03 in Communication Arts and Science than either of the preceding two years. While the total number of students taking the Math test decreased, the number of students *Nearing Proficiency* decreased by half. (Figures 6.9, 6.10, and 6.11)<br><br>• Only 16% of the Little River third graders scored at *Proficient* and above in Communication Arts. (Figure 6.8)<br><br>• Little River scored lower than the district in all but Science. (Figure 6.8)<br><br>• The disaggregations for Communication Arts by ethnicity show that there are very few African-Americans and Hispanics scoring in the *Proficient* and *Advanced* levels. Only one Caucasian male scored in the *Advanced* level in Communication Arts in 2002-03. (Figure 6.9)<br><br>• The majority of African-American students fall in the *Progressing* and *Nearing Proficient* categories of the Mathematics test. (Figure 6.10)<br><br>• Only Caucasians scored at the *Advanced* level of the Science and Social Studies tests in 2002-03. (Figures 6.11 and 6.12)<br><br>• Over one-third of the African-American students at Little River scored at the *Step 1* level in Social Studies in 2002-03. (Figure 6.12)<br><br>• Over one-half of the African-American female and male students at Little River scored at the *Step 1* or *Progressing* levels in Science in 2002-03. Seventy-five percent of the African-American females scored at *Level 1* or Progressing. Only five percent of the African-American males scored at *Proficiency* or higher. The story is similar in all areas. (Figure 6.11)<br><br>• Looking at the same grade level over time, although comparing different students, it looks as though there have not been changes made to the curriculum and instructional strategies over time, related to SAP.<br><br>• There is a big gap between African-American and Caucasians, and free/reduced and paid lunch students on the COGAT, which is consistent with the scores on the SAP test.<br><br>• The higher scores on the COGAT for Little River non-free/reduced lunch students than the district implies that Little River's SAP scores should be higher than the district's SAP scores for this category. (Figure 6.14) |

## What are some implications for their school improvement plan?

- Staff needs to look at the data—both at the school and classroom levels. They would be changing processes if they were analyzing and using the data. With only a third and fourth-grade criterion-referenced test, Little River is at a true disadvantage in basing decisions only on student learning data.
- Little River needs to figure out how to bring up all scores, especially for students who are African-American and who qualify for free/reduced lunch.
- If not already, teachers need to teach to the standards and talk with one another across grade levels to create and implement a continuum of learning that makes sense for the students. Teachers need to know what is being expected of students in the grade before coming to their classrooms and after leaving.
- This school might consider early intervention programs.

## Other desired data or information

Little River Elementary School provided some basic analyses of its student achievement results. Other data that would be helpful in understanding the school results include:

- Other measures of student learning. One measure for different subjects at two grade levels does not provide nearly enough information to know which students are not progressing and what to improve to get better results, or even when we are "losing" the students academically.
- What happens to the students' achievement when they go to the middle school and high school?
- Are students who went to preschool more successful than those who did not go to preschool?
- How are the students taught to read, write, and learn Mathematics, Science, and Social Studies?

## Summary

Answering the question, *Where are we now?*, takes the data analysis work into the student learning realm. Analyzing required norm-referenced and/or criterion-referenced tests and disaggregating by grade level, gender, ethnicity, lunch status, and special education is an excellent way to begin answering the question, *How are we doing?* Looking across measures can be useful and informative—another way to think about what students know and are able to do, giving us a glimpse at *how* students learn.

As one looks at the trends, she/he can begin to see discrepancies and areas for further and deeper analyses, which we follow in the next chapter. The study questions can help guide one to these next levels.

*Analyzing required norm-referenced and/or criterion-referenced tests and disaggregating by grade level, gender, ethnicity, and lunch status is an excellent way to begin answering the question, "How are we doing?"*

## On the CD Related to this Chapter

▼ Study Questions Related to *Where Are We Now?* (Ch6Qs.pdf)
These study questions will help you understand the information provided in Chapter 6. This file can be printed for use with staff as you begin to explore your own student learning results.

▼ *Arguments For and Against Standardized Testing* (TestArgu.pdf)
This table summarizes the most common arguments for and against the use of standardized testing.

▼ *Standardized Test Score Terms, Their Most Effective Uses, and Cautions for Their Uses* (TestTerm.pdf)
This table shows the different standardized testing terms, their effective uses, and cautions for their uses.

▼ *Arguments For and Against Performance Assessments* (PerfArgu.pdf)
This table shows the most common arguments for and against the use of performance assessments.

▼ *Arguments For and Against Teacher Grading* (GradeArg.pdf)
This table shows the most common arguments for and against the use of teacher grading.

▼ *Terms Related to Analyzing Student Achievement Results, Descriptively, Their Most Effective Uses, and Cautions for Their Uses* (SAterms1.pdf)
This table shows the different terms related to analyzing student achievement results, descriptively, their effective uses, and cautions for their uses.

▼ *Terms Related to Analyzing Student Achievement Results, Inferentially,*
  *Their Most Effective Uses, and Cautions for Their Uses* (SAterms2.pdf)
  This table shows the different terms related to analyzing student
  achievement results, inferentially, their effective uses, and cautions for
  their uses.

▼ *What I Saw in Example One* (Ch6Saw.pdf)
  *What I Saw in Example One* is a file, organized by the student learning
  study questions, that summarizes what I saw in the student learning data
  provided by Little River Elementary School.

▼ Student Achievement Graphing Templates (ElemSA.xls)
  All of the *Microsoft Excel* files that were used to create the student
  achievement graphs in the Little River example (Chapter 6) appear on the
  CD. Use these templates by putting your data in the data table and
  changing the title/labels to reflect your data. The graphs will build
  automatically. This file also explains how to use the templates.

▼ Student Achievement Data Table Templates (ElemSA.doc)
  All of the *Microsoft Word* files that were used to create the student
  achievement data tables in the Little River example (Chapter 6)
  appear on the CD. Use these templates by putting your data in the
  data table and changing the title/labels to reflect your data.

▼ *Questions to Guide the Analysis of Student Achievement Data* (QsStachv.doc)
  This *Microsoft Word* file consists of questions to guide the interpretation
  of your student learning data. You can write your responses into this file.

# Analyzing the Data:
## *What Are the Gaps? and What Are the Root Causes of the Gaps?*

## Chapter 7

Gaps are the differences between *where the school wants to be* and *where the school is right now*. *Where the school wants to be* can be defined through the school's vision and goals.

A *vision* is what the school would look like, sound like, and feel like when it is carrying out its purpose. To be effective in getting all staff members implementing the same concepts, a vision must be spelled-out in specific terms that everyone can understand in the same way. (*The School Portfolio Toolkit: A Planning, Implementation, and Evaluation Guide for Continuous School Improvement* [Bernhardt, 2002], Chapter 5, beginning on page 97.)

*Goals* are the outcomes of the vision. Goals are stated in broad, general, abstract, and non-measurable terms. *Objectives* are much more narrow and specific and require data to create so they can be measured. Schools often want to attempt many goals, and very few get implemented. There should be only two to three school goals that reflect the results the school wants to achieve by implementing the vision. (See *Goal Setting* and *Gap Analysis and Objectives Activities* on CD. )

*Where the school is right now* are the results—specifically what the data say about strengths, challenges, and areas for improvement. To uncover *gaps*, one must review the data and dig deeper. Just looking at one level of analysis could be misleading. One must dig deeper to uncover those students not meeting the standards and where they rank on the scoring scale. The reason for digging deeper is that a large gap may not seem as large as a smaller gap when one discovers that the students in the area with the largest gap scored only one or two points away from mastery, while the students not mastering the subtest with the smallest gap could be on the very bottom of the distribution—a long way from mastery.

Once school personnel see the gaps, they typically want to start implementing solutions *without discovering the root causes.*

*Root causes* are real reasons that "problems" or "challenges" exist. Schools must uncover the root causes of their undesirable results to alleviate the problem or to get desirable results that will last over time. If they do not understand the root causes, schools could be merely treating a symptom and never get to the real reason for the results. On the pages that follow are gap and root cause analyses completed for Little River Elementary School. On the CD are several activities/processes for working with staff to uncover root causes.

Please note the study questions on page 146 to assist in studying the data. Also note that there is space in the margins on the data pages to write your impressions as you review the data. At the end of the chapter, I have shared what I saw in the data.

## Example One: Little River Elementary School

One of Little River Elementary School's goals is for all students to achieve proficiency on the State Assessment Program (SAP), a criterion-referenced test. Using the analyses conducted in Chapter 6, one can regroup the most recent year's results. The scores of the most recent year are used because:

1. the measures and the SAP are not consistent across grade levels, so there are no cohorts to follow; and

2. there are no real differences in the results over time.

To learn about Little River's gaps and root causes, the school's results were synthesized around these questions:

▼ *What are the gaps?*

▼ *How did these students score?*

▼ *Who are the students who are not achieving?* (What are their common characteristics?)

▼ *What do they know? What do they not know?*

▼ *How were they taught?*

*What are the Gaps?* On the SAP, as shown below in Figure 7.1, 84% and 75% of the third graders did not meet proficiency on the Communication Arts and Science tests, respectively. In Mathematics and Social Studies, 71% and 68% of fourth graders did not meet proficiency levels. The third grade scores have larger percentages of students not meeting proficiency, although the fourth-grade scores are close behind. Gaps appear on all subtests.

> *Where the school is right now are the results—specifically what the data say about strengths, challenges, and areas for improvement.*

> *Root causes are real reasons that "problems" or "challenges" exist.*

### Figure 7.1

#### Percentage of Little River Students Not Meeting Proficiency on the SAP, 2002-03

| Communication Arts Grade Three | Science Grade Three | Mathematics Grade Four | Social Studies Grade Four |
|---|---|---|---|
| 84% | 75% | 71% | 68% |

WHAT ARE THE GAPS? AND WHAT ARE THE ROOT CAUSES OF THE GAPS?

*How did the students score?* How many students were in the very lowest group (*Step 1*), how many were *Progressing*, and how many were *Nearing Proficient?* Figure 7.2 shows the number and percentage of students in each achievement level on the SAP. The figure indicates that roughly a quarter to one third of the students in each content area were *Nearing Proficient*—and close to one-third was *Progressing*. At the third grade level, 20% of the students were at *Step 1* in Communication Arts and Science; 7% of the fourth graders were at *Step 1* in Mathematics; and 17% were at *Step 1* in Social Studies.

### Figure 7.2

### Number and Percentage of Little River Elementary School Students By Achievement Levels on the SAP, 2002-03

|  | Step 1 | Progressing | Nearing Proficient | Proficient | Advanced |
|---|---|---|---|---|---|
| **Communication Arts** Grade Three | 20% (*n*=16) | 32% (*n*=26) | 32% (*n*=26) | 15% (*n*=12) | 1% (*n*=1) |
| **Science** Grade Three | 20% (*n*=16) | 27% (*n*=22) | 28% (*n*=23) | 22% (*n*=18) | 4% (*n*=3) |
| **Math** Grade Four | 7% (*n*=4) | 40% (*n*=24) | 28% (*n*=17) | 23% (*n*=14) | 2% (*n*=1) |
| **Social Studies** Grade Four | 17% (*n*=11) | 30% (*n*=19) | 22% (*n*=14) | 19% (*n*=12) | 13% (*n*=8) |

Figure 7.3 begins to answer the question, *Who are the students who are not achieving?* The majority of students at *Step 1* were African-American females. At the *Progressing* level, most of the students were African-American males. Caucasian females had the highest percentage of occurrence in the *Nearing Proficient* level. Looking at the percentage of students by free/reduced lunch, shown as Figure 6.13 in Chapter 6, one can see that students qualifying for free/reduced lunch did have lower scores than the other students. Looking at the scores of students suspended for behaviors versus those who had not been suspended did *not* show a difference in performance (figure not shown here). Additionally, looking at the names of the students scoring in the lowest categories, by grade level, one can see that the same students who scored at *Step 1* in one subject area scored at *Step 1* or *Progressing* in the other subject area (not shown here). One must be aware that conclusions can be misleading by the size of overall groups (i.e., 43 African-Americans versus 37 Caucasians taking the third-grade Communications testing, and so on).

# Figure 7.3

## Number and Percentage of Little River Elementary School Students Scoring in SAP Achievement Levels by Ethnicity and Gender, 2002-03

| Subject and Grade Level | Ethnicity | Step 1 | | Progressing | | Nearing Proficient | | Proficient | | Advanced | |
|---|---|---|---|---|---|---|---|---|---|---|---|
| | | Male | Female | Male | Female | Male | Female | Male | Female | Male | Female |
| Communication Arts Grade Three n=81 | African-American | 4 5% | 9 11% | 11 14% | 8 10% | 4 5% | 6 7% | | 1 1% | | |
| | Caucasian | 2 2% | 1 1% | 3 4% | 3 4% | 7 9% | 9 11% | 6 7% | 5 6% | 1 1% | |
| | Asian | | | 1 1% | | | | | | | |
| Science Grade Three n=82 | African-American | 2 2% | 9 11% | 11 13% | 9 11% | 6 7% | 6 7% | 1 1% | | | |
| | Caucasian | 2 2% | 3 4% | 1 1% | | 5 6% | 6 7% | 9 11% | 8 10% | 2 2% | 1 1% |
| | Asian | | | 1 1% | | | | | | | |
| Mathematics Grade Four n=65 | African-American | 1 2% | 2 3% | 12 18% | 5 8% | 2 3% | 6 9% | | | | |
| | Caucasian | 1 2% | | 3 5% | 4 6% | 2 3% | 6 9% | 5 8% | 8 12% | 2 3% | 1 2% |
| | American Indian | | | | | | | 1 2% | | | |
| | Hispanic | | | | | 1 2% | 1 2% | 1 2% | 1 2% | | |
| Social Studies Grade Four n=65 | African-American | 5 8% | 5 8% | 8 12% | 5 8% | 2 3% | 2 3% | | 1 2% | | |
| | Caucasian | 1 2% | | 3 5% | 3 5% | 2 3% | 6 9% | 3 5% | 6 9% | 4 6% | 4 6% |
| | American Indian | | | | | | | 1 2% | | | |
| | Hispanic | | | | | 1 2% | 1 2% | 1 2% | | | 1 2% |

*What do the students know? What do they not know?* Analyzing the results by standards, one can see the average percentage of total points earned on any of the standards (that are tested on the subtests) to be about the same each year. Few standards stick out as being a lot lower or higher than others. Figures 7.4 and 7.5 show the standards for each subtest and the average percentage of total points earned for each standard over the past three years. (Social Studies was tested only for two years.) At grade three, the lowest total scores (below 50% correct) in 2002-03 in Communication Arts were related to the following three standards:

▼ Plan and make presentations for a variety of purposes and audiences (Improvement over 2001-02 scores)

▼ Reading nonfiction (Increase or improvement over previous years)

▼ Writing formally and informally (Improvement over 2001-02 scores)

## Figure 7.4

## Little River Elementary School
## Average Percentage of Total Points Earned

| Grade Three Communication Arts Standards, 2000-01 to 2002-03 | Average Percentage of Total Points Earned | | |
|---|---|---|---|
| | 2000-01 | 2001-02 | 2002-03 |
| Comprehend and evaluate written, visual, and oral presentations | 68.3 | 61.1 | 68.1 |
| Discover and evaluate patterns and relationships in information | 71.1 | 54.8 | 52.0 |
| Plan and make presentations for a variety of purposes and audiences | 47.1 | 39.3 | 44.7 |
| Review and revise communications to improve accuracy and clarity | 60.5 | 51.7 | 61.5 |
| Combined reading | 63.4 | 56.1 | 55.9 |
| Reading fiction, poetry, and drama | 62.6 | 54.3 | 59.8 |
| Reading nonfiction | 62.1 | 55.6 | 47.4 |
| Speaking and writing English | 55.4 | 49.3 | 61.5 |
| Writing formally and informally | 47.1 | 38.8 | 44.7 |

| Grade Three Science Standards, 2000-01 to 2002-03 | Average Percentage of Total Points Earned | | |
|---|---|---|---|
| | 2000-01 | 2001-02 | 2002-03 |
| Science and technology | 52.1 | 46.5 | 57.4 |
| Earth process | 64.5 | 44.0 | 38.8 |
| The universe | 65.8 | 54.5 | 66.7 |
| Inquiry | 81.5 | 71.6 | 54.7 |
| Ecology | 71.2 | 42.6 | 58.6 |
| Living organisms | 75.3 | 56.0 | 53.9 |
| Force and motion | 61.8 | 62.9 | 52.4 |
| Matter and energy | 70.0 | 49.9 | 68.3 |
| Apply acquired information, ideas, and skills to different contexts | 63.6 | 51.0 | 57.7 |
| Comprehend and evaluate written, visual, and oral presentations and works | 68.1 | 55.5 | 59.7 |
| Discover and evaluate patterns and relationships in information, ideas, and structures | 65.2 | 50.8 | 59.9 |
| Plan and make written, oral, and visual presentations for a variety of purposes and audiences | 57.0 | 54.7 | 54.4 |
| Reason inductively from a set of specific facts and deductively from general premises | 66.5 | 43.7 | 47.4 |

## Figure 7.5

## Little River Elementary School
## Average Percentage of Total Points Earned

| Grade Four Mathematics Standards, 2000-01 to 2002-03 | Average Percentage of Total Points Earned | | |
|---|---|---|---|
| | 2000-01 | 2001-02 | 2002-03 |
| Data analysis probability | 65.7 | 82.2 | 68.9 |
| Discrete math | 58.6 | 52.9 | 58.9 |
| Mathematical systems | 52.9 | 61.7 | 54.4 |
| Number sense | 72.8 | 58.3 | 59.0 |
| Patterns and relationships | 80.0 | 62.1 | 64.7 |
| Geometric spatial sense | 69.5 | 59.2 | 63.7 |
| Apply acquired information, ideas, and skills to different contexts | 73.9 | 66.2 | 60.5 |
| Comprehend and evaluate written, visual, and oral presentations and works | 66.1 | 72.4 | 64.1 |
| Discover and evaluate patterns and relationships in information, ideas, and structures | 78.2 | 63.5 | 63.3 |
| Organize data, information, and ideas into useful forms for analysis or presentation | 64.3 | 73.3 | 73.5 |
| Identify problems and define their scope and elements | 56.0 | 41.4 | 47.8 |
| Develop and apply the processes used in recognizing and solving problems | 41.3 | 47.4 | 65.0 |

| Grade Four Social Studies Standards, 2001-02 to 2002-03 | Average Percentage of Total Points Earned | |
|---|---|---|
| | 2001-02 | 2002-03 |
| Continuity and change in history | 43.9 | 53.7 |
| Democratic principles | 57.6 | 50.8 |
| Economic concepts | 48.7 | 54.7 |
| Elements of geography | 56.2 | 61.6 |
| Governance systems | 68.6 | 65.1 |
| Institutions and culture | 80.1 | 60.7 |
| Social Science inquiry | 70.0 | 64.8 |
| Apply acquired information, ideas, and skills to different contexts | 51.8 | 66.8 |
| Comprehend and evaluate written, visual, and oral presentations and works | 70.3 | 65.6 |
| Discover and evaluate patterns and relationships in information, ideas, and structures | 60.8 | 55.2 |
| Identify, analyze, and compare institutions, traditions, and art forms of societies | 60.8 | 55.2 |
| Reason inductively from a set of specific facts and deductively from general premises | 42.6 | 59.8 |
| Explain reasoning and identify information used to support decisions | 53.8 | 57.0 |

The lowest scores in 2002-03 in Science at grade three were related to the following two standards:

▼ Earth process (Decrease from 2001-02, and a large decrease from 2000-01)

▼ Reason inductively from a set of specific facts and deductively from general premises (Decrease from 2001-02 scores)

At grade four, the lowest score in 2002-03 in Mathematics was related to the standard:

▼ Identify problems and define their scope and elements (Increase from 2001-02 scores)

In grade four Social Studies, the lowest score was related to the standard:

▼ Democratic principles (Decrease from 2001-02 scores)

There were increases in 2002-03 from 2001-02. In grade three Communication Arts, increases were seen in these standards:

▼ Comprehend and evaluate written, visual, and oral presentations

▼ Plan and make presentations for a variety of purposes and audiences

▼ Review and revise communications to improve accuracy and clarity

▼ Reading fiction, poetry, and drama

▼ Speaking and writing English

▼ Writing formally and informally

In grade three Science, increases in 2002-03 were seen in the following standards:

▼ Science and technology; the universe; ecology; and matter and energy

▼ Apply acquired information, ideas, and skills to different contexts

▼ Comprehend and evaluate written, visual, and oral presentations and works

▼ Discover and evaluate patterns and relationships in information, ideas, and structures

▼ Reason inductively from a set of specific facts and deductively from general premises

Increases in grade four 2002-03 Mathematical Standards were seen in:

▼ Discrete math; numbers sense; patterns and relationships; and geometric spatial sense

▼ Organize data, information, and ideas into useful forms for analysis or presentation

▼ Identify problems and define their scope and elements

▼ Develop and apply the processes used in recognizing and solving problems

In grade four Social Studies standards, increases were seen in:

▼ Continuity and change in history

▼ Economic concepts; elements of geography

▼ Apply acquired information, ideas, and skills to different contexts

▼ Reason inductively from a set of specific facts and deductively from general premises

▼ Explain reasoning and identify information used to support decisions

Performance on some standards decreased during the same time period. In grade three Communication Arts, decreases were seen in two standards:

▼ Discover and evaluate patterns and relationships in information

▼ Combined reading and reading nonfiction

In grade three Science, decreases were seen in the following standards:

▼ Earth process

▼ Inquiry

▼ Living organisms; force and motion

▼ Plan and make written, oral, and visual presentations for a variety of purposes and audiences

Decreases in grade four Mathematics standards for 2002-03 were seen in:

▼ Data analysis probability; mathematical systems

▼ Apply acquired information, ideas, and skills to different contexts

▼ Comprehend and evaluate written, visual, and oral presentations and works

▼ Discover and evaluate patterns and relationships in information, ideas, and structures

In grade four Social Studies, decreases were seen in the following standards:

▼ Democratic principles, governance systems, and institutions and culture

▼ Social Science inquiry

▼ Comprehend and evaluate written, visual, and oral presentations and works

▼ Discover and evaluate patterns and relationships in information, ideas, and structures

▼ Identify, analyze, and compare institutions, traditions, and art forms of societies

*How were they taught?* According to the principal, students were assigned to teachers in a fairly random fashion. This means that the starting achievement levels and aptitudes of students in all classrooms were essentially the same.

## Figure 7.6

## Number and Percentage of Little River Students Scoring in SAP Achievement Levels By Teacher and Subject, 2002-03

| Teacher | Subject | Step 1 | | Progressing | | Nearing Proficient | | Proficient | | Advanced | |
|---|---|---|---|---|---|---|---|---|---|---|---|
| | | Number | Percent | Number | Percent | Number | Percent | Number | Percent | Number | Percent |
| Grade 3 A 2 Years Experience | Communication Arts | 1 | 13% | 3 | 38% | 4 | 50% | | | | |
| | Science | 1 | 25% | 1 | 25% | 2 | 50% | | | | |
| Grade 3 B 4 Years Experience | Communication Arts | 2 | 22% | 5 | 56% | 1 | 11% | 1 | 11% | | |
| | Science | 3 | 30% | 4 | 40% | 2 | 20% | 1 | 10% | | |
| Grade 3 C 5 Years Experience | Communication Arts | 1 | 10% | 1 | 10% | 7 | 70% | | | 1 | 10% |
| | Science | 1 | 10% | 1 | 10% | 3 | 30% | 5 | 50% | | |
| Grade 3 D 8 Years Experience | Communication Arts | | | | | 2 | 29% | 5 | 71% | | |
| | Science | | | 2 | 18% | 2 | 18% | 5 | 45% | 2 | 18% |

| Teacher | Subject | Step 1 | | Progressing | | Nearing Proficient | | Proficient | | Advanced | |
|---|---|---|---|---|---|---|---|---|---|---|---|
| | | Number | Percent | Number | Percent | Number | Percent | Number | Percent | Number | Percent |
| Grade 4 A 29 Years Experience | Mathematics | | | 5 | 33% | 6 | 40% | 4 | 27% | | |
| | Social Studies | | | 5 | 31% | 6 | 38% | 3 | 19% | 2 | 13% |
| Grade 4 B 13 Years Experience | Mathematics | 1 | 9% | 6 | 55% | | | 3 | 27% | 1 | 9% |
| | Social Studies | 3 | 27% | 3 | 27% | 2 | 18% | 2 | 18% | 1 | 1% |
| Grade 4 C 8 Years Experience | Mathematics | 2 | 17% | 3 | 25% | 4 | 33% | 2 | 17% | 1 | 8% |
| | Social Studies | 3 | 25% | 4 | 33% | 1 | 8% | 2 | 17% | 2 | 17% |

Figure 7.6 shows the number and percentage of students by achievement levels, organized by teacher and subject tested. It appears that the students in classrooms with teachers with the most years of experience performed better on the subtests. Teachers with one or two years of experience, especially at grade three, did not have any students scoring at the *Advanced* level, and the two-year veteran had only one student score at the *Proficient* level in Science and in Communication Arts. The three-year veteran had one student score in the *Advanced* category in Communication Arts and none in the *Proficient* category. At the same time, she/he had five students score *Proficient* in Science. Fourth-grade teachers with more experience had more students scoring across the distributions in both subjects.

Looking at the standards data by teacher, grade three students with teachers with one to three years of experience have average percentages of points earned in the 30s and 40s. The experienced teachers have average percentages of points earned in the 60s and 70s.

## Summary:  What Are the Root Causes of Little River's Gaps?

After analyzing Little River's data, the gaps, and digging deeper to discover root causes, one comes up with the idea that there are contributing causes. However, one major contributing cause needs to be addressed before different results can be achieved—the way teachers are teaching in Little River Elementary School! There are differences in the results teachers are getting. All we know with the data we have is that there are differences related to the number of years the teachers have been teaching. We do not know what happened in grades pre-kindergarten, kindergarten, one, and two. The school and the teachers are in complete control of the way in which instruction is delivered, and they must learn to teach to the standards and to whom they have as students. It is not who the kids are—or where they come from—the school has no control over that. Some of the experienced teachers seem to have developed successful strategies for the Little River students. They must share these strategies with all teachers in the school and help all teachers implement a continuum of learning that makes sense for all students in the school.

## Study Questions for *What Are the Gaps?* and *What Are the Root Causes of the Gaps?* 💿

As you review Little River's data, use either the margins in the text, this page, or print this page from the CD, to write down your early thinking. These notes, of course, are only hunches or placeholders until all the data are analyzed.

| |
|---|
| **1. What are Little River's *gaps*?** |
| |
| **2. Do you feel that the *root causes* of their student learning results were uncovered? If the answer is *no*, what other analyses would you perform?** |
| |
| **3. What are the *implications* for the school improvement plan?** |
| |
| **4. What other data would you want to consider?** |
| |

## What I Saw in Example One:
## Little River Elementary School 💿

Using the study questions as an outline, what I saw in the data for Chapter 7 appears below. When applicable, I have referenced the figure that gave me my first impression of strengths and challenges.

### What are the gaps?

Figures 7.1 and 7.2 show that all subject areas tested on the SAP have very few students meeting proficiency. Figure 7.3 shows that gaps exist between Caucasians and the other ethnicities, particularly African-Americans. A large gap in performance centers on how the students are being taught at the different grade levels, as shown in Figure 7.6.

### What are the root causes of the gaps?

In this chapter, we can see that a major contributing cause of the discrepancies might be the way teachers are teaching in Little River Elementary School. While there are some differences in scores by ethnicity and free/reduced lunch status, one can see there are teachers who can deal with the population and some who cannot. At least a contributing cause appears to be how teachers are teaching.

### Implications for the school improvement plan

What about what the pre-kindergarten through grade two teachers do in these same subject areas? With only some subtests administered in grades three and four, we have no way of knowing to what degree the pre-kindergarten through grade two teachers are contributing to the positive and negative results.

We can see differences by teacher. However, how much are the curriculum and instructional strategies impacting the results? How much is discipline impacting the results?

*Strategies to Support New Teachers*

* Teachers might need professional development training for:
    * bringing up the scores of African-American students, children living in poverty, and English Learners
    * working with families living in poverty and students of backgrounds different from the teachers
    * mentoring new teachers
    * teaching to and implementing the standards
* Perhaps spread some of the veteran teachers in the upper grades across all grade levels—start the primary grades with strong, veteran teachers
* Create a leadership structure to share decisions and ownership for implementation and the results within and across grade levels
* Make time to study the student achievement results when the SAP results come in
* Systematically and deeply review the gaps and root causes
* Look at the curriculum and materials being used across grade levels
* Flowchart current processes

### Other desired data or information

* Need to study the results on other measures as well
* It would be good to know who is teaching which students, and what students are being taught in grades kindergarten through five
* We need to keep digging deeper and asking why these students are not achieving, and why all teachers are not getting positive results

> *Gap analyses help schools see the difference between where they are (current results) and where they want to be (vision and goals).*

> *To find a root cause, one often has to ask "Why?" at least five levels down to uncover the root reason for the symptom.*

## Summary

Gap analyses are critical for answering the question, *What are the gaps?* Gap analyses help schools see the difference between where they are (current results) and where they want to be (vision and goals). To be effective, gap analyses must dig layers deep into the data to truly understand the results and to begin to uncover root causes.

Root causes, as used in this continuous school improvement planning model, refer to the deep underlying reasons for the occurrence of a specific situation, the gap. While a symptom may become evident from a needs assessment or gap analysis—the symptom (low student scores) is not the cause. To find a root cause, one often has to ask *Why?* at least five levels down to uncover the root reason for the symptom. One will know if she/he found the root cause when she/he can answer *no* to the following questions:

▼ Would the problem have occurred if the cause had not been present?

▼ Will the problem reoccur if the cause is corrected? (Preuss, 2003)

If the answers to these questions are *maybe*, you are probably looking at contributing causes, not one root cause. Most problems within schools are caused by systems rather than people. Improvement of the system will result in reduction or removal of the problem. Teams that include processes in their analyses tend not to jump to solutions or conclusions as quickly as those who do not. At some point, when searching for the root cause, one must realize that the "problem" is really a result. What we are trying to do with these analyses is to uncover how we get our results. These very same processes can be used to uncover how we get our successes.

Root causes are not easy to uncover, but the information that is uncovered is well worth the effort.

# On the CD Related to this Chapter

▼ *Goal Setting Activity* (ACTGoals.pdf)

By setting goals, a school can clarify its end targets for the school's vision. This activity will help a school set goals for the future.

▼ *Gap Analysis and Objectives Activity* (ACTGap.pdf)

The purpose of this activity is to look closely at differences between current results and where the school wants to be in the future. It is this gap that gets translated into objectives that guide the development of the action plan.

▼ *Root Cause Analysis Activity* (ACTRoot.pdf)

Root causes are the real causes of our educational problems. We need to find out what they are so we can eliminate the true cause and not just address the symptom. This activity asks staff teams to review and analyze data and ask probing questions to uncover the root cause(s).

▼ *Cause and Effect Analysis Activity* (ACTCause.pdf)

This activity will help teams determine the relationships and complexities between an effect or problem and all the possible causes.

▼ *Problem-Solving Cycle Activity* (ACTCycle.pdf)

The purpose of the *Problem-Solving Cycle Activity* is to get all staff involved in thinking through a problem before jumping to solutions. This activity can also result in a comprehensive data analysis design.

▼ Study Questions Related to the Gaps and the Root Causes of the Gaps (Ch7Qs.pdf)

These study questions will help you better understand the information provided in Chapter 7. This file can be printed for use with staffs as you analyze their data to determine the gaps and the root causes of the gaps.

▼ *What I Saw in Example One* (Ch7Saw.pdf)

*What I Saw in Example One* is a file, organized by the student learning study questions, that summarizes what I saw in the student learning data provided by Little River Elementary School.

▼ *Gap Analyses Data Table Templates* (ElemGaps.doc)

All of the *Microsoft Word* files that were used to create the gap analyses data tables in the Little River example (Chapter 7) appear on the CD. Use these templates by putting your data in the data table and changing the title/labels to reflect your data.

WHAT ARE THE GAPS? AND WHAT ARE THE ROOT CAUSES OF THE GAPS?

149

▼ *No Child Left Behind* (NCLB) Templates

Table templates for analyzing student learning data for NCLB are provided on the CD.

◆ *NCLB Language Scores Template* (LangTbl.doc)

This *Microsoft Word* file is a table template to use in capturing your NCLB Language scores analysis.

◆ *NCLB Reading Scores Template* (ReadTbl.doc)

This *Microsoft Word* file is a table template to use in capturing your NCLB Reading scores analysis.

◆ *NCLB Math Scores Template* (MathTbl.doc)

This *Microsoft Word* file is a table template to use in capturing your NCLB Math scores analysis.

◆ *NCLB Student Achievement Reading Results Template* (ProfLaEl.doc)

This *Microsoft Word* file is a table template to use in summarizing your NCLB disaggregated student achievement Reading proficiency results.

◆ *NCLB Student Achievement Math Results Template* (ProfMaEl.doc)

This *Microsoft Word* file is a table template to use in summarizing your NCLB disaggregated student achievement Math proficiency results.

▼ Group Process Tools and Activities

The files include read-only documents, examples, templates, tools, activities, and strategy recommendations. Many of the group process tools and activities can be used throughout the analysis of data.

◆ *Affinity Diagram Activity* (ACTAfnty.pdf)

The affinity diagram encourages honest reflection on the real underlying root causes of a problem and its solutions, and encourages people to agree on the factors. This activity assists teams in discussing and resolving problems, using a nonjudgmental process.

◆ *Fishbowl Activity* (ACTFish.pdf)

This activity can be used for dynamic group involvement. The most common configuration is an inner ring, which is the discussion group, surrounded by an outer ring, which is the observation group. Just as people observe the fish in the fishbowl, the outer ring observes the inner ring.

◆ *Forcefield Analysis Activity* (ACTForce.pdf)

The *Forcefield Analysis Activity* helps staffs think about the ideal state for the school and the driving and restraining forces regarding that ideal state.

◆ *Placemat Activity* (ACTPlace.pdf)

The *Placemat Activity* was developed to invite participants to share their knowledge about the school portfolio, data, a standard, an instructional strategy, a concept, etc.

◆ *T-Chart Activity* (ACTTChrt.pdf)

A *T-Chart* is a simple tool to organize material into two columns. Use a T-Chart to compare and contrast information or to show relationships. Use it to help people see the opposite dimension of an issue.

◆ *"X" Marks the Spot Activity* (ACTXSpot.pdf)

This activity helps staff understand levels of expertise or degrees of passion about a topic.

◆ *Quadrant Diagram Activity* (ACTQuadr.pdf)

A *quadrant diagram* is a method to determine which solution best meets two goals at once, such as low cost and high benefit.

# Analyzing the Data:
## *How Can We Get to Where We Want to Be?*

Chapter 8

We know a little more about the gaps in Little River's student achievement results, and we have a better idea of the root causes. So now, *How can we get to where we want to be?* The answer to this question is the key to unlocking how the vision will be implemented and how gaps will be eliminated. An action plan consisting of strategies, actions, person(s) responsible, due dates, timelines, and resources needs to be created to achieve the vision and goals and to eliminate the root causes of the gaps.

Action plans need to clarify how decisions will be made, identify professional development required to learn new skills and gain new knowledge, and clarify the use of partners to achieve the vision. A school's leadership structure, professional development strategies, and partnership development plan are important components of the answer to the question, *How can we get to where we want to be?*

This chapter shows how Little River Elementary School created a school improvement plan using the data gathered and analyzed.

We start by reviewing the implications for the school improvement plan determined through the data analyses that were presented in Chapters 4 through 7 of this book.

# Implications for the Little River Elementary School Improvement Plan

Studying the data and pulling together the implications for the school improvement plan derived from the data shown in Chapters 4 through 7, one would want to see the following strategies and activities addressed in the Little River school improvement plan.

Strategies to:

▼ align curriculum to the state standards

▼ improve the scores of all students, no matter what ethnicity, social economic status, or background

▼ implement a schoolwide discipline plan with total staff involvement

▼ welcome new students and their parents to the school

▼ work with the students who are absent, and their parents

Study groups to:

▼ practice and share effective strategies

▼ read, practice, and share best practices

▼ develop quarterly benchmarks and assessments at every grade level

▼ analyze the results of quarterly standards assessments

Professional development training for:

▼ working with Special Education and English learning students, and developing strategies that will ensure their achievement

▼ working with families living in poverty and students of backgrounds different from the teachers

▼ assuring that new teachers, in fact, all teachers, incorporate best practices into their teaching

Support structures to:

▼ review data and student work

▼ analyze and utilize data, and student work

▼ mentor new teachers

▼ improve and allow quality conversations about standards implementation

▼ implement standards and align curriculum

▼ ensure best practices for teaching reading, math, science, and social studies

*A school's leadership structure, professional development strategies, and partnership development plan are important components of the answer to the question, "How can we get to where we want to be?"*

- ▼ train leaders, including classroom teachers
- ▼ involve parents
- ▼ expand knowledge of Behavior Modification/Conflict Resolution, etc.
- ▼ train supervisors of the playground, the lunchroom, and before and after school activities

Reorganize the school to:

- ▼ teach to the standards
- ▼ spread some of the veteran teachers in the upper grades across all grade levels—start the primary grades with strong, veteran teachers
- ▼ revisit the mission and vision for the school
- ▼ create a leadership structure to share decisions and ownership for standards implementation and the results within and across grade levels, and to improve communication of teachers across grade levels
- ▼ bring in partners to assist with the implementation of student learning standards

Annually:

- ▼ administer student, staff, and parent questionnaires
- ▼ schedule time to assess on the *Continuous Improvement Continuums* and determine next steps, preferably twice a year—ask for facilitation assistance if the intended way to assess on the *Continuous Improvement Continuums* is too difficult for an in-house person
- ▼ set aside time to study the student achievement results as soon as possible when the SAP results come in
- ▼ systematically and deeply review the gaps and root causes
- ▼ determine if strategies are having an impact on gaps and root causes

Other things:

- ▼ ask why morale is down to understand about the root causes, and then include ways to improve the school climate and morale— perhaps social activities, celebration events, or staff meetings for "fun"
- ▼ gather and study the data to know more about the discipline issues; when do they occur and with which students?
- ▼ start believing *all* students can learn
- ▼ show students that teachers have faith in the students' abilities to learn

## Little River's School Improvement Plan

Little River's staff determined their number one goal had to be—

**To ensure *all* students are proficient in all subject areas.**

Staff's review of data indicated that they had a long way to go. Staff looked for pathways to improvement by reviewing the research on performance improvement, the implications for school improvement that came from their data analysis study, and by committing to improvement.

Staff acknowledged that they needed—

1. *Instructional coherence*—to have all teachers teaching to the state standards and creating a continuum of learning for all students.

2. *A shared vision for school improvement*—staff agreed it was time to revisit the vision in such a way that all staff members could and would commit to teaching consistencies and school improvement.

3. *Data-driven decision making*—at all points along the way, staff would gather data to know if they were making progress with moving all students to proficiency in all subject areas. It was no longer an option not to use data, and not to know if all students are learning as the year progresses.

The first draft of the Little River School Plan is shown in Figure 8.1, which staff felt covered the major implications that came from their data analysis study, and built upon what many had already started—specifically standards alignment and *Character Counts* training.

# Figure 8.1

## Little River Elementary School Plan for Improvement

**GOAL 1:** *Ensure that all students are proficient in all state standard subject areas.*

**BASELINE PROFICIENCY 2002-03:**

*Grade Three*
Communication Arts: 16%
Science: 25%

*Grade Four*
Mathematics: 29%
Social Studies: 32%

**OBJECTIVES:**

▼ By 2013-14, all Little River students will be proficient in every standard subject area, as measured by the SAP test.

▼ By the end of 2004, all teachers will be implementing the state standards in their classrooms, as measured through classroom observations, the standards implementation tools, lesson plans, and SAP results.

▼ Staff will continuously improve the learning organization, as measured by the *Continuous Improvement Continuums* assessments, questionnaire results, and the SAP results.

| Strategy/Action | Person Responsible | Measurement | Resources Needed | Due Date | Aug | Sept | Oct | Nov | Dec | Jan | Feb | Mar | Apr | May | Jun | Jul |
|---|---|---|---|---|---|---|---|---|---|---|---|---|---|---|---|---|
| **I. Implement the Standards** | | | | | | | | | | | | | | | | |
| *Make sure every teacher has knowledge of the standards* | | | | | | | | | | | | | | | | |
| ◆ Get copies of the standards to all staff members | Principal | Teachers' knowledge of standards, attendance at professional development meetings, and evidence that they are beginning to implement the standards in their classrooms | Standards | Back-to-school mailing | X | | | | | | | | | | | |
| ◆ View a professional development video to inform all about why standards are important | | | Video | August 21 | X | | | | | | | | | | | |
| ◆ Use grade level meetings to review the standards and support the understanding of the standards | | | No cost | Ongoing | X | X | X | X | X | X | X | X | X | X | X | X |
| *Create a vision and mission, based on the purpose of the school, values and beliefs of the staff, and standards* | Everyone | | | | | | | | | | | | | | | |
| ◆ Setup a professional development day | Professional Development Coordinator | Creation of a shared vision, mission based on values and beliefs | $$ for a full staff day with facilitator | August 22 | X | | | | | | | | | | | |
| ◆ Hire a facilitator | Professional Development Coordinator | | Facilitator fee | By August 15 | X | | | | | | | | | | | |
| *Support the implementation of the standards* | | | | | | | | | | | | | | | | |
| ◆ Create a self-assessment tool that will assist teachers in assessing the degree to which they are implementing their vision and standards | Leadership Team Leader | The tool is created | Time | December 17 | | | | | X | | | | | | | |
| ◆ All teachers measure on the self-assessment tool | | Teachers use the tool | | | | | | | | X | X | X | X | | | |
| ◆ View professional development videos that show teachers implementing the standards, facilitated by teachers from neighboring school districts known to be implementing the state standards with success | Professional Development Coordinator | Professional development sessions Support structures in place to support the implementation Teachers' attendance at grade-level and cross-grade-level meetings | $$ for snacks | September 10 | | X | | | | | | | | | | |

# Figure 8.1 (Continued)

## Little River Elementary School Plan for Improvement (Continued)

### I. Implement the Standards (Continued)

| Strategy/Action | Person Responsible | Measurement | Resources Needed | Due Date | Aug | Sept | Oct | Nov | Dec | Jan | Feb | Mar | Apr | May | Jun | Jul |
|---|---|---|---|---|---|---|---|---|---|---|---|---|---|---|---|---|
| • Share *Best Practices* in staff meetings (teachers sharing research and how they have learned to enjoy teaching the standards and seeing success) | Team Leaders | Meeting minutes | | Ongoing | X | X | X | X | X | X | X | X | X | X | X | X |
| • Demonstration lessons and classroom observations so each teacher knows what it will look like, sound like, feel like when she/he is teaching to the standards | Team Leaders | Demo lessons and class observations | Sub-time | Ongoing, structured, and reinforced by grade-level and subject-area leaders | X | X | X | X | X | X | X | X | X | X | X | X |
| • Peer coaching to support the implementation in every classroom | Team Leaders | Peer coaching being implemented | Sub-time | Ongoing 1st and 3rd Wednesdays | X | X | X | X | X | X | X | X | X | X | X | X |
| • Grade-level meetings focused on standards | Team Leaders | Teachers' attendance | Time | 1st and 3rd Wednesdays | X | X | X | X | X | X | X | X | X | X | X | X |
| • Cross-grade-level meetings focused on standards | Team Leaders | Teachers' attendance | Time | 2nd and 4th Wednesdays | X | X | X | X | X | X | X | X | X | X | X | X |
| • Leadership team meeting focused on standards and progress schoolwide | Team Leaders | Leadership Team attendance | Time | 1st Tuesday and 3rd Wednesday | X | X | X | X | X | X | X | X | X | X | X | X |
| • Map the curriculum<br>• Language Arts<br>• Mathematics<br>• Social Studies<br>• Science<br>  * Determine where the curriculum is right now<br>  * Establish benchmarks<br>  * Align curriculum to the benchmarks<br>  * Review and use state practice tests, teach concepts before the test is given | Principal and grade-level leaders lead all the staff | Mapping finished | Some sub-time | Ongoing until completed | X | X | X | X | X | X | X | X | X | | | |
|   * Develop lessons and activities to achieve the benchmarks and to integrate technology | Technology Coordinator | | Time | | | | | | | | | | | | | |
| • Review student work in standards mapping areas across grades | Principal | Assessment is completed | Some materials | Quarterly | | | X | | | X | | | X | | X | |
| • Review state assessment results | Principal | | | Annually | | | | | | | | | | X | X | |

HOW CAN WE GET TO WHERE WE WANT TO BE?

**Figure 8.1** (Continued)

## Little River Elementary School Plan for Improvement (Continued)

| Strategy/Action | Person Responsible | Measurement | Resources Needed | Due Date | Aug | Sept | Oct | Nov | Dec | Jan | Feb | Mar | Apr | May | Jun | Jul |
|---|---|---|---|---|---|---|---|---|---|---|---|---|---|---|---|---|
| **I. Implement the Standards** *(Continued)* | | | | | | | | | | | | | | | | |
| ◆ Create a website to support the knowledge and implementation of the standards and vision | | | | | | | | | | | | | | | | |
| • Have students create and maintain the website | Technology Coordinator | Website created and used | Technology class time | Get it started in September | X | X | | | | | | | | | | |
| • Establish a system for teachers and others to submit items to post on the website (particularly, example lessons taught to the standards) | Website Committee | | | Ongoing | X | X | X | X | X | X | X | X | X | X | X | X |
| *Assess the standards* | | | | | | | | | | | | | | | | |
| ◆ Develop the rubrics to assess benchmarks | Content area leaders will lead the charge—all teachers will participate | Rubrics created | Some materials Sub-time | | | | X | | X | | X | | X | | X | |
| ◆ Assess where the students are with respect to the standards, using the standard rubrics | Content Leaders | Rubrics used | Some materials Sub-time | As they are completed and then quarterly | | | X | | X | | X | | X | | | |
| • As a baseline to use as diagnostics | | | | September 15 | | X | | | | | | | | | | |
| ◆ Assess learning styles/teaching styles preferences of teachers | Principal | Learning styles assessed | Learning styles inventory | By early October | | | X | | | | | | | | | |
| **II. Improve Teachers' Knowledge of *Best Practices*** | | | | | | | | | | | | | | | | |
| ◆ Professional development in meeting the educational needs of students who live in poverty and have backgrounds different from ours | Professional Development Coordinator | Session setup | Facilitators as needed | November with follow-up | | | | X | | X | | X | | | | |
| ◆ Grade-level and cross-grade-level meetings will ensure the implementation of ideas along with standards | Team Leaders | Part of meeting | | Ongoing | X | X | X | X | X | X | X | X | X | X | X | X |
| **III. Continuously Improve the Learning Organization** | | | | | | | | | | | | | | | | |
| ◆ Assess on the *Continuous Improvement Continuums* | Leadership Team Leader | CIC report is completed with next steps | Cross-grade time | | | X | | | | | | | X | | | |
| ◆ Administer Student, Staff, and Parent questionnaires | Leadership Team Leader | Questionnaire graphs are completed | Time to administer and analyze | | | | X | | | | | | | | | |

Figure 8.1 (Continued)

# Little River Elementary School Plan for Improvement (*Continued*)

**GOAL 2:** *Nurture characteristics in students that are respectful of themselves and others, nonviolent, and conducive to learning.*

**OBJECTIVES:**
- By the end of the 2003-04 school year, the number of behavorial interventions will decrease by ten percent.
- By the end of Fall 2003, all teachers will be trained in programs to support respectful and nonviolent behaviors in students.
- By the middle of Fall 2003, all parents will know how to support their children's learning at home.

| Strategy/Action | Person Responsible | Measurement | Resources Needed | Due Date | Timeline | | | | | | | | | | | |
|---|---|---|---|---|---|---|---|---|---|---|---|---|---|---|---|---|
| | | | | | Aug | Sept | Oct | Nov | Dec | Jan | Feb | Mar | Apr | May | Jun | Jul |
| **I. Learn How to Encourage/Support Desired Behaviors in Students** | | | | | | | | | | | | | | | | |
| Create a committee responsible for goal | Principal | Committee created | | September | | X | | | | | | | | | | |
| Investigate *when* behavior is a problem | Behavior Committee | Behavior study | Some sub-time | Late October | | | X | | | | | | | | | |
| Create a protocol for studying and taking action on behavior | Behavior Committee | Behavior study | Some sub-time | Late October | | | X | | | | | | | | | |
| *Implement "No Violence" Curriculum* | | | | | | | | | | | | | | | | |
| Train all staff K-6 (September 13-14) | Behavior Team Leader | Reduce the number of behavioral interventions by 10% each year | Training Facilitation | September | | X | | | | | | | | | | |
| Work with teachers to implement | Behavior Team Leader | | | Ongoing | | | | | X | X | X | X | X | X | X | X |
| *Implement "Character Education" Curriculum* | | | | | | | | | | | | | | | | |
| Train all staff K-6 | Behavior Training Leader | Evidence of students caring | Facilitator | October | | | X | | | | | | | | | |
| Implement in every classroom and on playground | Grade-level Leaders | Fewer discipline referrals | | Ongoing | | | | | X | X | X | X | X | X | X | X |
| **II. Actively Involve Students and Parents in Students' Learning and Behavior** | | | | | | | | | | | | | | | | |
| Notify all students and parents about how to use the website to clarify standards and expectations | Grade-level Leaders | | | By the time the website is up | | | X | | | | | | | | | |
| Establish programs and partnerships with parents and community to assist with the learning standards | Partnership Team | | | | | | | | | | | | | | | |

## Implementing the Plan: The Leadership Structure

It is hard to create a comprehensive plan—no doubt. Making sure everyone on staff implements the plan in the manner intended is even harder. A leadership structure can ensure that a plan is truly implemented. Leadership structures must look like the vision. In this case, Little River's vision is in the planning stage. In the meantime, their new leadership structure looks like their plan and will help them implement that shared vision they need.

The Little River Leadership Structure emerged from the plan as follows, shown in Figure 8.2. (This information is in the plan; it has been extracted from the plan to clarify roles, responsibilities, and meeting times.)

From the overall action plan, Little River staff was able to create a leadership structure and commit to the following meeting times, roles, and responsibilities.

### Figure 8.2

### Little River Leadership Structure

#### Meeting Times for Staff

All staff members have committed to meet on Wednesdays after school, with the Leadership Team meeting additionally on the first Tuesday of each month and the third Wednesday after the grade-level meeting. Our focus is *standards*—learning them, implementing, assessing, and understanding the impact of teaching to them. Since grade-level and cross-grade-level team meetings are one hour in length, an agenda will be provided beforehand. The dates and times are as follows:

| Day | Time | Teams |
|---|---|---|
| 1st Tuesday | 3:45 to 5:00 | Leadership |
| 1st Wednesday | 3:45 to 4:45 | Grade Level |
| 2nd Wednesday | 3:45 to 4:45 | Cross-Grade Level by Subject |
| 3rd Wednesday | 3:45 to 4:45 | Grade Level |
| 3rd Wednesday | 4:50 to 5:30 | Leadership |
| 4th Wednesday | 3:45 to 4:45 | Cross-Grade Level K-6 |
| 5th Wednesday | 3:45 to 4:45 | Celebration of Progress |

#### Roles and Responsibilities

It is each staff member's responsibility to implement the standards in her/his classroom. All staff members will meet in grade-level teams, cross-grade-level subject-area teams, or as a whole staff every week. In addition, some staff members will participate on the Leadership Team. The roles and responsibilities of each team are defined below.

*Grade-level Teams*

The purposes of grade-level teams are to maintain unity of curriculum, instruction, assessment, and to implement the standards at each grade level.

♦ Every teacher will participate in meetings with her or his grade level.

♦ Teachers will coach and support the implementation of the standards and the vision in each other's classrooms.

♦ Grade-level teams will seek support from the subject-area teams.

♦ Teachers will study and support each other's implementation of best practices.

♦ Support staff will be assigned to appropriate grade level teams.

♦ Grade level meetings will take place in the grade leader's classroom.

Figure 8.2 (Continued)

## Little River Leadership Structure

*Cross-grade-level Teams*

Cross-grade-level meetings will take place in the subject area leader's classroom. The purposes of the cross-grade-level teams are to maintain unity of curriculum, instruction, and assessment in each subject area, specifically to:

- improve instruction and student achievement results schoolwide
- ensure the implementation of standards within subject areas and across the grade levels
- advise the leadership team of progress and concerns of grade-level and cross-grade-level team meetings
- coach and support the quality implementation of subject areas
- demonstrate the implementation of subject standards for teachers in each subject area
- review data and plan for improvement
- disseminate subject information from the school, district, state, and federal government

*Purposes of the Grade-level and Cross-grade-level Meetings Include:*

- review and clarify standards
- implement the state standards
- support the implementation of the standards in every classroom
- share best practices
- share examples
- review data (student learning, questionnaire, demographics, school process, student learning style preferences)
- review student work
- develop rubrics for student work related to the standards
- map the curriculum
- help teachers format classroom tests to resemble the state assessment
- develop standards assessments and benchmarks

*Leadership Team*

The Leadership Team will meet on the first Tuesday of each Month, from 3:35 to 5:00, the third Wednesday after the grade-level meetings from 4:50 to 5:30, and other times as necessary. The purposes of the Leadership Team are to:

- improve instruction and student achievement results schoolwide
- guide, enforce, and reinforce the school plan
- assist with the development of agendas for the grade level and cross-grade level meetings
- ensure the implementation of standards and the vision within and across the grade levels
- monitor progress and address concerns
- be a resource for the implementation of standards and district curriculum
- review data and plan for improvement
- disseminate content information from the district, state, and federal government
- troubleshoot the concerns of teams
- enable others to act and model the way
- encourage the heart

*Celebrations of Progress*

Whenever there is a fifth Wednesday of the month, staff will meet to celebrate and/or to assess progress. The Leadership Team will determine from staff what the celebrations will include.

## Implementing the Plan:
### The Professional Development Schedule/Plan

The professional development schedule that reinforces the Leadership Structure and overall plan can help staff know if the plan is possible and what adjustments are necessary. It also serves as a document of commitment. It is one thing to see the activities in a plan; it is another thing to see the activities listed in chronological order, with the time commitments and expectations clearly laid out. Below is Little River's Professional Development Calendar for Fall 2003, extracted from the overall plan (Figure 8.3). The entire 2003-04 Professional Development Calendar is shown on the CD.

Also on the CD is a table of *Powerful Professional Development Designs* and a folder of activities related to these designs.

Figure 8.3

## Little River Professional Development Calendar

| Fall 2003 | | |
|---|---|---|
| August 21-22<br>8:00 to 3:00 | Professional development for all staff | Inservice: *What are standards and why are they important?*<br>Expectations for the year.<br>Create a shared vision.<br>Select team members and leaders.<br>Review standards and grade level preparation. |
| September 2<br>3:45 to 5:00 | Leadership Team | Planning for the year. |
| September 3<br>3:45 to 4:45 | Grade Level | Map Language Arts standards to the curriculum. |
| September 10<br>3:45 to 4:45 | Cross Grades | Inservice: *Standards Implementation.* |
| September 17<br>3:45 to 4:45 | Grade Level | Continue mapping Language Arts standards to the curriculum. |
| September 17<br>4:50 to 5:30 | Leadership Team | Review progress and recommend agenda for cross-grade-level meetings. |
| September 24<br>3:45 to 4:45 | Cross Grades | Review and revise Language Arts standards mapping:<br>Grade levels present highlights. |
| October 1<br>3:45 to 4:45 | Grade Level | Continue mapping Language Arts standards.<br>Begin developing benchmarks and rubrics. |
| October 7<br>3:45 to 5:00 | Leadership Team | Next steps in supporting cross-grade level implementation of the standards. |
| October 8<br>3:45 to 4:45 | Cross Grades | Continue mapping Language Arts standards, with grade level highlights, and subject area calibration of benchmarks and rubrics. |
| October 15<br>3:45 to 4:45 | Grade Level | Review benchmarks and rubrics. Report on implementation of standards; prepare to assess students on rubrics and to identify anchor papers. |
| October 15<br>4:50 to 5:30 | Leadership Team | Review progress and assist with the assessment of standards and identification of anchor papers. |
| October 22<br>3:45 to 4:45 | Cross Grades | Inservice: *Best Practice* for working with students living in poverty and with backgrounds different from teachers. |
| October 29<br>3:45 to 4:45 | Celebration of Progress | Assess on *Continuous Improvement Continuums.* |
| November 3 | Everyone | Administer questionnaires this week. |
| November 4<br>3:45 to 5:10 | Leadership Team | Review progress/make any recommendations to grade-level teams about Language Arts implementation. Start mapping of Math standards. |
| November 5<br>3:45 to 4:45 | Grade Level | Map Math standards to curriculum. |
| November 12<br>3:45 to 4:45 | Cross Grades | Continue mapping Math standards to the curriculum. |
| November 19<br>3:45 to 4:45 | Grade Level | Continue mapping Math standards to the curriculum; identifying benchmarks and rubrics. |
| November 19<br>4:50 to 5:30 | Leadership Team | Review progress: *How is the curriculum mapping going?* |
| **November 26** | **No Meeting** | **Happy Thanksgiving** |
| December 2<br>3:45 to 5:10 | Leadership Team | Review progress and make recommendations. |
| December 3<br>3:45 to 4:45 | Grade Level | Review benchmarks and rubrics. Report on implementation of standards; prepare to assess students on rubrics and to identify anchor papers. |
| December 10<br>3:45 to 4:45 | Cross Grades | Review questionnaire results.<br>Review student work. |
| December 17<br>3:45 to 4:45 | Grade Level | Recalibrate the standards and benchmarks, if necessary. |
| December 17<br>4:50 to 5:30 | Leadership Team | Review progress for the year. |

HOW CAN WE GET TO WHERE WE WANT TO BE?

## Implementing the Plan:
### The Partnership Plan

Similar to the leadership structure, professional development, and evaluation plans, a partnership plan can be extracted from the overall plan.

When extracting the partnership plan from the overall plan, Little River realized they did not have enough meaningful partnerships. They reviewed their goals and objectives and brainstormed how they could work with parents, business, and the community to achieve their main goal to have all students proficient in the standards. They came up with these ideas:

We need to let students, their parents, and the community know that we are implementing standards.

A couple of teachers wrote an article for the *newspaper*, similar to one they saw in a neighboring town, that staff agreed should be published at the beginning of the year. The article lists the student standards at each grade level. The article specifies that every student will be held accountable to these standards and offers suggestions for parents to support their students' achievement of the standards. The article also indicated how every teacher would be teaching to these standards. Joy and Cindy agreed to create periodic newspaper articles that will show the progress of our work with standards.

The school website will archive newspaper articles, the entire set of standards, and everything else that will help everyone understand the standards and their uses. The website will have a section for students, parents, staff, and everybody. Schedules and announcements will be accessible to everyone. Lessons that teachers are willing to share with each other will be on the teacher site. Suggestions for students to do their best will be on the student website, along with articles from students and student work. Suggestions for how parents can support their students' achievement of standards will be in the parent section. This website will grow and evolve throughout the year.

Just in case some parents neither get the newspaper nor have access to the Internet, our *school newsletter* will carry similar articles about standards and will summarize questionnaire results.

We do want to hear from students, staff, and parents about our learning environment. *Questionnaires* will be administered to parents in November at Parent-Teacher Conferences, both of which will be student-led this year. We will follow-up on any parents who do not appear at the conferences. We will get 100% response rates from students and staff. The results will be published in articles for the newspaper, newsletter, and website.

In talking about how they could have fun with parents getting their students to read and write, elementary teachers came up with *Muffins for Moms* and *Donuts for Dads,* and *e-mail buddies.* Moms and Dads (or Grandmas and Grandpas) will be invited at different times to come to school to read with their children. Additionally, the teachers want to set up e-mail buddies with parents, high school students, professionals, and other grade levels. Perhaps the high school will want to follow suit for career awareness.

Some teachers want to experiment with *student learning contracts,* and even student-parent-teacher contracts, to heighten the awareness of the role each party must take in the achievement of standards.

## Evaluating the Plan

Also in the Little River Elementary School Action Plan is a column indicating how strategies and activities will be evaluated. By condensing the measurement column into a comprehensive evaluation plan (Figure 8.4), the persons responsible for the measurement of the plan can see the overall evaluation and plan accordingly. If one looks only at the measurement of individual strategies and activities in isolation of each other, she/he could miss ways to efficiently measure the entire plan.

## Figure 8.4

## Little River Evaluation Plan

The evaluation of the Little River Elementary School action plan is designed around achieving adequate yearly progress toward 100% proficiency of all students in all subject areas, and the measurement of the strategies and activities to achieve the school's two main goals, which are to:

- ◆ Ensure that all students are proficient in all state standard subject areas.
- ◆ Nurture characteristics in students that are respectful of themselves and others, nonviolent, and conducive to learning.

### Evaluation of the Plan

**Goal 1:** *Ensure that all students are proficient in all state standard subject areas.*

**Objective 1:** *By 2013-14, all Little River students will be proficient in every standard subject area, as measured by the SAP test.*

The gaps related to all students and subgroups meeting proficiency include:

Overall:

| Grade Three | Grade Four |
|---|---|
| Communication Arts: 84% | Mathematics: 75% |
| Science: 74% | Social Studies: 68% |

By subgroups:

*Grade Three Communication Arts:*

| African-American: 98% | Free/Reduced Lunch Students: 95% |
|---|---|
| Caucasian: 68% | |

*Grade Three Science:*

| African-American: 98% | Free/Reduced Lunch Students: 94% |
|---|---|
| Caucasian: 46% | |

*Grade Four Mathematics:*

| African-American: 100% | Free/Reduced Lunch Students: 82% |
|---|---|
| Caucasian: 50% | |

*Grade Four Social Studies:*

| African-American: 96% | Free/Reduced Lunch Students: 89% |
|---|---|
| Caucasian: 47% | |

Figure 8.4 (Continued)

## Little River Evaluation Plan

To meet the requirements of *No Child Left Behind,* Little River will move 9% of its students from non-proficient to proficient each year, as measured by the SAP, since they had subgroups of students not scoring in the proficient or advanced categories in the baseline year. Little River will also need to organize its data system so student learning results can be disaggregated by special education.

**Objective 2:** *By the end of 2004, all teachers will be implementing the state standards in their classrooms, as measured through classroom observations, standards implementation tools, lesson plans, and student work.*

The degree to which teachers implement the vision and the standards will be measured as follows:

♦ Each teacher will be an "X" by the end of the 2004 school year as measured by the Little River Shared Vision Self-assessment Tool. This level will be maintained or increased throughout the 2004-05 school year.

♦ The collective assessment measured by the Little River Shared Vision Self-assessment Tool of all Little River teachers will be a "Y" for each grade level and the total school by the end of the 2004 school year, and maintained or increased throughout the 2004-05 school year.

♦ Minutes of grade-level team, cross-grade-level, and leadership team meetings will show productive discussions about implementing the standards and the vision. The minutes will also show that teachers are in attendance at their respective meetings. Teachers' lesson plans will show the implementation of the standards and the vision.

♦ Informal assessments at leaders' meetings will show the areas that need improvement on an ongoing basis.

♦ Student work will show what students know and are able to do.

♦ Principal's classroom observations will show that teachers know the standards and are implementing the standards and the vision

♦ Principal's classroom observations will show that students know what they are supposed to be learning and are learning these things.

♦ All teachers will be in attendance at all professional development sessions.

♦ All teachers will observe demonstration lessons provided by colleagues and will demonstrate at least one lesson that incorporates standards during 2003-04.

♦ All teachers will participate in peer coaching to implement the standards.

♦ The Language Arts curriculum will be aligned to the standards by October 2003; Math by January 2004; Social Studies by April 2004; and most, if not all, of Science by July 2004.

**Objective 3:** *Staff will improve the learning organization, as measured by the Continuous Improvement Continuums, questionnaires, and other evaluations.*

♦ The school will improve from the baseline assessment on the *Education for the Future Continuous Improvement Continuums* at least one level in all areas by December 2003, and increase another level by December 2004.

♦ The *Education for the Future* staff questionnaire will show, by the end of school year 2003-04, that all staff agree there is a shared vision, one plan to get to the shared vision, strong communication, and an effective leadership structure. The staff questionnaire will also show that teachers believe teaching to the state standards will increase student learning.

♦ The *Education for the Future* student questionnaire will show that students feel cared for and challenged. The questionnaire will also indicate that students know what they are supposed to be learning, that they are challenged by the work, and are trying as hard as they can to learn.

♦ The *Education for the Future* parent questionnaire will show that parents feel welcome at the school, that they know about their child's progress, and that school-home communications are effective.

**Figure 8.4** (Continued)

## Little River Evaluation Plan

**Goal 2:**    *Promote behavior characteristics in students that are respectful of themselves and others, nonviolent, and conducive to learning.*

**Objective 1:**    *By the end of the 2003-04 school year, the number of behavioral interventions will decrease by ten percent.*

- By October 2003, the Behavior Committee will determine what causes the behavior issues with students, and when.
- The number of behavioral interventions will decrease by 10% by May 2004.
- Teachers will acknowledge students' acts of caring on the website and in assemblies. This caring will lead to fewer discipline referrals than in 2002-03.

**Objective 2:**    *By the end of Fall 2003, all teachers will be trained in programs to support respectful and nonviolent behaviors in students.*

- The training on *No Violence* and *Character Education* will be complete as of October 2003. All teachers will show evidence of implementing these concepts in their classrooms.

**Objective 3:**    *By the middle of Fall 2003, all parents will know how to support their children's learning at home.*

Evidence of parent involvement and communication will be assessed as follows:

- Parents' perceptions of home-school communications will improve by Fall 2003, as measured by the *Education for the Future* Parent Questionnaire.
- The number of parents attending parent events at the school, such as *Muffins for Moms,* and *Donuts for Dads,* will be steady and high.
- Evaluations of parent events will be satisfactory as measured by instruments developed to assess the quality of the event.
- Many parents and students will be accessing the website.
- Evaluations of the school website will be positive.
- Ultimately, student learning will increase because of parent involvement.

## Summary

With the strengths, challenges, gap analyses, and root cause analyses complete, one can integrate findings to create a continuous school improvement plan that is informed by the data, and that will lead to student achievement increases. A continuous school improvement plan that is based on quality data can eliminate root causes. Identifying and then eliminating the root causes of the gaps in student achievement by using the data will almost surely guarantee student learning increases.

A continuous school improvement plan includes objectives for reaching the school goals, strategies, and actions to achieve the objectives, person responsible, how each strategy and action will be measured, resources needed, due date, and timeline.

From the overall continuous school improvement plan, one can pull out a leadership structure, evaluation plan, professional development schedule/plan, and even a partnership plan that will reinforce roles, responsibilities, meeting times, and the overall approach to continuous improvement and evaluation.

## On the CD Related to this Chapter

▼ *Little River School Plan for Improvement* (SchlPlan.pdf)

This read-only graphic is the first draft of the Little River Elementary School Plan and is shown as Figure 8.1 in Chapter 8.

▼ *Planning Template* (APForm.doc)

A quality action plan to implement the vision consists of goals, objectives, strategies, actions, persons responsible, resources required, due dates, and timelines. A template with these components is provided in *Microsoft Word*, ready to be completed.

▼ *Little River Leadership Structure* (LeadStruc.pdf)

This read-only graphic is the Little River Leadership Structure, created from the overall action plan, and is shown as Figure 8.2 in Chapter 8.

▼ *Little River Professional Development Calendar* (PrDevCal.pdf)

This read-only graphic is the uncut 2003-04 Fall/Spring Little River Professional Development Calendar.

▼ *Little River Professional Development Calendar Template* (PrDevCal.doc)

This *Microsoft Word* document is a template for creating your school Professional Development Calendar.

▼ *Little River Partnership Plan* (PartPlan.pdf)

This read-only graphic is the Little River Partnership Plan, created from the overall action plan, and is shown on pages 166-167 in Chapter 8.

▼ *Establishing a Partnership Plan* (EstPPlan.pdf)

This read-only file describes the steps in creating a partnership plan that will become a part of the continuous school improvement plan.

▼ *Little River Evaluation Plan* (EvalPlan.pdf)

This read-only graphic, the Little River Evaluation Plan, condenses the measurement column of the action plan into a comprehensive evaluation plan, and is shown as Figure 8.4 in Chapter 8.

▼ *Powerful Professional Development Designs* (Designs.pdf)

This read-only file describes numerous ways to embed professional development into the learning community.

▼ *Powerful Professional Development Designs*

Powerful Professional Development Designs are those that are embedded into the daily operations of a staff. They are ongoing and lead to improvement of instruction and increases in student learning.

◆ *Action Research Activity* (ACTRsrch.pdf)

Teachers and/or administrators raise questions about the best way to improve teaching and learning, systematically study the literature to answer the questions, implement the best approach, and analyze the results.

◆ *Cadres or Action Teams Activity* (ACTCdres.pdf)

Organizing cadres or teams allows for the delegation of responsibilities so teams of educators can study new approaches, plan for the implementation of new strategies or programs, and get work done without every staff member's involvement.

◆ *Case Studies Activity* (ACTCases.pdf)

Staff members review case studies of student work, and/or of another teacher's example lessons, which can lead to quality discussions and improved practices.

◆ *Coaching Activity* (ACTCoach.pdf)

Teachers form teams of two or three to observe each other, plan together, and to talk and encourage each other in meaningful ways, while reflecting on continuously improving instructional practices.

◆ *Examining Student Data: Teacher Analysis of Test Scores Table One* (Table1.doc)

Examining student data consists of conversations around individual student data results and the processes that created the results. This approach can be a significant form of professional development when skilled team members facilitate the dialogue.

◆ *Examining Student Work Activity* (ACTSWork.pdf)
Examining student work as professional development ensures that what students learn is aligned to the learning standards. It also shows teacher the impact of their actions.

◆ *Example Lessons: Birds of a Feather Unit Example* (UnitEx.pdf)
Some teachers need to see what a lesson that implements all aspects of the school vision would look like. Providing examples for all teachers to see can reward the teacher who is doing a good job of implementing the vision and provide a template for other teachers. It is very effective to store summary examples in a binder for everyone to peruse at any time.

◆ *Example Lessons: Unit Template* (UnitTmpl.doc)
This *Microsoft Word* template provides the outline for creating instructional units that implement the vision.

◆ *Immersion Activity* (ACTImrsn.pdf)
Immersion is a method for getting teachers engaged in different content through hands-on experiences as a learner.

◆ *Journaling Activity* (ACTJourn.pdf)
Journal writing helps teachers construct meaning for, and reflect on, what they are teaching and learning.

◆ *Listening to Students Activity* (ACTListn.pdf)
Students' perceptions of the learning environment are very important for continuous improvement. Focus groups, interviews, and questionnaires can be used to discover what students are perceiving.

◆ *Needs Assessment: Professional Development Needs Related to Technology Example* (TechnEx.pdf)
Needs assessments help staff understand the professional development needs of staff. At the same time, if done well, a tool can lead to quality staff conversations and sharing of knowledge.

◆ *Needs Assessment: Professional Development Plan Related to Technology Template* (TechTmpl.doc)
This template provides the outline for doing your own professional development needs assessment.

◆ *Networks Activity* (ACTNtwrk.pdf)
Purposeful grouping of individuals/schools to further a cause or commitment.

◆ *Partnerships: Creating Partnerships Activity* (ACTParts.pdf)
Teachers partnering with businesses in the community, scientists, and/or university professors can result in real-world applications for student learning and deeper understandings of content for the teacher.

◆ *Process Mapping: Charting School Processes Activity* (ACTProcs.pdf)
School processes are instruction, curriculum, and assessment strategies used to ensure the learning of all students. Mapping or flowcharting school processes can help staff objectively look at how students are being taught.

◆ *Reflection Log Activity* (ACTLog.pdf)
Reflective logs are recordings of key events in the educators' work days to reflect on improvement and/or to share learnings with colleagues.

◆ *Scheduling Activity* (ACTSchdl.pdf)
A real test for whether or not a vision is realistic is to have teachers develop a day's schedule. This would tell them immediately if it is doable, or what needs to change in the vision and plan to make it doable.

◆ *School Meetings: Running Efficient Meetings* (Meetings.pdf)
Staff, department, grade level, and cross-grade level meetings can promote learning through study or sharing best practice, while focusing on the implementation of the vision.

◆ *Self-Assessment: Teacher Assessment Tool Related to the Central City School Vision* (AssessEx.pdf)
Staff self-assessments on tools to measure progress toward the vision, such as the *Continuous Improvement Continuums*, will help them see where their school is as a system and what needs to improve for better results.

◆ *Self-Assessment: Teacher Assessment Tool Related to Our School Vision* (AssessEx.doc)
This template file for staff self-assessments on tools to measure progress toward the vision, such as the *Continuous Improvement Continuums*, will help them see where their school is as a system and what needs to improve for better results.

◆ *Self-Assessment: Our School Shared Vision Implementation Rubric Example* (StRubric.pdf)

Staff self-assessments on tools to measure progress toward the vision, such as the *Continuous Improvement Continuums*, will help them see where their school is as a system and what needs to improve for better results.

◆ *Self-Assessment: Our School Shared Vision Implementation Rubric Template* (StRubric.doc)
This template file for staff self-assessments on tools to measure progress toward the vision, such as the *Continuous Improvement Continuums*, will help them see where their school is as a system and what needs to improve for better results.

- *Self-Assessment: Staff-Developed Rubric Activity* (ACTRubric.pdf)
  This activity for staff self-assessments on tools to measure progress toward the vision, such as the *Continuous Improvement Continuums,* will help them see where their school is as a system and what needs to improve for better results.

- *Shadowing Students Activity* (ACTShadw.pdf)
  Purposefully following students and systematically recording the student's instructional experiences is a wonderful job-embedded approach to understanding what students are experiencing in school.

- *Storyboarding Activity* (ACTStory.pdf)
  Storyboarding is an activity that will allow participants to share previous knowledge, while reflecting on the topic. It is a structure for facilitating conversations.

- *Study Groups Activity* (ACTStudy.pdf)
  Groups of educators meet to learn new strategies and programs, to review new publications, or to review student work together.

- *Teacher Portfolio Activity* (ACTTcher.pdf)
  Teacher portfolios can be built to tell the story of implementing the vision in the classroom, and its impact on student learning. Portfolios are excellent for reflection, understanding, and showing progress. Portfolios can be used for many things including self-assessment, employment, supervision to replace traditional teacher evaluation, and peer collaboration.

- *Train the Trainers Activity* (ACTTrain.pdf)
  Train the Trainers is an approach to saving time and money. Individuals are trained and return to the school or school district to train others.

- *Tuning Protocols Activity* (ACTTune.pdf)
  A tuning protocol is a formal process for reviewing, honoring, and fine tuning colleagues' work through presentation and reflection.

# Analyzing the Data:
## Example Two – Blue Bird Elementary School

## Chapter 9

Chapters 4 through 8 show data analysis for one elementary school with a state *criterion-referenced* test. The data analysis for Blue Bird Elementary School, a school with four years of *norm-referenced* testing, is shown in this chapter. Please note the study questions on pages 229-232 to assist in looking at the data. Also note that there is space in the margins on the data pages to write your impressions as you review the data. At the end of the chapter, I have shared what I saw in the Example Two data for Blue Bird School. (Graphing templates are included on the CD.)

## Example Two: Blue Bird Elementary School

### *Who Are We?*

Blue Bird Elementary School is a kindergarten through grade six school in a multicultural, metropolitan area situated on the southern edge of the west coast. The city's population has increased from 27,331 in 1992, to 31,711 in 2002 (*www.census.gov*). The census data also show that the average household income in 1992 was about $32,000, while in 2002, the average household income was approximately $46,000. There are no major businesses in the city. Many of the residents of this area commute to work in other locations in the county.

### Great View Elementary School District

Blue Bird Elementary is one of eight schools in the Great View Elementary School District. The district has five elementary schools that serve kindergarten through grade six: one school offers kindergarten through grade three; one school consists of grades four through six; and one middle school serves grades seven and eight. The total district enrollment is approximately 6,000 students. The children who come to Great View schools are from first generation immigrant families as well as established residents of the area.

The district reached a peak enrollment of 7,016 students in 1970. A gradual decline in student enrollment began in 1971, that continued through the mid 1980's to approximately 3,900 students. Since then there has been an increasing enrollment trend. Approximately 5,706 students were enrolled in the district during 1999-00; 5,804 in 2000-01; 5,828 in 2001-02; and 6,117 in 2002-03. Projections indicate that enrollment will increase by approximately 1,100 students over the next several years. The increasing enrollment for the past nine years is shown in Figure 9.1.

Figure 9.1

**Great View Elementary School District Student Enrollment
1994-95 to 2002-03**

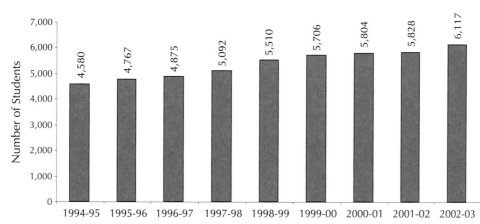

The district's enrollment is shown by grade levels in Figure 9.2. This figure shows
a fairly steady increase at each grade level.

Figure 9.2

**Great View Elementary School District
Student Enrollment by Grade Level
1994-95 to 2002-03**

| Grade Level | 1994-95 | 1995-96 | 1996-97 | 1997-98 | 1998-99 | 1999-00 | 2000-01 | 2001-02 | 2002-03 |
|---|---|---|---|---|---|---|---|---|---|
| Kindergarten | 573 | 599 | 626 | 653 | 735 | 705 | 695 | 701 | 723 |
| Grade One | 555 | 578 | 614 | 655 | 674 | 756 | 715 | 707 | 695 |
| Grade Two | 562 | 551 | 580 | 623 | 661 | 668 | 731 | 687 | 715 |
| Grade Three | 524 | 560 | 562 | 566 | 646 | 644 | 649 | 679 | 678 |
| Grade Four | 472 | 512 | 547 | 558 | 583 | 597 | 627 | 644 | 674 |
| Grade Five | 520 | 466 | 480 | 544 | 571 | 592 | 588 | 595 | 612 |
| Grade Six | 512 | 502 | 471 | 494 | 562 | 583 | 575 | 590 | 638 |
| Grade Seven | 380 | 418 | 390 | 363 | 447 | 496 | 504 | 499 | 513 |
| Grade Eight | 375 | 366 | 379 | 418 | 413 | 431 | 488 | 504 | 541 |
| Ungraded | 107 | 215 | 226 | 218 | 218 | 234 | 232 | 222 | 328 |
| **Totals:** | **4,580** | **4,767** | **4,875** | **5,092** | **5,510** | **5,706** | **5,804** | **5,828** | **6,117** |

## The School

Blue Bird Elementary School currently serves 851 students in kindergarten through grade six. Figure 9.3 shows how the enrollment has changed over time. After an increase to 888 students in 1998-99, enrollment decreased to 826 in 1999-00, increased to 857 and 871 in 2000-01 and 2001-02, respectively, and settled down to 851 in 2002-03.

### Figure 9.3

**Blue Bird Elementary School
Student Enrollment, 1997-98 to 2002-03**

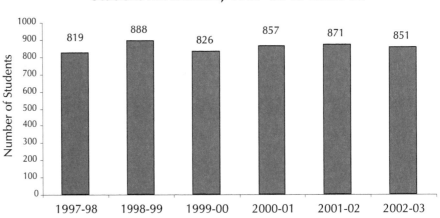

The majority of Blue Bird's current student population is Hispanic at 70%, followed by African-Americans at 14%; Caucasians, 10%; Asians, 3%; Pacific Islanders, 1%; American Indians, 1%; and Filipino, 1% (Figure 9.4).

### Figure 9.4

**Blue Bird Elementary School
Percent of Student Enrollment by Ethnicity
2002-03**

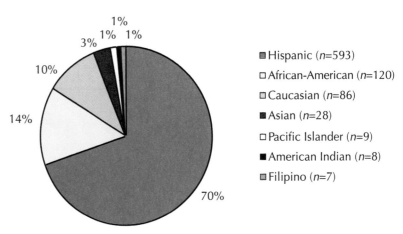

Figures 9.5 and 9.6 show the enrollment by numbers and percentages of ethnicity for the past six years. One can see that the percentage of Hispanic students has increased over time, while the other ethnicities' percentages are decreasing or essentially staying the same.

## Figure 9.5

### Blue Bird Elementary School
### Student Enrollment by Ethnicity
### 1997-98 to 2002-03

| Ethnicity | 1997-98 | | 1998-99 | | 1999-00 | | 2000-01 | | 2001-02 | | 2002-03 | |
|---|---|---|---|---|---|---|---|---|---|---|---|---|
| Hispanic | 438 | 53.5% | 506 | 57% | 503 | 60.9% | 539 | 62.9% | 576 | 66.1% | 593 | 69.7% |
| African-American | 182 | 22.2% | 194 | 21.8% | 169 | 20.5% | 171 | 20% | 137 | 15.7% | 120 | 14.1% |
| Caucasian | 137 | 16.7% | 125 | 14.1% | 106 | 12.8% | 98 | 11.4% | 92 | 10.6% | 86 | 10.1% |
| Asian | 49 | 6% | 41 | 4.6% | 29 | 3.5% | 26 | 3% | 35 | 4% | 28 | 3.3% |
| Pacific Islander | 4 | .5% | 6 | .7% | 3 | .4% | 8 | .9% | 12 | 1.4% | 8 | 1.1% |
| American Indian | 2 | .2% | 5 | .6% | 9 | 1.1% | 7 | .8% | 8 | .9% | 8 | .9% |
| Filipino | 7 | .9% | 11 | 1.2% | 7 | .8% | 8 | .9% | 11 | 1.3% | 8 | .9% |

## Figure 9.6

### Blue Bird Elementary School
### Student Enrollment by Ethnicity
### 1997-98 to 2002-03

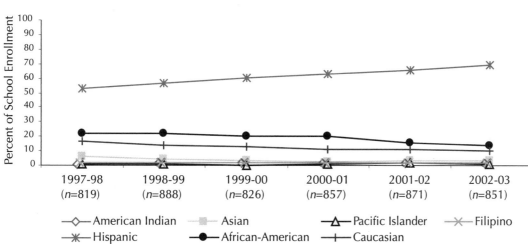

Figure 9.7 shows student enrollment by grade level, over time. There are some fluctuations over time, within grade levels.

Figure 9.7

**Blue Bird Elementary School
Student Enrollment by Grade Level
1997-98 to 2002-03**

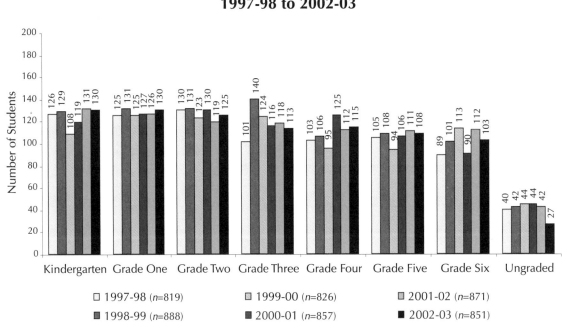

Reorganizing the data to follow the same groups of students over time, or cohorts, one can see fluctuations in their numbers as shown in Figure 9.8.

**Figure 9.8**

**Blue Bird Elementary School
Student Cohorts by Grade Level
1997-98 to 2002-03**

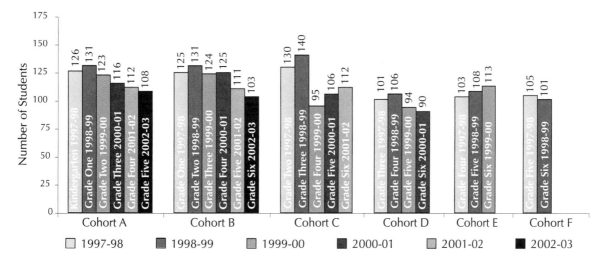

Figure 9.9 shows the enrollment by grade level, gender, and ethnicity for 2002-03.

## Figure 9.9

### Blue Bird Elementary School Student Enrollment
### By Grade Level, Gender, and Ethnicity, 2002-03 (N=851)

| Grade Level | Gender | Ethnicity | | | | | | | | | | | | | Total Number | |
|---|---|---|---|---|---|---|---|---|---|---|---|---|---|---|---|---|
| | | American Indian | | Asian | | Pacific Islander | | Filipino | | Hispanic | | African-American | | Caucasian | | | |
| | | Number | Percent | Number | Percent | Number | Percent | Number | Percent | Number | Percent | Number | Percent | Number | Percent | | |
| Kindergarten | Female | 1 | 1% | 2 | 2% | | | 2 | 2% | 59 | 45% | 8 | 6% | 3 | 2% | 75 | |
| | Male | | | 2 | 2% | | | | | 37 | 28% | 6 | 5% | 10 | 8% | 55 | 130 |
| Grade One | Female | 1 | 1% | 2 | 2% | | | | | 44 | 34% | 2 | 2% | 6 | 5% | 55 | |
| | Male | | | 4 | 3% | 1 | 1% | 1 | 1% | 55 | 42% | 6 | 5% | 8 | 6% | 75 | 130 |
| Grade Two | Female | 1 | 1% | 4 | 3% | | | 1 | 1% | 42 | 34% | 14 | 11% | 5 | 4% | 67 | |
| | Male | | | 2 | 2% | 3 | 2% | | | 42 | 34% | 5 | 4% | 6 | 5% | 58 | 125 |
| Grade Three | Female | | | 2 | 2% | 1 | 1% | | | 42 | 37% | 4 | 4% | 8 | 7% | 57 | |
| | Male | 2 | 2% | 2 | 2% | | | | | 35 | 31% | 12 | 11% | 5 | 4% | 56 | 113 |
| Grade Four | Female | 1 | 1% | | | 1 | 1% | | | 41 | 36% | 10 | 9% | 2 | 2% | 55 | |
| | Male | | | 1 | 1% | 1 | 1% | 1 | 1% | 42 | 37% | 7 | 7% | 8 | 7% | 60 | 115 |
| Grade Five | Female | | | 1 | 1% | 1 | 1% | | | 29 | 27% | 8 | 7% | 4 | 4% | 43 | |
| | Male | | | 4 | 4% | | | | | 46 | 43% | 10 | 9% | 5 | 5% | 65 | 108 |
| Grade Six | Female | 1 | 1% | 1 | 1% | 1 | 1% | | | 31 | 30% | 10 | 10% | 5 | 5% | 49 | |
| | Male | | | 1 | 1% | | | 2 | 2% | 36 | 35% | 10 | 10% | 5 | 5% | 54 | 103 |
| Ungraded | Female | 1 | 4% | | | | | | | 2 | 7% | 3 | 11% | 1 | 4% | 7 | |
| | Male | | | | | | | | | 10 | 37% | 5 | 19% | 5 | 19% | 20 | 27 |
| Total Numbers | Female | 6 | | 12 | | 4 | | 3 | | 290 | | 59 | | 34 | | 408 | |
| | Male | 2 | | 16 | | 5 | | 4 | | 303 | | 61 | | 52 | | 443 | |
| | All | 8 | | 28 | | 9 | | 7 | | 593 | | 120 | | 86 | | | 851 |

Figure 9.10 shows the number and percentage of students by native language between 2000-01 and 2002-03. Over one-half of the current school population are native Spanish speakers (52%), followed by 44% English, and 2.8% native speakers of Vietnamese.

## Figure 9.10

### Blue Bird Elementary School
### Number and Percentage of Students
### By Native Language, 2000-01 to 2002-03

| Native Language | 2000-01 | | 2001-02 | | 2002-03 | |
|---|---|---|---|---|---|---|
| | Number | Percent | Number | Percent | Number | Percent |
| English | 389 | 47% | 368 | 45% | 371 | 44% |
| Spanish | 412 | 49% | 421 | 51% | 437 | 52% |
| Vietnamese | 23 | 2.8% | 21 | 2.5% | 24 | 2.8% |
| Tagalog | 1 | 1% | 4 | .5% | 1 | .1% |
| Arabic | 2 | 2% | 3 | .4% | 6 | .7% |
| Hindu | 1 | 1% | | | | |
| Urdu | 2 | 2% | 1 | .1% | | |
| Other Chinese | 1 | 1% | 1 | .1% | 2 | .2% |
| Other | 1 | 1% | 1 | .1% | 2 | .2% |

Figure 9.11 shows the numbers and percentage of students classified as English speakers, fluent English, limited English, and redesignated by grade level for 2000-01 through 2002-03. English-only students are native speakers of English. Fluent-English students are non-native English speakers who speak English fluently. Limited-English students are non-native English speakers who are learning English. Redesignated students are those who moved from non-English to limited-English speaking status. In 2002-03, 37% of all kindergarten students were English Learners (EL). Almost one-half of the first-graders were EL. Forty-two percent of second graders were English learners. The other grades ranged from 34% to 47% EL.

## Figure 9.11

### Blue Bird Elementary School Students
### By Grade Level and Language Designation
### 2000-01 to 2002-03

| Grade Level | Language Designation | 2000-01 | | 2001-02 | | 2002-03 | |
|---|---|---|---|---|---|---|---|
| | | Number | Percent | Number | Percent | Number | Percent |
| Kindergarten | English Only | 54 | 46% | 41 | 33% | 47 | 38% |
| | Fluent English | 18 | 15% | 21 | 17% | 31 | 25% |
| | Limited English | 46 | 39% | 61 | 50% | 45 | 37% |
| Grade One | English Only | 51 | 43% | 55 | 45% | 41 | 33% |
| | Fluent English | 15 | 13% | 20 | 16% | 22 | 18% |
| | Limited English | 53 | 45% | 47 | 39% | 60 | 49% |
| Grade Two | English Only | 58 | 45% | 47 | 40% | 54 | 45% |
| | Fluent English | 19 | 15% | 22 | 19% | 16 | 13% |
| | Limited English | 52 | 40% | 48 | 41% | 40 | 42% |
| Grade Three | English Only | 46 | 37% | 51 | 45% | 48 | 45% |
| | Fluent English | 13 | 10% | 18 | 16% | 22 | 21% |
| | Limited English | 59 | 47% | 39 | 34% | 36 | 34% |
| | Redesignated | 8 | 6% | 6 | 5% | | |
| Grade Four | English Only | 53 | 43% | 41 | 38% | 52 | 44% |
| | Fluent English | 9 | 7% | 17 | 16% | 20 | 17% |
| | Limited English | 46 | 37% | 40 | 37% | 40 | 34% |
| | Redesignated | 15 | 12% | 10 | 9% | 6 | 5% |
| Grade Five | English Only | 63 | 52% | 44 | 41% | 44 | 40% |
| | Fluent English | 16 | 13% | 10 | 9% | 17 | 15% |
| | Limited English | 34 | 28% | 41 | 38% | 33 | 30% |
| | Redesignated | 8 | 7% | 13 | 12% | 16 | 15% |
| Grade Six | English Only | 46 | 50% | 53 | 47% | 42 | 38% |
| | Fluent English | 15 | 16% | 25 | 22% | 17 | 15% |
| | Limited English | 16 | 17% | 12 | 11% | 18 | 16% |
| | Redesignated | 15 | 16% | 22 | 20% | 35 | 31% |
| Total Number of Students | | 828 | | 804 | | 802 | |

Figure 9.12 shows how the number of students qualifying for free/reduced lunch has been high for all three years—between 93% (2001-02) to 97% (2000-01). Ninety-six percent of all students at Blue Bird qualified for free/reduced lunch in 2002-03.

Figure 9.12

**Blue Bird Elementary School
Students Qualifying for Free/Reduced
Lunch Status, 2000-01 to 2002-03**

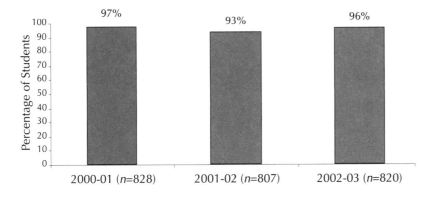

Figure 9.13 shows the number of students qualifying for free/reduced lunch has not changed a great deal within grade levels over the past two years, with the exception of kindergarten and grades four and six, which saw increases of students qualifying for free/reduced lunch at around 10% or higher. The percentage of total students enrolled for that particular subgroup is below the number value.

Figure 9.13

**Blue Bird Elementary School
Students Qualifying for Free/Reduced Lunch
By Grade Level, 2001-02 to 2002-03**

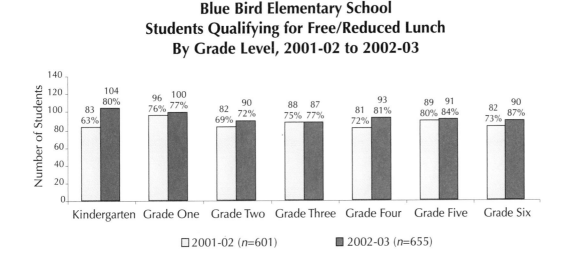

## Mobility

Figure 9.14 shows the number and percentage of students who transferred in or out of Blue Bird Elementary over the past three years. In 2002-03, 113 students moved in or out, representing a 13% mobility rate. In 2001-02 and 2000-01, there were 54 and 84 students, respectively, who moved in or out of the school, representing 6% and 10%, respectively. (*Transfer from in state* means students transferred from another school within the state; *transfer from out-of-state* means students transferred from a school in another state; *previously in school* means that the students moved out of Blue Bird and back in that noted year; *in-district moved* indicates the student moved from Blue Bird to another school in the district; *in-state moved* students left Blue Bird to attend school somewhere else in the state; and *out-of-state moved* are students who left Blue Bird to attend school in another state.) The percentage of total students enrolled for that particular subgroup is below the number value.

Figure 9.14

### Blue Bird Elementary School Student Mobility 2000-01 to 2002-03

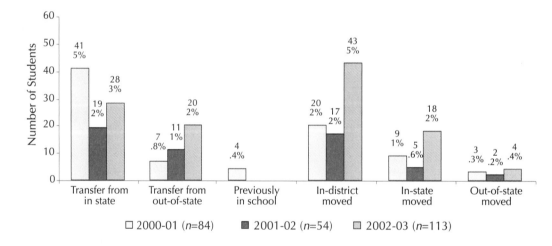

## Attendance and Per Pupil Expenditure

The average daily student attendance was 94.8% in 2002-03. The average per pupil expenditure was $4,299.86 in 2002-03.

## Retentions

The number of Blue Bird Elementary School students retained in a grade level increased since 2000-01, with the highest retention being in 2001-02. In 2000-01, 11 students in the school were retained in a grade—four in grade three, one in grade four, two in grade five, and four in grade six. In 2001-02, 32 students were retained—seven in kindergarten, nine in grade one, nine in grade two, four in grade three, one in grade four, and two in grade five; and in 2002-03, there were 19—three in kindergarten, four in grade one, six in grade two, two in grade three, two in grade four, and two in grade five. No students were retained in kindergarten through grade two in 2000-01, and none in grade six in 2001-02 and 2002-03. Figure 9.15 indicates that the number of students retained by grade level during this time period was highest at the kindergarten, first, second, and third-grade levels, with a high of 32 students retained in 2001-02 before dropping back to 19 in 2002-03.

### Figure 9.15

**Blue Bird Elementary School
Students Retained by Grade Level
2000-01 to 2002-03**

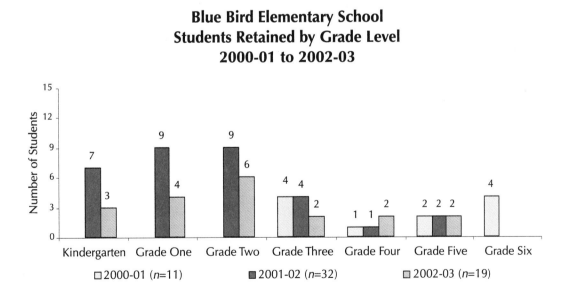

Retentions by gender and ethnicity are shown in Figure 9.16. Over time, Hispanic males have been retained the most. In 2002-03, ten Hispanic males were retained, five Hispanic females, two African-American males, one Caucasian male, and one African-American female. In 2001-02, twelve Hispanic males, ten Hispanic females, two African-American males, three African-American females, three Caucasian males, one Caucasian female, and one Asian male were retained. In 2000-01, five Hispanic males, two African-American males, two Hispanic females, one Asian male, and one Caucasian male were retained. The rates for all of these are small.

Figure 9.16

## Blue Bird Elementary School
## Number of Students Retained by
## Grade Level, Gender, and Ethnicity
## 2000-01 to 2002-03

| Grade Level | Gender | Ethnicity | 2000-01 (N=11) | 2001-02 (N=32) | 2002-03 (N=19) |
|---|---|---|---|---|---|
| Kindergarten | Female | Hispanic | | 2 | |
| | Male | African-American | | 1 | |
| | | Hispanic | | 4 | 3 |
| Grade One | Female | African-American | | 1 | |
| | | Hispanic | | 4 | 2 |
| | Male | African-American | | | 1 |
| | | Hispanic | | 2 | 1 |
| | | Caucasian | | 2 | |
| Grade Two | Female | African-American | | 1 | 1 |
| | | Hispanic | | 4 | 3 |
| | Male | Asian | | 1 | |
| | | Hispanic | | 2 | 2 |
| | | Caucasian | | 1 | |
| Grade Three | Female | African-American | | 1 | |
| | | Hispanic | 1 | | |
| | | Caucasian | | 1 | |
| | Male | Asian | 1 | | |
| | | African-American | | 1 | 1 |
| | | Hispanic | 2 | 1 | 1 |
| Grade Four | Male | African-American | 1 | | |
| | | Hispanic | | 1 | 1 |
| | | Caucasian | | | 1 |
| Grade Five | Male | Hispanic | 1 | 2 | 2 |
| | Female | Hispanic | 1 | | |
| Grade Six | Male | African-American | 1 | | |
| | | Hispanic | 2 | | |
| | | Caucasian | 1 | | |
| | | Total Students | 11 | 32 | 19 |

## Discipline and Climate for Learning

The staff at Blue Bird Elementary School believe that a nurturing and supportive environment is a key element in meeting the changing needs of all students. This is what they say about discipline and climate for learning:

> Students deserve to be educated in a safe place where individuals are treated with respect and where a quality educational program is offered. The school has a system-wide plan of positive incentives and accountability for students not meeting school and classroom expectations. Staff provide programs that offer students an opportunity to feel connected at school. Some of the activities offered before, during, and after school are noontime sports, student council, after-school specials, and newspaper club. Monthly awards assemblies honor students for high achievement, improvement, and citizenship. A full-time counselor facilitates *Character Counts,* a schoolwide program emphasizing important character qualities such as respect, trustworthiness, and responsibility. When students do not meet school expectations, teachers implement fair and consistent consequences for unacceptable behaviors. One of the most effective strategies employed is to maintain consistent communication with parents, keeping them informed and asking them to work together with the school on improving student behaviors. Each teacher is expected to have a plan for classroom environment. There is also a plan for playground behavior. Administrators are always available to counsel students causing disruption to a class or when they just need a place to talk about issues or restart the day with a positive tone. The school's motto is, "We believe we *can* and *do* make a difference in our children's lives."

The number of Blue Bird students suspended (Figure 9.17) has decreased dramatically over the past three years, from almost 99 students (11.6%) in 2000-01, to 26 (3%) in 2002-03. The discipline plan seems to be having a positive impact on suspension rates.

## Figure 9.17

### Blue Bird Elementary School
### Number of Students Suspended
### 2000-01 to 2002-03

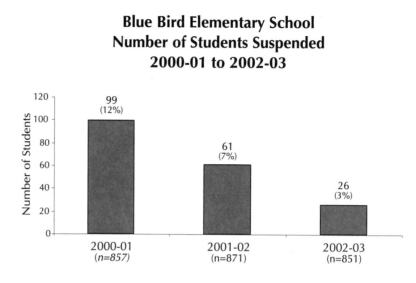

## Special Education

In the two most recent years for which we have data, 2001-02 and 2002-03, the number of students classified as needing special education has decreased by one at Blue Bird Elementary School from 71 to 70. The majority of students classified as receiving special education assistance were speech and language impaired and learning disabled. As shown in Figure 9.18, a total of 141 students were classified as special education in 2001-02 and 2002-03.

## Figure 9.18

### Blue Bird Elementary School
### Special Education
### 2001-02 to 2002-03

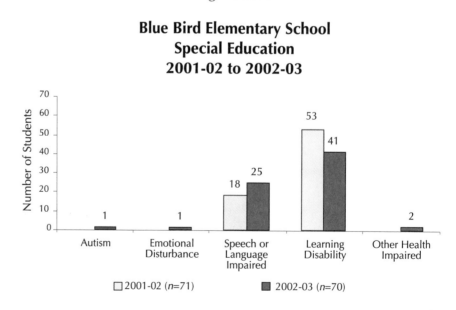

Figure 9.19, which shows the number of students classified as receiving special education services by gender, indicates that more than twice the number of males than females were receiving special education services in 2001-02, and four times the number of males were receiving special education services in 2002-03.

Figure 9.19

**Blue Bird Elementary School
Special Education Status by Gender
2001-02 to 2002-03**

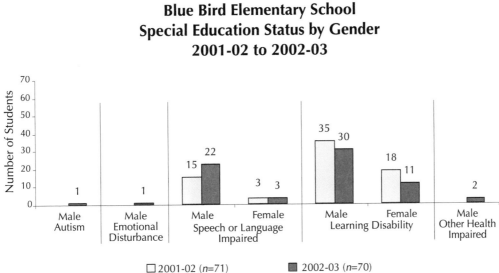

□ 2001-02 (*n*=71)     ■ 2002-03 (*n*=70)

Figure 9.20 shows special education learning impairments by gender and ethnicity. Hispanics were more likely than any other ethnicity to be classified as needing special education. They also represent the greatest percentage of the total school population.

## Figure 9.20

### Blue Bird Elementary School
### Special Education by Gender and Ethnicity
### 2001-02 to 2002-03

| Learning Impairment | Gender | Ethnicity | 2001-02 | 2002-03 |
|---|---|---|---|---|
| Autism | Male | Caucasian | | 1 |
| Emotional disturbance | Male | Caucasian | | 1 |
| Learning disability | Female | American Indian | 1 | 1 |
| | | Asian | 1 | |
| | | African-American | 7 | 3 |
| | | Hispanic | 8 | 7 |
| | | Caucasian | 1 | |
| | Male | African-American | 10 | 6 |
| | | Filipino | 1 | |
| | | Hispanic | 20 | 20 |
| | | Caucasian | 4 | 4 |
| Speech/Language impaired | Female | Hispanic | 2 | 2 |
| | | Caucasian | 1 | 1 |
| | Male | African-American | | 1 |
| | | Filipino | 1 | |
| | | Hispanic | 13 | 17 |
| | | Caucasian | | 2 |
| | | Pacific Islander | 1 | 1 |
| | | Ethnicity Unknown | | 1 |
| Other health impaired | Male | Hispanic | | 2 |

The number of students receiving special education services by free/reduced lunch status appears in Figure 9.21. Most of the schools' special education students also qualify for free/reduced lunch, as does the majority of Blue Bird's enrollment.

## Figure 9.21

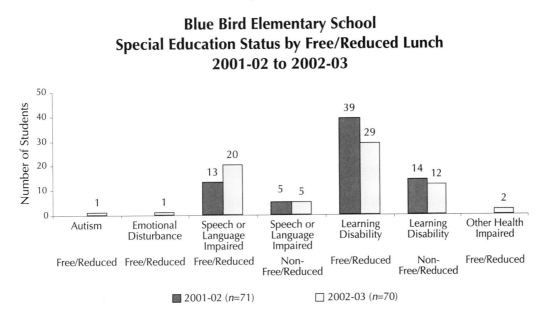

**Blue Bird Elementary School
Special Education Status by Free/Reduced Lunch
2001-02 to 2002-03**

## Staff

Blue Bird Elementary School staff is made up of:

▼ 36 Classroom Teachers

▼ 24 Classified Support Staff

▼ 2 Special Day Class Teachers

▼ 1 Resource Specialist Teacher

▼ 1 Psychologist

▼ 1 Speech/Language Specialist

▼ 1 Nurse

▼ 1 Adaptive P.E. Specialist

▼ 1 Language Arts Specialist

▼ Noon Duty and After-school Staff

All Blue Bird School teachers are assigned to teach within their certificated subject/grade areas, with the exception of three teachers with emergency credentials. Figure 9.22 shows the number of years each teacher has taught.

## Figure 9.22

### Blue Bird Elementary School
### Teaching Experience by Grade Level, Gender, and Teacher, 2002-03

| Grade Level | Gender | Teacher | Other Language | Years of Experience |
|---|---|---|---|---|
| Kindergarten (Average=10.8 years) | Female | Kinder A | Spanish | 14 |
| | | Kinder B | | 23 |
| | | Kinder C | | 12 |
| | | Kinder D | | 7 |
| | | Kinder E | Spanish | 5 |
| | | Kinder F | Spanish | 5 |
| | | Kinder G | | 10 |
| Grade One (Average=6.3 years) | Female | One A | | 1 |
| | | One B | | 5 |
| | | One C | | 3 |
| | | One D | Chinese | 2 |
| | | One E | | 12 |
| | | One F | | 15 |
| Grade Two (Average=8.1 years) | Female | Two A | | 6 |
| | | Two B | | 11 |
| | | Two C | | 25 |
| | | Two D | | 4 |
| | | Two E | | 7 |
| | | Two F | Spanish | 5 |
| | | Two G | | 1 |
| | | Two H | | 6 |
| Grade Three (Average=5.3 years) | Female | Three A | Vietnamese | 8 |
| | | Three B | | 9 |
| | | Three D | | 6 |
| | | Three E | Chinese | 3 |
| | | Three F | | 5 |
| | Male | Three C | Korean | 1 |
| Grade Four (Average=8.2 years) | Female | Four A | | 18 |
| | | Four B | | 9 |
| | | Four C | Chinese | 3 |
| | | Four D | | 3 |
| Grade Five (Average=11.0 years) | Female | Five A | Spanish | 25 |
| | | Five B | | 11 |
| | | Five C | | 3 |
| | Male | Five D | | 5 |
| Grade Six (Average=8.0 years) | Female | Six A | Spanish | 2 |
| | | Six B | | 6 |
| | | Six C | | 16 |

## Student to Teacher Ratios

During the past five years, staff at Blue Bird have worked hard to decrease the student-to-teacher ratio. For the past two years, the school has achieved and maintained a 20-to-1 ratio in kindergarten through grade three. Grades four, five, and six are still 29 or 30-to-1. The average class size by grade level in 2002-03, is shown below in Figure 9.23.

**Figure 9.23**

**Blue Bird Elementary School
Average Class Size 2002-03**

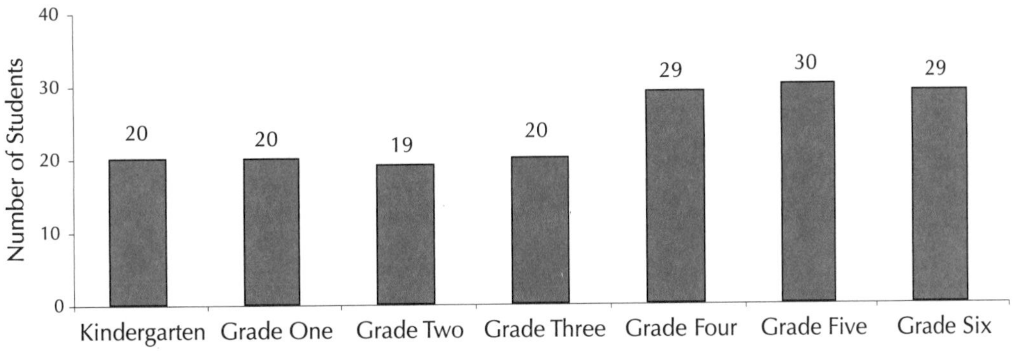

## Special Student Programs

Some of the special programs at Blue Bird Elementary include:

- ▼ Classroom Library K-4
- ▼ Safe & Drug Free
- ▼ Tobacco Use Prevention Education (TUPE)
- ▼ School Library
- ▼ Pupil Block Grant
- ▼ Economic Impact Aid (EIA)/State Compensatory Education (SCE)
- ▼ Economic Impact Aid (EIA)/Bilingual (BIL)
- ▼ English Language Acquisition Program (ELAP)
- ▼ Gifted and Talented Education (GATE)
- ▼ Title 1, Title VI
- ▼ Miller-Unruh (Language Arts Specialists)
- ▼ Emergency Immigrant Education Program (EIEP)
- ▼ School Improvement Program (SIP)

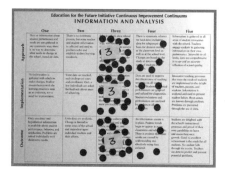

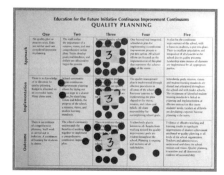

## How Do We Do Business?

To get a better understanding of the learning environment at Blue Bird Elementary School, staff assessed where they felt the school ranked on the *Education for the Future Continuous Improvement Continuums* (CICs). A summary of the CIC results follow. The complete assessment is also located on the CD, along with tools to assist schools in doing this assessment. *Education for the Future* student, staff, and parent questionnaires were administered in December 2002. Student questionnaires were administered in May 2003, as well. The questionnaire results are shown on the CD.

### Continuous Improvement Continuum Baseline Results

In December 2002, staff members of the Blue Bird Elementary School conducted their baseline self-assessment of where their school is, using the *Education for the Future Continuous Improvement Continuums.*

After reading a *Continuum,* each staff member placed a dot on the *Continuum* to represent where she/he thinks the school is with respect to *Approach, Implementation,* and *Outcome.*

Staff members discussed why they thought the school is where they rated it. Following the discussion, the staff came to consensus on a number that represented where the school is for each element, and created "Next Steps" for moving up the *Continuum.* The ratings and brief discussions for each *Continuous Improvement Continuum* follow.

## Information and Analysis

*Blue Bird Elementary School staff rated their school 3s in Approach, Implementation, and Outcome with respect to Information and Analysis. Staff agreed that there are some data collected. It is neither systematic nor analyzed effectively to be used to improve instruction. Staff have become more effective at collecting data and charting data. Staff has tracked SAT 9 (Stanford Achievement Test, Version 9) data over the past three years and have become good at looking at successes and areas of concern in achievement testing. Some of these results can be seen in the analysis of SAT 9 data found in the Student Achievement section of the Blue Bird School Portfolio. Teachers and staff have used these data to assist in guiding instruction—especially in finding the gaps in instruction. This use of data has been especially effective in math instruction. Teachers have analyzed the data to make certain they are teaching all of the components of the SAT 9 before students take the actual test.*

### INFORMATION AND ANALYSIS

| | One | Two | Three | Four | Five |
|---|---|---|---|---|---|
| **Approach** | Data or information about student performance and needs are not gathered in any systematic way; there is no way to determine what needs to change at the school, based on data. | There is no systematic process, but some teacher and student information is collected and used to problem-solve and establish student learning standards. | School collects data related to student performance (e.g., attendance, achievement) and conducts surveys on student, teacher, and parent needs. The information is used to drive the strategic quality plan for school change. | There is systematic reliance on hard data (including data for subgroups) as a basis for decision making at the classroom level as well as at the school level. Changes are based on the study of data to meet the needs of students and teachers. | Information is gathered in all areas of student interaction with the school. Teachers engage students in gathering information on their own performance. Accessible to all levels, data are comprehensive in scope and an accurate reflection of school quality. |
| **Implementation** | No information is gathered with which to make changes. Student dissatisfaction with the learning process is seen as an irritation, not a need for improvement. | Some data are tracked, such as drop-out rates and enrollment. Only a few individuals are asked for feedback about areas of schooling. | School collects information on current and former students (e.g., student achievement and perceptions), analyzes and uses it in conjunction with future trends for planning. Identified areas for improvement are tracked over time. | Data are used to improve the effectiveness of teaching strategies on all student learning. Students' historical performances are graphed and utilized for diagnostics. Student evaluations and performances are analyzed by teachers in all classrooms. | Innovative teaching processes that meet the needs of students are implemented to the delight of teachers, parents, and students. Information is analyzed and used to prevent student failure. Root causes are known through analyses. Problems are prevented through the use of data. |
| **Outcome** | Only anecdotal and hypothetical information is available about student performance, behavior, and satisfaction. Problems are solved individually with short-term results. | Little data are available. Change is limited to some areas of the school and dependent upon individual teachers and their efforts. | Information collected about student and parent needs, assessment, and instructional practices is shared with the school staff and used to plan for change. Information helps staff understand pressing issues, analyze information for "root causes," and track results for improvement. | An information system is in place. Positive trends begin to appear in many classrooms and schoolwide. There is evidence that these results are caused by understanding and effectively using data collected. | Students are delighted with the school's instructional processes and proud of their own capabilities to learn and assess their own growth. Good to excellent achievement is the result for all students. No student falls through the cracks. Teachers use data to predict and prevent potential problems. |

*Next Steps:*

▼ *There is a need to gather information about former students.*

▼ *There is a need to survey students about their attitudes toward school.*

## Student Achievement

*Blue Bird Elementary School staff rated their school 3s in Approach and Implementation and a 4 in Outcome with respect to Student Achievement. Staff does some following of student achievement data, but it is neither systematic nor exhaustive. It is much improved, and teachers are using achievement data to identify students at risk. The data have also proved useful in identifying specific areas of instruction that need to be emphasized both for individual students and for whole groups of students. For example, there seems to be a concern for the English Learners, especially in the upper grades. Achievement data have assisted in identifying this need and in planning accordingly.*

### STUDENT ACHIEVEMENT

| | One | Two | Three | Four | Five |
|---|---|---|---|---|---|
| **Approach** | Instructional and organizational processes critical to student success are not identified. Little distinction of student learning differences is made. Some teachers believe that not all students can achieve. | Some data are collected on student background and performance trends. Learning gaps are noted to direct improvement of instruction. It is known that student learning standards must be identified. | Student learning standards are identified, and a continuum of learning is created throughout the school. Student performance data are collected and compared to the standards in order to analyze how to improve learning for all students. | Data on student achievement are used throughout the school to pursue the improvement of student learning. Teachers collaborate to implement appropriate instruction and assessment strategies for meeting student learning standards articulated across grade levels. All teachers believe that all students can learn. | School makes an effort to exceed student achievement expectations. Innovative instructional changes are made to anticipate learning needs and improve student achievement. Teachers are able to predict characteristics impacting student achievement and to know how to perform from a small set of internal quality measures. |
| **Implementation** | All students are taught the same way. There is no communication with students about their academic needs or learning styles. There are no analyses of how to improve instruction. | Some effort is made to track and analyze student achievement trends on a school-wide basis. Teachers begin to understand the needs and learning gaps of students. | Teachers study effective instruction and assessment strategies to implement standards and to increase their students' learning. Student feedback and analysis of achievement data are used in conjunction with implementation support strategies. | There is a systematic focus on implementing student learning standards and on the improvement of student learning schoolwide. Effective instruction and assessment strategies are implemented in each classroom. Teachers support one another with peer coaching and/or action research focused on implementing strategies that lead to increased achievement and the attainment of the shared vision. | All teachers correlate critical instructional and assessment strategies with objective indicators of quality student achievement. A comparative analysis of actual individual student performance to student learning standards is utilized to adjust teaching strategies to ensure a progression of learning for all students. |
| **Outcome** | There is wide variation in student attitudes and achievement with undesirable results. There is high dissatisfaction among students with learning. Student background is used as an excuse for low student achievement. | There is some evidence that student achievement trends are available to teachers and are being used. There is much effort, but minimal observable results in improving student achievement. | There is an increase in communication between students and teachers regarding student learning. Teachers learn about effective instructional strategies that will implement the shared vision, including student learning standards, and meet the needs of their students. They make some gains. | Increased student achievement is evident schoolwide. Student morale, attendance, and behavior are good. Teachers converse often with each other about preventing student failure. Areas for further attention are clear. | Students and teachers conduct self-assessments to continuously improve performance. Improvements in student achievement are evident and clearly caused by teachers' and students' understandings of individual student learning standards, linked to appropriate and effective instructional and assessment strategies. A continuum of learning results. No students fall through the cracks. |

*Teachers have also been able to measure what has been working, as the school scores have improved dramatically during the last school year. Teachers have used a portfolio of schoolwork and assessment that follows each student as she/he moves from grade to grade. This is a helpful tool as it provides other ways to measure student achievement besides the SAT 9.*

*The teaching staff spend a great deal of time discussing current instructional practices with one another. There is a spirit of cooperation and a real desire on the part of staff to achieve best practices. Teachers are concerned for every student and try not to let any child fall through the crack. Teachers, for example, spend many hours tutoring students before and after school and trying to meet the needs of students through various interventions.*

*Teachers spend a great deal of time in contact with parents about student achievement. In addition to three report cards, three progress reports, and two parent conferences annually, there are a variety of opportunities for parents to discuss with teachers the success and struggles of their students. Teachers, in a student study team format, discuss concerns about the progress of individual students.*

*Next Steps:*

▼ *Some teachers feel the need to have a staff inservice on the possible effects of poverty on student achievement.*

▼ *There is a need for further discussion about teachers' beliefs about all that students can do as opposed to what they can't do. There is a concern that we sometimes do not have high enough expectations for our students and thus limit what they can achieve.*

▼ *Some teachers feel that multi-age classrooms and looping might serve the best interest of the students, making it easier to track student progress. However, there has been resistance to combination classes by parents who are concerned that teachers cannot effectively serve two grades in one classroom. If multi-age classrooms or looping are going to occur, staff believe it would be most effective in early years such as a kindergarten-first grade or a first-second grade combination.*

▼ *There is a need to have consistent rubrics used by all teachers for students. This is currently being done in writing. The district has a pre and post-writing assessment with a rubric that it uses to assess all students in writing proficiency. The rubric supplied has been helpful; however, in the opinion of many staff, it still needs to be further modified.*

▼ *The number of computers in the school has increased, and teachers have begun to teach students the skills necessary to use the computer. There is still a need for staff and students to learn how to use technology as a means for students to acquire information and to present that data collection in reports that are effective means of communication.*

*Quality Planning*

*Blue Bird Elementary School Staff rated their school 3s in Approach, Implementation, and Outcome with respect to Quality Planning.*

## QUALITY PLANNING

| | One | Two | Three | Four | Five |
|---|---|---|---|---|---|
| **Approach** | No quality plan or process exists. Data are neither used nor considered important in planning. | The staff realize the importance of a mission, vision, and one comprehensive action plan. Teams develop goals and timelines, and dollars are allocated to begin the process. | A comprehensive school plan to achieve the vision is developed. Plan includes evaluation and continuous improvement. | One focused and integrated schoolwide plan for implementing a continuous improvement process is put into action. All school efforts are focused on the implementation of this plan that represents the achievement of the vision. | A plan for the continuous improvement of the school, with a focus on students, is put into place. There is excellent articulation and integration of all elements in the school due to quality planning. Leadership team ensures all elements are implemented by all appropriate parties. |
| **Implementation** | There is no knowledge of or direction for quality planning. Budget is allocated on an as-needed basis. Many plans exist. | School community begins continuous improvement planning efforts by laying out major steps to a shared vision, by identifying values and beliefs, the purpose of the school, a mission, vision, and student learning standards. | Implementation goals, responsibilities, due dates, and timelines are spelled out. Support structures for implementing the plan are set in place. | The quality management plan is implemented through effective procedures in all areas of the school. Everyone commits to implementing the plan aligned to the vision, mission, and values and beliefs. All share responsibility for accomplishing school goals. | Schoolwide goals, mission, vision, and student learning standards are shared and articulated throughout the school and with feeder schools. The attainment of identified student learning standards is linked to planning and implementation of effective instruction that meets students' needs. Leaders at all levels are developing expertise because planning is the norm. |
| **Outcome** | There is no evidence of comprehensive planning. Staff work is carried out in isolation. A continuum of learning for students is absent. | The school community understands the benefits of working together to implement a comprehensive continuous improvement plan. | There is evidence that the school plan is being implemented in some areas of the school. Improvements are neither systematic nor integrated schoolwide. | A schoolwide plan is known to all. Results from working toward the quality improvement goals are evident throughout the school. Planning is ongoing and inclusive of all stakeholders. | Evidence of effective teaching and learning results in significant improvement of student achievement attributed to quality planning at all levels of the school organization. Teachers and administrators understand and share the school mission and vision. Quality planning is seamless and all demonstrate evidence of accountability. |

*There is evidence of schoolwide planning. The school has focused primarily on literacy and technology for the last five years and has seen significant gains in these areas. There have been ongoing discussions of goals in these areas. Literacy scores have improved, and there is clear evidence that the number of fluent readers in grades three through six has increased dramatically. The school staff recognizes the need to improve comprehension, both in the areas of fiction and content-area reading. Staff also recognizes the need to serve more effectively the needs of English Learners.*

*The school has a comprehensive school plan that meets the needs of federal requirements and is consistent with schoolwide goals. It is available to staff but needs to be shared more consistently with the total staff. The plan needs to be reviewed and revised yearly by a committee such as the staff curriculum committee.*

*Next Steps:*

▼ *There is a need for everyone on staff to know the school plan and to be involved in the carrying out of the plan.*

▼ *There is a need to publicize the plan to the staff and community in the form of a brochure or a pamphlet.*

▼ *The plan needs to be comprehensive with clear timelines.*

▼ *There is a need to articulate a clear and concise vision statement that is motivating and can be articulated by all members of the school community.*

▼ *A plan needs to be developed that provides for a response to school concerns and goals.*

## *Professional Development*

*Blue Bird Elementary School staff rated their school 3s in Approach and Implementation and a 4 in Outcome with respect to Professional Development.*

### PROFESSIONAL DEVELOPMENT

| | One | Two | Three | Four | Five |
|---|---|---|---|---|---|
| **Approach** | There is no professional development. Teachers, principals, and staff are seen as interchangeable parts that can be replaced. Professional development is external and usually equated to attending a conference alone. Hierarchy determines "haves" and "have-nots." | The "cafeteria" approach to professional development is used, whereby individual teachers choose what they want to take, without regard to an overall school plan. | The shared vision, school plan and student needs are used to target focused professional development for all employees. Staff is inserviced on relevant instructional and leadership strategies. | Professional development and data-gathering methods are used by all teachers and are directed toward the goals of the shared vision and the continuous improvement of the school. Teachers have ongoing conversations about student achievement data. Other staff members receive training in their content areas. Systems thinking is considered in all decisions. | Leadership and staff continuously improve all aspects of the learning organization through an innovative, data-driven, and comprehensive continuous improvement process that prevents student failures. Effective job-embedded professional development is ongoing for implementing the vision for student success. Traditional teacher evaluations are replaced by collegial coaching and action research focused on student learning standards. Policies set professional development as a priority budget line-item. Professional development is planned, aligned, and lead to the achievement of student learning standards. |
| **Implementation** | Teacher, principal, and staff performance is controlled and inspected. Performance evaluations are used to detect mistakes. | Teacher professional development is sporadic and unfocused, lacking an approach for implementing new procedures and processes. Some leadership training begins to take place. | Teachers are involved in year-round quality professional development. The school community is trained in shared decision making, team building concepts, effective communication strategies, and data analysis at the classroom level. | Teachers, in teams, continuously set and implement student achievement goals. Leadership considers these goals and provides necessary support structures for collaboration. Teachers utilize effective support approaches as they implement new instruction and assessment strategies. Coaching and feedback structures are in place. Use of new knowledge and skills is evident. | Teams passionately support each other in the pursuit of quality improvement at all levels. Teachers make bold changes in instruction and assessment strategies focused on student learning standards and student learning styles. A teacher as action researcher model is implemented. Staffwide conversations focus on systemic reflection and improvement. Teachers are strong leaders. |
| **Outcome** | No professional growth and no staff or student performance improvement. There exists a high turnover rate of employees, especially administrators. Attitudes and approaches filter down to students. | The effectiveness of professional development is not known or analyzed. Teachers feel helpless about making schoolwide changes. | Teachers, working in teams, feel supported and begin to feel they can make changes. Evidence shows that shared decision making works. | A collegial school is evident. Effective classroom strategies are practiced, articulated schoolwide, are reflective of professional development aimed at ensuring student achievement, and the implementation of the shared vision, that includes student learning standards. | True systemic change and improved student achievement result because teachers are knowledgeable of and implement effective, differentiated teaching strategies for individual student learning gains. Teachers' repertoire of skills are enhanced and students are achieving. Professional development is driving learning at all levels. |

EXAMPLE TWO

201

*Professional development in Blue Bird School takes on many forms. There are districtwide inservices and schoolwide inservices (this year focusing on the issue of comprehension and language development for English Learners). Professional development follows the school plan and focuses primarily on literacy and technology. During the 2001-02 school year, districtwide training has been conducted for the new social studies textbooks. Between 10-15 teachers have been involved in the Disney grant training that involved year-long exposure to Different Ways of Knowing (DWOK) strategies and its project-based model, using the arts as a tool to assist achievement. Two teachers have been involved in yearlong Lucent training that emphasizes algebra as a gateway skill in the area of mathematics. Teachers in their first two years of teaching have been provided a Beginning Teacher Support and Assessment Support Provider who serves as a mentor during what can be difficult beginning experiences.*

*The staff pride themselves on their sense of sharing and peer dialogue. The teaching staff work very well together, and teachers regularly plan together and freely share ideas. There is a sense of reflection on instructional practices and a willingness to try new ideas in a safe environment. The school attempts to focus primarily on the area of literacy. It has worked to develop teacher skills in this area and to develop assessment to measure student progress. There is still a need to develop effective coaching models and to find ways to formalize dialogue, for example, a critical friends' group.*

*Next Steps:*

▼ *There is a need to provide more training to the instructional assistants.*

▼ *There is a need to look at peer coaching to assist the professional development of the teaching staff.*

▼ *Some feel that a way to formalize dialogue, such as a critical friends' group, would assist in the teachers' professional development.*

▼ *Some feel the need to modify the evaluation process in order to assist in teachers' professional development.*

▼ *Some feel the need to explore the concept of teacher as action researcher.*

## Leadership

*Blue Bird School staff rated their school 4s in Approach, Implementation, and Outcome with respect to Leadership.*

### LEADERSHIP

|  | One | Two | Three | Four | Five |
|---|---|---|---|---|---|
| **Approach** | Principal as decision maker. Decisions are reactive to state, district, and federal mandates. There is no knowledge of continuous improvement. | A shared decision-making structure is put into place and discussions begin on how to achieve a school vision. Most decisions are focused on solving problems and are reactive. | Leadership team is committed to continuous improvement. Leadership seeks inclusion of all school sectors and supports study teams by making time provisions for their work. | Leadership team represents a true shared decision-making structure. Study teams are reconstructed for the implementation of a comprehensive continuous improvement plan. | A strong continuous improvement structure is set into place that allows for input from all sectors of the school, district, and community, ensuring strong communication, flexibility, and refinement of approach and beliefs. The school vision is student focused, based on data and appropriate for school/community values, and meeting student needs. |
| **Implementation** | Principal makes all decisions, with little or no input from teachers, the community, or students. Leadership inspects for mistakes. | School values and beliefs are identified; the purpose of school is defined; a school mission and student learning standards are developed with representative input. A structure for studying approaches to achieving student learning standards is established. | Leadership team is active on study teams and integrates recommendations from the teams' research and analyses to form a comprehensive plan for continuous improvement within the context of the school mission. Everyone is kept informed. | Decisions about budget and implementation of the vision are made within teams, by the principal, by the leadership team, and by the full staff as appropriate. All decisions are communicated to the leadership team and to the full staff. | The vision is implemented and articulated across all grade levels and into feeder schools. Quality standards are reinforced throughout the school. All members of the school community understand and apply the quality standards. Leadership team has systematic interactions and involvement with district administrators, teachers, parents, community, and students about the school's direction. Necessary resources are available to implement and measure staff learning related to student learning standards. |
| **Outcome** | Decisions lack focus and consistency. There is no evidence of staff commitment to a shared vision. Students and parents do not feel they are being heard. Decision-making process is clear and known. | The mission provides a focus for all school improvement and guides the action to the vision. The school community is committed to continuous improvement. Quality leadership techniques are used sporadically. | Leadership team is seen as committed to planning and quality improvement. Critical areas for improvement are identified. Faculty feel included in shared decision making. | There is evidence that the leadership team listens to all levels of the organization. Implementation of the continuous improvement plan is linked to student learning standards and the guiding principles of the school. Leadership capacities for implementing the vision among teachers are evident. | Site-based management and shared decision making truly exists. Teachers understand and display an intimate knowledge of how the school operates. Teachers support and communicate with each other in the implementation of quality strategies. Teachers implement the vision in their classrooms and can determine how their new approach meets student needs and leads to the attainment of student learning standards. Leaders are standards-driven at all levels. |

*The staff feel involved in the school vision and seem to have a solid trust of the school administration. There is a need to more clearly articulate and publicize the school's vision.*

*Decisions about the school are usually made with the input of all components of the school community. The school plan is a working tool that has been modified, but it needs to be shared more consistently with all components of the school community. Parents are involved in school decisions through the school site council and the PTA. However, there is a need to involve more parents in the process. The use of parent questionnaires was a good way to obtain parent input.*

*A schoolwide curriculum committee will be formed to assist in the implementation of the school's vision, schoolwide goals, and the school plan. As the school goes on a year-round format, it will be important to develop communication systems so that all staff and parents feel involved in Blue Bird School decisions.*

*Next Steps:*

- ▼ *There are systems in place for involving community, but the community is not involved enough.*
- ▼ *Share the school portfolio and the school plan with all components of the school community.*
- ▼ *Develop and share the school's vision.*

*Partnership Development*

*Blue Bird School staff rated their school 3s in Approach, Implementation, and Outcome with respect to Partnership Development.*

## PARTNERSHIP DEVELOPMENT

| | One | Two | Three | Four | Five |
|---|---|---|---|---|---|
| **Approach** | There is no system for input from parents, business, or community. Status quo is desired for managing the school. | Partnerships are sought, but mostly for money and things. | School has knowledge of why partnerships are important and seeks to include businesses and parents in a strategic fashion related to student learning standards for increased student achievement. | School seeks effective win-win business and community partnerships and parent involvement to implement the vision. Desired outcomes are clearly identified. A solid plan for partnership development exists. | Community, parent, and business partnerships become integrated across all student groupings. The benefits of outside involvement are known by all. Parent and business involvement in student learning is refined. Student learning regularly takes place beyond the school walls. |
| **Implementation** | Barriers are erected to close out involvement of outsiders. Outsiders are managed for least impact on status quo. | A team is assigned to get partners and to receive input from parents, the community, and business in the school. | Involvement of business, community, and parents begins to take place in some classrooms and after school hours related to the vision. Partners begin to realize how they can support each other in achieving school goals. School staff understand what partners need from the partnership. | There is a systematic utilization of parents, community, and businesses schoolwide. Areas in which the active use of these partner-ships benefit student learning are clear. | Partnership development is articulated across all student groupings. Parents, community, business, and educators work together in an innovative fashion to increase student learning and to prepare students for the 21st Century. Partnerships are evaluated for continuous improvement. |
| **Outcome** | There is little or no involvement of parents, business, or community at-large. School is a closed, isolated system. | Much effort is given to establishing partner-ships. Some spotty trends emerge, such as receiving donated equipment. | Some substantial gains are achieved in implementing partnerships. Some student achievement increases can be attributed to this involvement. | Gains in student satisfaction with learning and school are clearly related to partner-ships. All partners benefit. | Previously non-achieving students enjoy learning with excellent achievement. Community, business, and home become common places for student learning, while school becomes a place where parents come for further education. Partnerships enhance what the school does for students. |

*The school does participate in a number of partnerships that have been very helpful. Staff has in place programs that involve adults and partners from outside the school community. These include career day, a health fair, a read-in, and a school carnival. Staff has received donations that helps support the school's program from the Optimist Club, Chevron, and other companies.*

*However, these partnerships are not systematic. They are not coordinated by any one person, but tend to develop when the school happens on them. Staff has not developed ways to measure the effectiveness of partnerships.*

*Next Steps:*

▼ *Develop a coordinated school partnership program focused on*
*increasing student learning.*

## Continuous Improvement and Evaluation

*Blue Bird School staff rated their school a 3 in Approach, and 4s in Implementation*
*and Outcome with respect to Continuous Improvement and Evaluation.*

### CONTINUOUS IMPROVEMENT AND EVALUATION

| | One | Two | Three | Four | Five |
|---|---|---|---|---|---|
| **Approach** | Neither goals nor strategies exist for the evaluation and continuous improvement of the school organization or for elements of the school organization. | The approach to continuous improvement and evaluation is problem-solving. If there are no problems, or if solutions can be made quickly, there is no need for improvement or analyses. Changes in parts of the system are not coordinated with all other parts. | Some elements of the school organization are evaluated for effectiveness. Some elements are improved on the basis of the evaluation findings. | All elements of the school's operations are evaluated for improvement and to ensure congruence of the elements with respect to the continuum of learning students experience. | All aspects of the school organization are rigorously evaluated and improved on a continuous basis. Students, and the maintenance of a comprehensive learning continuum for students, become the focus of all aspects of the school improvement process. |
| **Implementation** | With no overall plan for evaluation and continuous improvement, strategies are changed by individual teachers and administrators only when something sparks the need to improve. Reactive decisions and activities are a daily mode of operation. | Isolated changes are made in some areas of the school organization in response to problem incidents. Changes are not preceded by comprehensive analyses, such as an understanding of the root causes of problems. The effectiveness of the elements of the school organization, or changes made to the elements, is not known. | Elements of the school organization are improved on the basis of comprehensive analyses of root causes of problems, client perceptions, and operational effectiveness of processes. | Continuous improvement analyses of student achievement and instructional strategies are rigorously reinforced within each classroom and across learning levels to develop a comprehensive learning continuum for students and to prevent student failure. | Comprehensive continuous improvement becomes the way of doing business at the school. Teachers continuously improve the appropriateness and effectiveness of instructional strategies based on student feedback and performance. All aspects of the school organization are improved to support teachers' efforts. |
| **Outcome** | Individuals struggle with system failure. Finger pointing and blaming others for failure occurs. The effectiveness of strategies is not known. Mistakes are repeated. | Problems are solved only temporarily and few positive changes result. Additionally, unintended and undesirable consequences often appear in other parts of the system. Many aspects of the school are incongruent, keeping the school from reaching its vision. | Evidence of effective improvement strategies is observable. Positive changes are made and maintained due to comprehensive analyses and evaluation. | Teachers become astute at assessing and in predicting the impact of their instructional strategies on individual student achievement. Sustainable improvements in student achievement are evident at all grade levels, due to continuous improvement. | The school becomes a congruent and effective learning organization. Only instruction and assessment strategies that produce quality student achievement are used. A true continuum of learning results for all students and staff. The impact of improvements is increasingly measurable. |

*In the past few years, the school has focused on assessment as a means of following*
*student performance. A portfolio that houses student assessment data is kept in each*
*student's cumulative record. Based on norms established by the district, students are*
*identified early in the year if the teacher sees that they are at-risk.*

*Trends in testing data have also been considered. The school portfolio discusses in*
*other sections how the school has attempted to look at SAT 9 data as a way of*
*prioritizing schoolwide goals. The question remains—how rigorous and systematic*
*is this look at individual and schoolwide data?*

*Next Steps:*

▼ *The staff believes that there is a great deal of assessment in place, especially in Language Arts. The question is how rigorous is it and how well used is it to identify needs in every classroom? This needs to be monitored by the curriculum instructional committee.*

▼ *Develop assessments in each of the content areas, not just in Language Arts.*

## Analyzing School-level Data with a Norm-referenced Test

Like all schools and districts in this state, Blue Bird Elementary School and Great View Elementary School District use, and have used, the *Stanford Achievement Test* (SAT 9), ninth edition, for the past four years, at all grade levels starting with grade two. This use of a consistent measure at every grade level, over time, makes it possible to understand progress at the school, classroom, and individual student levels. What follows are analyses made for Blue Bird Elementary using four years of SAT 9 results.

To get a clear view of how the school has performed on the SAT 9 over time, Figure 9.24 gives an overall school average for 1999-00 through 2002-03, using normal curve equivalent (NCE) scores. These graphs show fairly consistent improvement in every subtest over time, with the exception of Language, Language Mechanics, and Language Expression, which generally stayed the same in the past two years, although up from the previous two years.

Figure 9.24

# Blue Bird Elementary School
## SAT9 NCE Scores
## Overall School Averages, 1999-00 to 2002-03

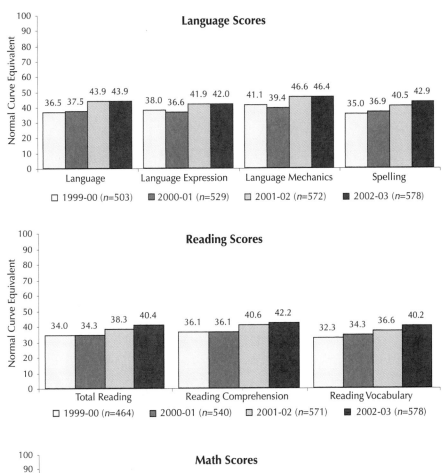

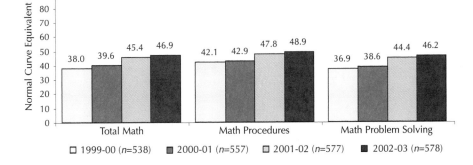

## Grade-level Analyses

Grade-level analyses show the average NCE scores for each subtest, over time. These analyses can help uncover inconsistencies in the curriculum. Focusing on the language and spelling subtests by grade level, Figure 9.25 shows that the 2002-03 averages were the same or higher than the three years prior, in all but grades two and three in Language, grade four in Language Expression and Language Mechanics, and grade six in Language, Language Expression, and Language Mechanics. Therefore, the students did not improve the average for one-half the subsets from 2001-02 to 2002-03. Furthermore, grade six Spelling in 2002-03 was lower than in 2000-01.

# Figure 9.25

## Blue Bird Elementary School
## SAT9 NCE Language Scores by Grade Level
## 1999-00 to 2002-03

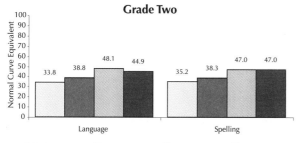

**Grade Two**

1999-00 (n=121) ■ 2000-01 (n=127) ■ 2001-02 (n=117) ■ 2002-03 (n=120)

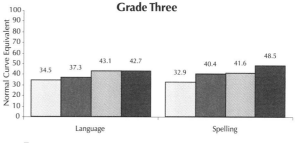

**Grade Three**

1999-00 (n=120) ■ 2000-01 (n=119) ■ 2001-02 (n=114) ■ 2002-03 (n=106)

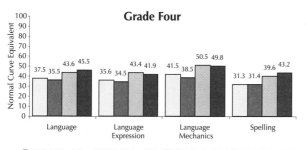

**Grade Four**

1999-00 (n=94) ■ 2000-01 (n=112) ■ 2001-02 (n=107) ■ 2002-03 (n=117)

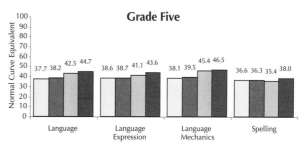

**Grade Five**

1999-00 (n=93) ■ 2000-01 (n=107) ■ 2001-02 (n=107) ■ 2002-03 (n=108)

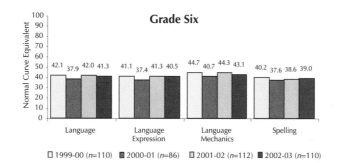

**Grade Six**

1999-00 (n=110) ■ 2000-01 (n=86) ■ 2001-02 (n=112) ■ 2002-03 (n=110)

Focusing on the reading subtests by grade level, Figure 9.26 shows all Reading scores higher or the same than the previous year for grades two through four. At grade five, Reading Vocabulary and Total Reading dropped slightly in 2001-02, with 2002-03 being the highest scoring year. At grade six, Total Reading scores improved every year. Reading Comprehension scores were down slightly in 2002-03, while Reading Vocabulary scores declined in 2001-02.

## Figure 9.26

### Blue Bird Elementary School
### SAT9 NCE Reading Scores by Grade Level
### 2000-01 to 2002-03

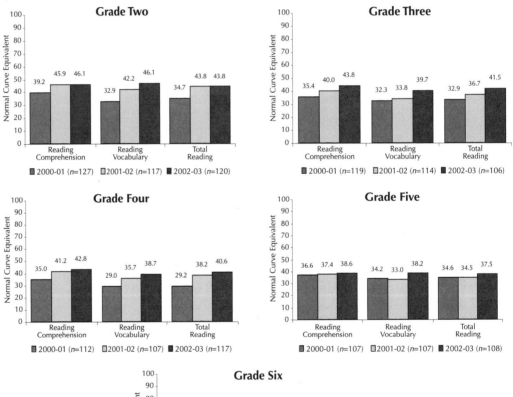

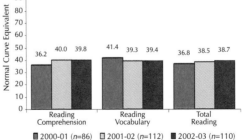

Focusing on the Mathematics subtests by grade level, Figure 9.27 shows that the 2002-03 scores were highest in all grade levels, except grade two. Grade two 2000-01 scores were lower than 1999-00 scores; both years were lower than the two more recent years. Grade two Math Procedures in 1999-00 was higher than 2002-03 Math Procedures. Student scores in 2001-02 showed the highest averages for each subtest. Grades three and four showed nice stair-step progressions over the four years in each subtest. Grade five subtest scores dipped briefly in 2000-01. Grade six scores were fairly consistent with 2002-03 showing the highest averages.

## Figure 9.27

## Blue Bird Elementary School
## SAT9 NCE Math Scores by Grade Level
## 1999-00 to 2002-03

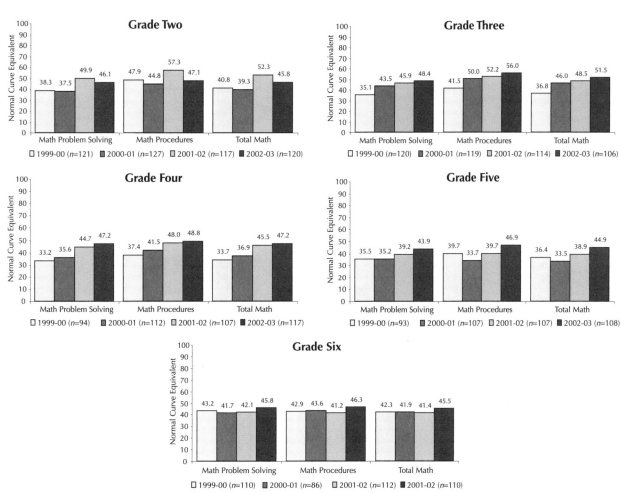

## Grade-level Analyses, Disaggregated by Gender

Due to space constraints, the analyses will show Reading subtests only. The full analyses of all subtests appear on the CD. Looking at the grade-level Reading scores by gender, one can see general differences in Figures 9.28. Female averages were generally higher than the males at all grade levels in all subtests.

### Figure 9.28

### Blue Bird Elementary School
### SAT9 NCE Reading Scores by Grade Level and Gender
### 2000-01 to 2002-03

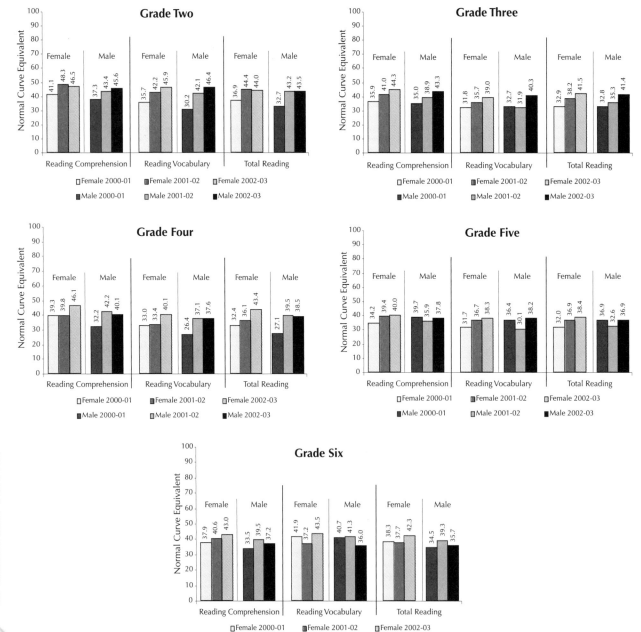

The fluctuations by grade level over time, to a great degree, reflect the performance of different students over time. Following cohorts, or the same groups of students over time, one should expect to see progress each year when using NCE scores. Figures 9.29 and 9.30 show that there was not necessarily progress in Reading subtests each year for each of the disaggregated cohorts. In fact, Cohort B generally shows decreases for each gender in each Reading subtest. Cohort C male scores dipped in 2002-03 in Reading Comprehension and Total Reading. Cohort D showed healthy increases each year. Cohort E also showed steady increases.

**Figure 9.29**

**Blue Bird Elementary School**
**SAT9 NCE Reading Score Cohorts by Gender**

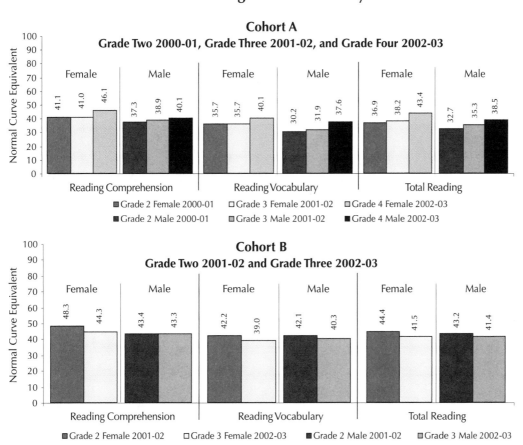

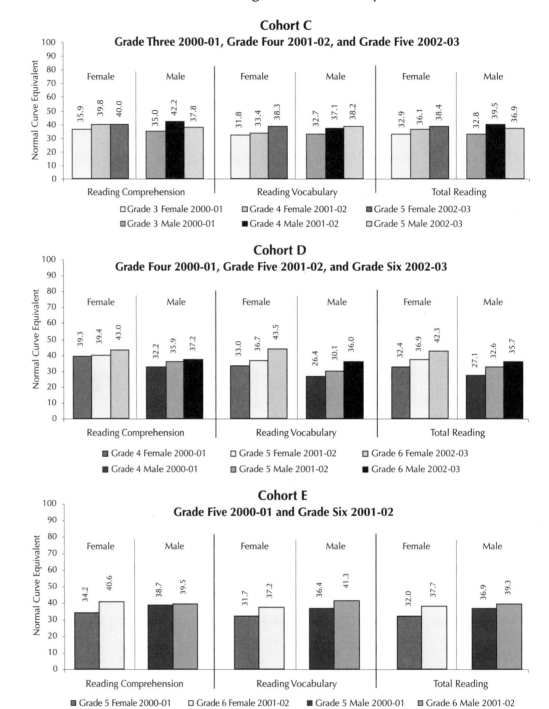

**Figure 9.30**

**Blue Bird Elementary School
SAT9 NCE Reading Score Cohorts by Gender**

**Cohort C**
Grade Three 2000-01, Grade Four 2001-02, and Grade Five 2002-03

□Grade 3 Female 2000-01    ■Grade 4 Female 2001-02    ■Grade 5 Female 2002-03
□Grade 3 Male 2000-01    ■Grade 4 Male 2001-02    □Grade 5 Male 2002-03

**Cohort D**
Grade Four 2000-01, Grade Five 2001-02, and Grade Six 2002-03

■ Grade 4 Female 2000-01    □ Grade 5 Female 2001-02    □ Grade 6 Female 2002-03
■ Grade 4 Male 2000-01    ■ Grade 5 Male 2001-02    ■ Grade 6 Male 2002-03

**Cohort E**
Grade Five 2000-01 and Grade Six 2001-02

■ Grade 5 Female 2000-01    □ Grade 6 Female 2001-02    ■ Grade 5 Male 2000-01    ■ Grade 6 Male 2001-02

NCE scores were also disaggregated by those students qualifying for free/reduced lunch (Figure 9.31). That disaggregation showed that, on the average, students who qualified for free/reduced lunch had lower scores than those not qualifying for free/reduced lunch, with the exception of grade two in 2002-03.

## Figure 9.31

### Blue Bird Elementary School
### SAT 9 NCE Scores by Grade Level and Free/Reduced Lunch Status
### 2000-01 to 2002-03

| Grade Level | Numbers | Year | Free/Reduced Lunch Status | Reading Comprehension | Reading Vocabulary | Total Reading |
|---|---|---|---|---|---|---|
| Grade Two | n=127 | 2000-01 | No Application | 39.5 | 33.7 | 35.8 |
| | n=35 | 2001-02 | | 49.7 | 49.4 | 48.9 |
| | n=29 | 2002-03 | | 44.7 | 47.4 | 43.6 |
| | n=64 | 2001-02 | Free Lunch | 44.2 | 39.4 | 42.0 |
| | n=76 | 2002-03 | | 46.5 | 47.0 | 45.0 |
| | n=18 | 2001-02 | Reduced Lunch | 44.7 | 40.9 | 43.3 |
| | n=13 | 2002-03 | | 48.7 | 42.1 | 42.6 |
| Grade Three | n=119 | 2000-01 | No Application | 35.4 | 32.6 | 33.2 |
| | n=26 | 2001-02 | | 44.2 | 37.6 | 41.1 |
| | n=21 | 2002-03 | | 48.0 | 46.6 | 46.9 |
| | n=72 | 2001-02 | Free Lunch | 37.0 | 31.4 | 33.7 |
| | n=64 | 2002-03 | | 41.4 | 36.3 | 38.6 |
| | n=16 | 2001-02 | Reduced Lunch | 46.5 | 38.5 | 43.3 |
| | n=21 | 2002-03 | | 46.8 | 42.9 | 44.8 |
| Grade Four | n=112 | 2000-01 | No Application | 35.0 | 33.1 | 33.3 |
| | n=28 | 2001-02 | | 46.2 | 44.7 | 45.0 |
| | n=26 | 2002-03 | | 44.9 | 41.1 | 42.8 |
| | n=64 | 2001-02 | Free Lunch | 38.9 | 32.2 | 35.6 |
| | n=78 | 2002-03 | | 44.4 | 38.7 | 41.9 |
| | n=15 | 2001-02 | Reduced Lunch | 42.1 | 36.0 | 39.0 |
| | n=13 | 2002-03 | | 42.3 | 42.8 | 41.7 |
| Grade Five | n=107 | 2000-01 | No Application | 36.6 | 34.2 | 34.6 |
| | n=19 | 2001-02 | | 37.1 | 29.6 | 32.7 |
| | n=21 | 2002-03 | | 45.7 | 45.0 | 44.9 |
| | n=70 | 2001-02 | Free Lunch | 37.4 | 34.2 | 35.2 |
| | n=71 | 2002-03 | | 38.0 | 38.3 | 36.9 |
| | n=18 | 2001-02 | Reduced Lunch | 38.0 | 34.0 | 35.6 |
| | n=15 | 2002-03 | | 39.9 | 36.8 | 37.9 |
| Grade Six | n=86 | 2000-01 | No Application | 36.2 | 41.9 | 37.3 |
| | n=31 | 2001-02 | | 48.9 | 46.8 | 48.0 |
| | n=24 | 2002-03 | | 43.7 | 47.7 | 44.9 |
| | n=70 | 2001-02 | Free Lunch | 35.2 | 36.5 | 34.4 |
| | n=69 | 2002-03 | | 38.0 | 36.2 | 36.4 |
| | n=11 | 2001-02 | Reduced Lunch | 48.8 | 46.3 | 47.5 |
| | n=17 | 2002-03 | | 41.5 | 43.2 | 41.5 |
| Grade Unknown | n=13 | 2001-02 | No Application | 42.5 | 35.1 | 38.2 |
| | n=5 | 2002-03 | | 50.7 | 47.2 | 50.3 |
| | n=2 | 2000-01 | Free Lunch | 27.1 | 39.0 | 28.9 |
| | n=1 | 2001-02 | | 33.7 | 41.3 | 35.1 |
| | n=1 | 2000-01 | Reduced Lunch | 18.9 | 21.8 | 18.9 |

## Deciles Analysis

Decile analyses allow one to see the spread of scores in groupings of ten. In other words, one can see the number of students who scored between 1 and 9 NCE, 10 and 19, 20 and 29, etc., for each year. When graphed, the results resemble a normal curve. Over time, one would want to see the resulting curves move to the right—as these show. In Figure 9.32, the Reading subtest decile scores are shown for the school from 1999-00 through 2002-03, and indicate that the distribution of scores is improving in all subtests. Language and Math subtest decile scores are shown on the CD.

Figure 9.32 indicates that Reading Vocabulary scores need the most improvement, since a large number of students scored in the lowest deciles. Over time, the number of students in the lowest deciles did decrease, while the number of students in the higher decile increased, as we would like to see.

Deciles were also created for cohorts over time. This cohort analysis showed that most cohorts improved over time, in step with the overall school analyses.

Figure 9.32

# Blue Bird Elementary School
## SAT 9 Reading Deciles, 1999-00 to 2002-03

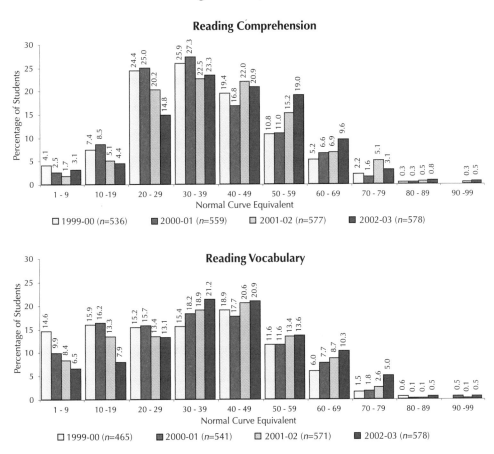

**Reading Comprehension**

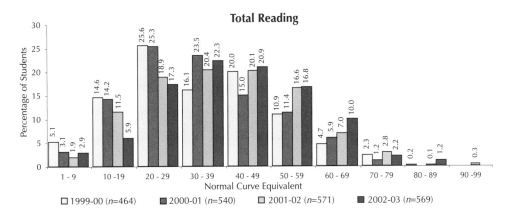

**Total Reading**

## Gaps and Root Causes

Blue Bird Elementary School's number one goal is for all students to score above 50 National NCE on the Stanford Achievement Test, Version 9 (SAT 9). Using the analyses conducted in Chapter 6, one can regroup and reanalyze the results to see the number of students who scored below 50 NCE—an indicator of non-proficiency on the SAT 9.

To learn about Blue Bird's gaps and root causes, the school's results were synthesized around these questions:

▼ *What are the gaps?*

▼ *How did these students score?*

▼ *Who are the students who are not achieving?*
   (What are their common characteristics?)

▼ *What do they know? What do they not know?*

▼ *How were they taught?*

*What are the gaps?* Figure 9.33 shows *the percentages of students who scored below 50 NCE* (national norms) on the SAT 9, schoolwide. Even though there has been tremendous progress made in increasing the numbers of students achieving above 50 NCE in all the subtests in the last three years, all subtests point to gaps. Reading subtests stand out as the school's greatest gaps, with 70% of the students scoring below 50 NCE in total Reading and Reading Vocabulary in 2000-01. Sixty-six percent scored below 50 NCE in Reading Comprehension in 2000-01. Figure 9.33 shows that the gap has decreased every year in each subtest, except for Math Procedures and Math Problem Solving. Both increased by 1% over the previous year (2001-02), although down 13% from the year before that (2000-01).

## Figure 9.33

### Blue Bird Elementary School
### Percentage of Students Scoring Below 50 NCE on SAT 9 Subtests
### 2000-01 to 2002-03

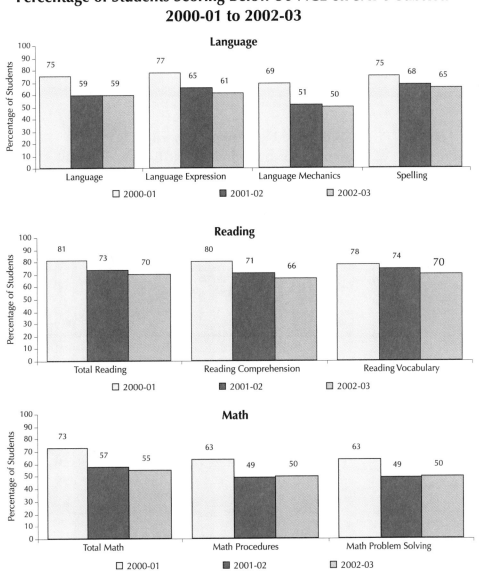

Looking at each grade level's most recent year of data (Figure 9.34), one can see the percentages of students scoring below 50 NCE for each subtest. The highest percentages of students scoring below 50 NCE was at grade five in the Language subtests; grade two in Spelling and Reading Comprehension; grade six in Reading Vocabulary, Total Math, and Math Problem Solving; and grade three for Math Problem Solving.

Figure 9.34

**Blue Bird Elementary School**
**Percentage of Students Scoring Below 50 NCE on SAT 9 Subtests**
**By Grade Level, 2002-03**

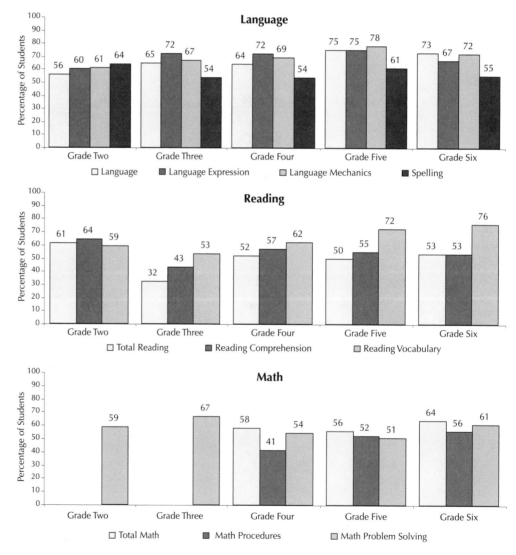

*How did the students score?* Our first hunch about the gaps was that the "Limited English Speaking" students scored below 50 NCE. Figure 9.35 shows, by grade level, the number and percentage of students whose SAT 9 Reading scores fell below 50 NCE by English Language Fluency—those who are speakers of "English Only," those who are "Fluent English" speakers, and those who have "Limited English" skills. The highest percentage of students, by grade level, scoring below 50 NCE were those students designated as "Limited English" speaking in grade two; "English Only" in the rest of the grades! (The data did *not* confirm our hunch.)

## Figure 9.35

### Number and Percentage of Blue Bird Students Scoring Below 50 NCE on SAT 9 Reading By Grade Level and English Language Proficiency, 2002-03

| Grade Level | English Fluency | Total Reading | | Reading Comprehension | | Reading Vocabulary | |
|---|---|---|---|---|---|---|---|
| | | Number | Percent | Number | Percent | Number | Percent |
| Grade Two | English Only | 34 | 47% | 34 | 44% | 28 | 39% |
| | Fluent English | 8 | 11% | 8 | 10% | 8 | 11% |
| | Limited English | 31 | 42% | 35 | 45% | 35 | 49% |
| Grade Three | English Only | 19 | 56% | 20 | 43% | 21 | 38% |
| | Fluent English | 6 | 18% | 8 | 17% | 14 | 25% |
| | Limited English | 9 | 26% | 18 | 39% | 21 | 38% |
| Grade Four | English Only | 31 | 52% | 30 | 45% | 29 | 41% |
| | Fluent English | 10 | 17% | 13 | 20% | 15 | 21% |
| | Limited English | 16 | 27% | 20 | 30% | 24 | 34% |
| | Redesignated English | 3 | 5% | 3 | 5% | 2 | 3% |
| Grade Five | English Only | 22 | 42% | 25 | 44% | 30 | 40% |
| | Fluent English | 8 | 15% | 9 | 16% | 13 | 37% |
| | Limited English | 20 | 38% | 21 | 37% | 25 | 33% |
| | Redesignated English | 2 | 4% | 2 | 4% | 7 | 9% |
| Grade Six | English Only | 23 | 40% | 25 | 43% | 36 | 43% |
| | Fluent English | 8 | 14% | 6 | 10% | 10 | 12% |
| | Limited English | 15 | 26% | 15 | 26% | 16 | 19% |
| | Redesignated English | 12 | 21% | 12 | 2% | 22 | 26% |

Looking at the number and percentage of students falling below 50 NCE on the SAT 9 Reading, by grade level, gender, and ethnicity (Figure 9.36), one can see that the largest ethnic population, Hispanic, also has the highest percentage of students at any grade level in the below 50 NCE categories on all the subtests. There were few differences by gender. All ethnicities had high percentages of students scoring below 50 NCE.

Figure 9.36

## Number and Percentage of Blue Bird Elementary School Students
## Scoring Below 50 NCE on SAT 9 Reading
## By Grade Level, Gender, and Ethnicity, 2002-03

| Grade Level | Gender | Ethnicity | Total Reading | | Reading Comprehension | | Reading Vocabulary | |
|---|---|---|---|---|---|---|---|---|
| | | | Number | Percent | Number | Percent | Number | Percent |
| Grade Two | Male | African-American | 3 | 38% | 3 | 38% | 2 | 25% |
| | | Hispanic | 22 | 31% | 25 | 33% | 26 | 37% |
| | | Caucasian | 3 | 25% | 4 | 33% | 5 | 42% |
| | | Asian | 2 | 33% | 2 | 33% | 2 | 33% |
| | Female | American Indian | | | | | 1 | 100% |
| | | African-American | 9 | 38% | 9 | 38% | 6 | 25% |
| | | Filipino | 1 | 33% | 1 | 33% | 1 | 33% |
| | | Hispanic | 27 | 34% | 28 | 35% | 25 | 31% |
| | | Caucasian | 4 | 40% | 4 | 40% | 2 | 20% |
| Grade Three | Male | African-American | 9 | 33% | 11 | 41% | 7 | 26% |
| | | Hispanic | 6 | 19% | 9 | 29% | 16 | 52% |
| | | Caucasian | 1 | 25% | 1 | 25% | 2 | 50% |
| | Female | African-American | | | | | 1 | 100% |
| | | Hispanic | 14 | 24% | 20 | 34% | 24 | 41% |
| | | Caucasian | 2 | 29% | 2 | 29% | 3 | 43% |
| | | Asian | 1 | 33% | 1 | 33% | 1 | 33% |
| Grade Four | Male | African-American | 3 | 33% | 3 | 33% | 3 | 33% |
| | | Hispanic | 24 | 32% | 25 | 33% | 26 | 35% |
| | | Caucasian | 6 | 32% | 6 | 32% | 7 | 37% |
| | | Asian | | | 1 | 50% | 1 | 50% |
| | Female | American Indian | 1 | 33% | 1 | 33% | 1 | 33% |
| | | African-American | 7 | 37% | 7 | 37% | 5 | 26% |
| | | Hispanic | 18 | 28% | 22 | 34% | 25 | 38% |
| | | Caucasian | | | | | 1 | 100% |
| | | Asian | 1 | 33% | 1 | 33% | 1 | 33% |
| Grade Five | Male | African-American | 5 | 28% | 6 | 33% | 7 | 39% |
| | | Hispanic | 21 | 25% | 26 | 31% | 38 | 45% |
| | | Caucasian | 2 | 33% | 2 | 33% | 2 | 33% |
| | Female | African-American | 5 | 31% | 5 | 31% | 6 | 38% |
| | | Hispanic | 18 | 33% | 17 | 31% | 19 | 35% |
| | | Caucasian | 1 | 33% | 1 | 33% | 1 | 33% |
| | | Asian | 1 | 33% | 1 | 33% | 1 | 33% |
| Grade Six | Male | African-American | 4 | 27% | 4 | 27% | 7 | 47% |
| | | Filipino | 2 | 33% | 2 | 33% | 2 | 33% |
| | | Hispanic | 23 | 31% | 21 | 28% | 30 | 41% |
| | | Caucasian | 5 | 28% | 6 | 33% | 7 | 39% |
| | Female | American Indian | 1 | 33% | 1 | 33% | 1 | 33% |
| | | African-American | 6 | 32% | 6 | 32% | 7 | 37% |
| | | Hispanic | 13 | 25% | 14 | 27% | 25 | 48% |
| | | Caucasian | 3 | 30% | 3 | 30% | 4 | 40% |

Figure 9.37 is an example created to understand how students of different ethnicities and gender scored on the SAT 9 Total Reading deciles. The table shows the percentages of ethnicities and gender falling into each decile.

## Figure 9.37

### Blue Bird Elementary School
### Percentage of Students Scoring in Deciles on SAT 9 Total Reading
### By Grade Level, Gender, and Ethnicity, 2002-03

| Grade Level | Gender | Ethnicity | 1–9 | 10–19 | 20–29 | 30–39 | 40–49 | 50–59 | 60–69 | 70–79 | 80–89 | 90–99 |
|---|---|---|---|---|---|---|---|---|---|---|---|---|
| Grade Two | Male | African-American | | 33% | | | 33% | 33% | | | | |
| | | Hispanic | | 10% | 13% | 23% | 20% | 13% | 23% | | | |
| | | Caucasian | 13% | | 25% | | | 38% | | 13% | 13% | |
| | | Asian | | | | | 67% | | | 33% | | |
| | Female | American Indian | | | | | | 100% | | | | |
| | | African-American | | | 17% | 17% | 25% | 33% | 8% | | | |
| | | Filipino | | | | 100% | | | | | | |
| | | Hispanic | | 3% | 23% | 28% | 15% | 23% | 8% | | 3% | |
| | | Caucasian | | | | 40% | 20% | | 40% | | | |
| Grade Three | Male | American Indian | | | | | 50% | | 50% | | | |
| | | African-American | 8% | 8% | 15% | 31% | 23% | 8% | 8% | | | |
| | | Hispanic | | 7% | 20% | 53% | 7% | 7% | | 7% | | |
| | | Caucasian | 20% | | | | 60% | | 20% | | | |
| | Female | African- | | | | | | 50% | | 50% | | |
| | | Hispanic | 5% | 8% | 23% | 20% | 10% | 28% | 5% | 3% | | |
| | | Caucasian | | 17% | | | 33% | | 17% | 17% | 17% | |
| | | Asian | | 100% | | | | | | | | |
| Grade Four | Male | African-American | | | 17% | 50% | 17% | | | 17% | | |
| | | Hispanic | 2% | 4% | 13% | 20% | 24% | 27% | 9% | | | |
| | | Caucasian | 11% | 11% | 11% | 33% | | 33% | | | | |
| | | Asian | | | 100% | | | | | | | |
| | Female | American Indian | | | | | 100% | | | | | |
| | | African-American | | | 13% | 63% | 13% | 13% | | | | |
| | | Hispanic | | | 13% | 18% | 38% | 21% | 5% | 5% | | |
| | | Caucasian | | | 33% | | | 33% | 33% | | | |
| | | Asian | | | | 100% | | | | | | |
| Grade Five | Male | African-American | 11% | 22% | 22% | 11% | 11% | 11% | 11% | | | |
| | | Hispanic | 2% | 15% | 25% | 17% | 23% | 6% | 8% | 2% | 2% | |
| | | Caucasian | | | 25% | 25% | | | 50% | | | |
| | Female | African- | | 11% | 33% | | 33% | | 22% | | | |
| | | Hispanic | 4% | | 21% | 32% | 21% | 11% | 7% | 4% | | |
| | | Caucasian | | | | | 50% | | | | 50% | |
| | | Asian | | 100% | | | | | | | | |
| Grade Six | Male | African-American | 14% | | 29% | 29% | 29% | | | | | |
| | | Filipino | | | 100 | | | | | | | |
| | | Hispanic | 8% | 5% | 13% | 33% | 10% | 23% | 8% | 3% | | |
| | | Caucasian | 22% | | | 22% | 33% | 11% | 11% | | | |
| | Female | American Indian | | | | 100% | | | | | | |
| | | African-American | 11% | 11% | 11% | 33% | 11% | | 22% | | | |
| | | Hispanic | | | 28% | 28% | 9% | 13% | 19% | 3% | | |
| | | Caucasian | | | 20% | | 40% | 20% | | | 20% | |
| | | Asian | | | | | | 100% | | | | |

How were they taught? Looking to see if there are differences by classrooms, the next level of data shows some interesting results. Figure 9.38 shows the number and percentage of students scoring below 50 NCE on the SAT 9 Reading subtests, organized by grade level and teacher. It appears that there are teachers whose students performed better on the subtests than others. Teachers with the highest percentages of students scoring below 50 NCE also had the fewest years of teaching in most cases, although not all cases.

**Figure 9.38**

**Blue Bird Elementary School**
**Number and Percentage of Students Scoring Below 50 NCE**
**on SAT 9 Reading By Grade Level and Teacher, 2002-03**

| Grade Level | Teacher | Number of Years Teaching Experience | Total Reading | | Reading Comprehension | | Reading Vocabulary | |
|---|---|---|---|---|---|---|---|---|
| | | | Below 50 | Percent | Below 50 | Percent | Below 50 | Percent |
| Grade Two | Two A | 4 | 15 | 28% | 16 | 28% | 16 | 29% |
| | Two B | 5 | 14 | 26% | 12 | 23% | 13 | 24% |
| | Two C | 1 | 16 | 30% | 17 | 32% | 17 | 31% |
| | Two D | 11 | 6 | 11% | 6 | 11% | 7 | 13% |
| | Two E | 25 | 2 | 4% | 2 | 4% | 2 | 4% |
| Grade Three | Three A | 3 | 8 | 40% | 11 | 44% | 8 | 29% |
| | Three B | 11 | 1 | 5% | 1 | 4% | 3 | 11% |
| | Three C | 5 | | | | | 1 | 4% |
| | Three D | 25 | 2 | 10% | 3 | 12% | 4 | 14% |
| | Three E | 7 | | | | | 1 | 4% |
| | Three F | 6 | 2 | 10% | 3 | 12% | 3 | 11% |
| | Three G | 1 | 5 | 25% | 3 | 12% | 4 | 14% |
| | Three H | 5 | 2 | 10% | 4 | 16% | 4 | 14% |
| Grade Four | Four A | 6 | 2 | 7% | 2 | 6% | 2 | 5% |
| | Four B | 9 | 9 | 32% | 10 | 32% | 14 | 37% |
| | Four C | 18 | 6 | 21% | 5 | 16% | 10 | 26% |
| | Four D | 5 | 3 | 11% | 5 | 16% | 5 | 13% |
| | Four E | 15 | 1 | 4% | 2 | 6% | 1 | 3% |
| | Four F | 3 | 4 | 14% | 4 | 13% | 2 | 5% |
| | Four G | 8 | 2 | 7% | 2 | 6% | 2 | 5% |
| | Four H | 6 | 1 | 4% | 1 | 3% | 2 | 5% |
| Grade Five | Four A | 6 | 8 | 25% | 8 | 24% | 8 | 17% |
| | Four B | 9 | 2 | 6% | 3 | 9% | 8 | 17% |
| | Four C | 3 | 9 | 28% | 8 | 24% | 14 | 30% |
| | Four D | 4 | 4 | 13% | 4 | 12% | 7 | 15% |
| | Four E | 3 | 9 | 28% | 10 | 30% | 9 | 20% |
| Grade Six | Four A | 9 | 9 | 23% | 10 | 23% | 15 | 26% |
| | Four B | 6 | 12 | 30% | 11 | 26% | 14 | 25% |
| | Four C | 18 | 7 | 18% | 7 | 16% | 7 | 12% |
| | Four D | 4 | 5 | 13% | 7 | 16% | 10 | 18% |
| | Four E | 1 | 7 | 18% | 8 | 19% | 9 | 16% |
| | Four F | 3 | | | | | 2 | 4% |

Figure 9.39 shows the results of Figure 9.38 in a scatterplot. With the scatterplot, one can see more vividly that the teachers with the least amount of experience had the greatest number of students scoring below 50 NCE.

**Figure 9.39**

**Percentage of Blue Bird Elementary School Students
Scoring Below 50 NCE on SAT 9 Reading
By Teachers' Years of Teaching Experience, 2002-03**

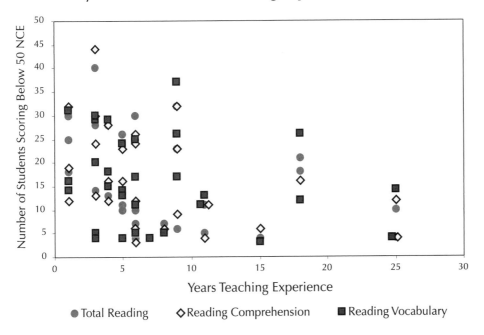

Figure 9.40, on the next two pages shows the number and percentage of students scoring below 50 NCE on the SAT 9 Reading, grouped by teacher and designated by "English Only," "Fluent English," and "Limited English." The calculated columns show the percentages of students, by language designation, scoring below 50 NCE, and the percentages of students of a language designation, by teacher, who scored below 50 NCE. These results show that there are differences by teacher.

# Figure 9.40

## Blue Bird Elementary School
## Number and Percentage of Students Scoring Below 50 NCE
## on SAT 9 Reading By Language Fluency and Teacher, 2002-03

| Grade Level | Teacher | English Fluency | Total Reading | | Reading Comprehension | | Reading Vocabulary | |
|---|---|---|---|---|---|---|---|---|
| | | | Below 50 | Percent | Below 50 | Percent | Below 50 | Percent |
| Grade Two | Two A | English Only | 4 | 8% | 4 | 7% | 3 | 5% |
| | | Fluent English | 2 | 4% | 2 | 4% | 2 | 4% |
| | | Limited English | 9 | 17% | 11 | 20% | 11 | 20% |
| | Two B | English Only | 6 | 11% | 4 | 7% | 4 | 7% |
| | | Limited English | 8 | 15% | 8 | 15% | 9 | 16% |
| | Two C | English Only | 8 | 15% | 9 | 17% | 8 | 15% |
| | | Fluent English | 2 | 4% | 2 | 4% | 2 | 4% |
| | | Limited English | 6 | 11% | 6 | 11% | 7 | 13% |
| | Two D | English Only | 2 | 4% | 2 | 4% | 3 | 5% |
| | | Limited English | 2 | 4% | 2 | 4% | 3 | 5% |
| | Two E | English Only | 4 | 8% | 4 | 7% | 4 | 7% |
| | | Limited English | 1 | 2% | 1 | 2% | 1 | 2% |
| Grade Three | Three A | English Only | 7 | 35% | 9 | 36% | 7 | 25% |
| | | Fluent English | 1 | 5% | 1 | 4% | 1 | 4% |
| | | Limited English | | | 1 | 4% | | |
| | Three B | English Only | 1 | 5% | 1 | 4% | 1 | 4% |
| | | Fluent English | | | | | 1 | 4% |
| | | Limited English | | | | | 1 | 4% |
| | Three C | English Only | | | | | 1 | 4% |
| | Three D | English Only | 2 | 10% | 3 | 12% | 4 | 14% |
| | Three E | English Only | | | | | 1 | 4% |
| | Three F | English Only | | | 1 | 4% | 2 | 17% |
| | | Limited English | 1 | 5% | 1 | 4% | | |
| | | Fluent English | 1 | 5% | 1 | 4% | 1 | 4% |
| | Three G | English Only | 5 | 25% | 3 | 12% | 2 | 7% |
| | | Fluent English | | | | | 1 | 4% |
| | | Limited English | | | | | 1 | 4% |
| | Three H | English Only | 1 | 5% | 1 | 4% | 1 | 4% |
| | | Fluent English | | | 1 | 4% | 1 | 4% |
| | | Limited English | 1 | 5% | 2 | 8% | 2 | 7% |
| Grade Four | Four A | English Only | 1 | 4% | 1 | 3% | 1 | 3% |
| | | Limited English | 1 | 4% | 1 | 3% | 1 | 3% |
| | Four B | English Only | 3 | 11% | 3 | 10% | 3 | 8% |
| | | Fluent English | 2 | 7% | 2 | 6% | 2 | 5% |
| | | Limited English | 2 | 7% | 3 | 10% | 7 | 18% |
| | | Redesignated | 2 | 7% | 2 | 6% | 2 | 5% |
| | Four C | English Only | 3 | 11% | 1 | 3% | 4 | 11% |
| | | Fluent English | 2 | 7% | 3 | 10% | 4 | 11% |
| | | Limited English | 1 | 4% | 1 | 3% | 2 | 5% |
| | | Redesignated | 3 | 11% | 5 | 16% | 5 | 13% |
| | Four D | Limited English | 1 | 4% | 2 | 6% | 1 | 3% |
| | Four E | English Only | 3 | 11% | 3 | 10% | 1 | 3% |
| | | Limited English | 1 | 4% | 1 | 3% | 1 | 3% |
| | Four F | English Only | 2 | 7% | 2 | 6% | 2 | 5% |
| | Four G | English Only | | | 1 | 3% | 1 | 3% |
| | | Limited English | 1 | 4% | | | 1 | 3% |

USING DATA TO IMPROVE STUDENT LEARNING IN ELEMENTARY SCHOOLS

Figure 9.40 (Continued)

## Blue Bird Elementary School
## Number and Percentage of Students Scoring Below 50 NCE
## on SAT 9 Reading By Language Fluency and Teacher, 2002-03

| Grade Level | Teacher | English Fluency | Total Reading | | Reading Comprehension | | Reading Vocabulary | |
|---|---|---|---|---|---|---|---|---|
| | | | Below 50 | Percent | Below 50 | Percent | Below 50 | Percent |
| Grade Five | Five A | English Only | 3 | 9% | 3 | 9% | 3 | 7% |
| | | Fluent English | | | 1 | 3% | 1 | 2% |
| | | Limited English | 5 | 16% | 4 | 12% | 3 | 7% |
| | | Redesignated FEP | | | | | 1 | 2% |
| | Five B | English Only | | | | | 1 | 2% |
| | | Fluent English | | | | | 2 | 4% |
| | | Limited English | 1 | 3% | 2 | 6% | 4 | 9% |
| | | Redesignated FEP | 1 | 3% | 1 | 3% | 1 | 2% |
| | Five C | English Only | 2 | 6% | 3 | 9% | 4 | 9% |
| | | Fluent English | | | | | 2 | 4% |
| | | Limited English | 7 | 22% | 5 | 15% | 8 | 17% |
| | Five D | English Only | 1 | 3% | 1 | 3% | 2 | 4% |
| | | Fluent English | | | | | 1 | 2% |
| | | Limited English | 3 | 9% | 3 | 9% | 4 | 9% |
| | Five E | English Only | 5 | 16% | 6 | 18% | 6 | 13% |
| | | Fluent English | 1 | 3% | 2 | 6% | | |
| | | Limited English | 3 | 9% | 2 | 6% | 2 | 4% |
| | | Redesignated FEP | | | | | 1 | 2% |
| Grade Six | Six A | English Only | 5 | 13% | 5 | 12% | 8 | 14% |
| | | Fluent English | 1 | 3% | 1 | 2% | 1 | 2% |
| | | Redesignated | 3 | 8% | 4 | 9% | 6 | 11% |
| | Six B | English Only | 3 | 8% | 3 | 7% | 5 | 9% |
| | | Fluent English | 3 | 8% | 2 | 5% | 2 | 4% |
| | | Limited English | 3 | 8% | 3 | 7% | 3 | 5% |
| | | Redesignated FEP | 3 | 8% | 3 | 7% | 4 | 7% |
| | Six C | English Only | 1 | 3% | 1 | 2% | 1 | 2% |
| | | Limited English | 2 | 5% | 2 | 5% | 2 | 4% |
| | | Redesignated FEP | | | | | | |
| | Six D | English Only | 1 | 3% | 1 | 2% | 1 | 2% |
| | | Fluent English | | | | | 1 | 2% |
| | | Limited English | 1 | 3% | 1 | 2% | 1 | 2% |
| | | Redesignated FEP | 2 | 5% | 2 | 5% | 1 | 2% |
| | Six E | English Only | 1 | 3% | 1 | 2% | 1 | 2% |
| | | Redesignated FEP | 1 | 3% | 1 | 2% | 1 | 2% |
| | Six F | English Only | 1 | 3% | 3 | 7% | 4 | 7% |
| | | Limited English | 1 | 3% | 1 | 2% | 1 | 2% |
| | | Redesignated FEP | 1 | 3% | 1 | 2% | 3 | 5% |
| | Six G | English Only | 1 | 3% | 1 | 2% | 1 | 2% |
| | | Limited English | 1 | 3% | 1 | 2% | 1 | 2% |
| | Six H | Fluent English | | | | | 1 | 2% |
| | Six I | English Only | | | | | 1 | 2% |
| | Six J | English Only | 1 | 3% | 1 | 2% | 2 | 4% |
| | | Fluent English | 1 | 3% | 1 | 2% | 1 | 2% |
| | | Limited English | 1 | 3% | 1 | 2% | 1 | 2% |
| | | Redesignated FEP | 2 | 5% | 2 | 5% | 2 | 4% |
| | Six K | English Only | | | 1 | 2% | 1 | 2% |

### What are the Root Causes of Blue Bird Elementary School Gaps?

Although this is a quick look at the gaps, when digging deeper, one comes up with the idea that there are many contributing causes, with one major root cause. The major root cause in this case may be the way teachers are teaching. The progress that has been made over time shows that when teaching strategies improve, so do the scores of students.

## Study Questions for Example Two

As you review Blue Bird Elementary School's data, use either the margins in the text, this page, or print this page from the CD to write down your early thinking. These notes, of course, are only hunches or placeholders until all the data are analyzed.

| 1.  What are the demographic *strengths* and *challenges* for Blue Bird? | |
|---|---|
| *Strengths* | *Challenges* |
| | |

**2.  What are some *implications* for the Blue Bird school improvement plan?**

**3.  Looking at the data presented, what other demographic data would you want to answer the question *Who are we?* for Blue Bird Elementary School?**

---

**4. What are the perceptual *strengths* and *challenges* for Blue Bird?**

| *Strengths* | *Challenges* |
|---|---|
| | |

---

**5. What are some *implications* for the Blue Bird school improvement plan?**



---

**6. Looking at the data presented, what other perceptual data would you want to answer the question *How do we do business?* for Blue Bird Elementary School?**

**7. What are the student learning *strengths* and *challenges* for Blue Bird?**

| *Strengths* | *Challenges* |
|---|---|
| | |

**8. What are some *implications* for the Blue Bird school improvement plan?**

**9. Looking at the data presented, what other student learning data would you want to answer the question *How are we doing?* for Blue Bird Elementary School?**

**10. Comments about the differences in what data the two schools had for analyzing *What are our results?***

11. What are Blue Bird's *gaps*?

12. Do you feel that the *root causes* of their student learning results were uncovered? If the answer is *no*, what other analyses would you perform?

13. What are the *implications* for the school improvement plan?

14. What other data would you want to consider?

# What I Saw in Example Two:
##     Blue Bird Elementary School

Using the study questions as an outline, what I saw in the data for Chapter 9 appears below. When applicable, I have referenced the figure that gave me my first impression of strengths and challenges.

---

## *WHO ARE WE?*

Blue Bird Elementary School provided an excellent summary of who they are with demographic data. Other data that would be helpful in understanding the context of the school might include:
- More about redesignated English Learners—language and programs.
- Average daily student and teacher attendance over time.
- Teachers' ethnicity.
- Gender and ethnicity of teachers by grade level.
- Information about the administrator.
- Teachers' years of experience by grade level.
- What happens to the students when they go to the next levels of schooling?
- How many students attended pre-school?
- Students' living conditions (i.e., being with one parent, a guardian).
- Parent education levels.

| *What are their strengths?* | *What are their challenges?* |
|---|---|
| • The school enrollment has stayed in the 800s over the past six years. (Figure 9.3)<br>• The school has an ethnic mix of students. (Figures 9.4 and 9.5)<br>• A large number of limited English-speaking students are redesignated in the fifth and sixth grades, generally increasing over the years. (Figure 9.11)<br>• With the increases in retentions in grades K-2 in recent years, it could suggest that the school is working to prevent failures later on. (Figures 9.15 and 9.16)<br>• Students start kingergarten here with experienced teachers. (Figure 9.22)<br>• Low class sizes in grades K-3. (Figure 9.23)<br>• It appears as though this school has done a good job of getting programs/grants to support their student population. (Page 190) | • Enrollment of the school will be increasing in the near future.<br>• There are some fluctuations by gender and ethnicity within grade levels. (Figure 9.9)<br>• There is a large English Learning population. (Figure 9.11)<br>• The number and percentage of students qualifying for free/reduced lunch are very large—nearly the entire student population. (Figures 9.12 and 9.13)<br>• Average daily student attendance could be better. (Page 187)<br>• Retentions—mostly in the early grades. (Figures 9.15 and 9.16)<br>• Three teachers are working under emergency credentials. (Page 194)<br>• There are only two male teachers. (Figure 9.22) |

## *What are some implications for their school improvement plan?*

- The school must be ready for increases in enrollment and possibly even higher free/reduced lunch percentages.
- The school will need to continue to hire teachers who speak more than English and who can effectively teach English Learners—and maybe more male teachers.
- The school might consider including strategies for improving attendance.
- There has to be a quality program for new teachers and emergency-credentialed teachers.

# What I Saw in Example Two:
## Blue Bird Elementary School (Continued)

## HOW DO WE DO BUSINESS?

Blue Bird Elementary School had one year of *Continuous Improvement Continuum* assessment data. It also had two years of student questionnaire data and one year of parent and staff questionnaire data. Additional data that will help in the future are annual assessments on student, staff, and parent questionnaires, and at least an annual assessment on the *Continuous Improvement Continuums*—preferably twice each year.

## Continuous Improvement Continuums Assessment

| *What are their strengths?* | *What are their challenges?* |
|---|---|
| • The school did an honest and thorough analysis of where the school is as a system. (Pages 197-205) | • Data collection is neither systematic nor balanced. (Page 197) |
| • Teachers and staff use data to guide instruction, making sure elements of SAT 9 are covered. (Pages 197-199) | • The use of data to guide instruction should be expanded to subject areas other than Math. (Page 197) |
| • Teachers are now able to measure what has been working; they are seeing scores improve. (Pages 198-199) | • Staff needs to take the data to the next level, including following former students into their next levels of schooling. (Page 197) |
| • Teachers have portfolios for students as they move from grade to grade. (Page 198-199) | • Staff wants to develop consistent rubrics to be used by all teachers for students like the one they are currently using in writing. (Pages 199) |
| • A spirit of cooperation and collaboration is evident; teachers meet regularly to discuss concerns about student progress and current instructional practices. (Pages 198-199) | • Some teachers feel that multi-age classrooms and looping might serve the best interests of students, making it easier to track student progress. There has been resistance to these class groupings by parents who are concerned that teachers cannot effectively service two grades in one classroom. If multi-age classrooms or looping are going to occur, staff believes it would be most effective in early years such as kindergarten-first grade or first-second grade combinations. (Page 199) |
| • It is wonderful that teachers are working with students before and after school, and through interventions to meet the needs of the students. (Pages 198-199) | |
| • Teachers communicate often with parents about student achievement. (Page 199) | |
| • Beneficial discussion is occurring about whether all teachers believe that all students *can do* as opposed to what they *can't do*. (Pages 198-199) | • Are expectations of students high enough? (Pages 199) |
| • The focus on literacy and technology the past five years is paying off with noticeable gains. (Pages 200) | • Staff needs to develop strategies to better serve the needs of English Learners. (Pages 198-199) |
| • The school has a comprehensive plan that meets federal requirements and is consistent with schoolwide goals. (Page 200) | • Publicize the school plan by developing a brochure or pamphlet. (Pages 201) |
| • Some teachers have been trained and are implementing *Different Ways of Knowing* (DWOK). (Page 202) | |
| • Professional development follows the school plan and focuses this year primarily on literacy and technology. (Pages 201-202) | |

## Continuous Improvement Continuums Assessment (Continued)

| *What are their strengths?* | *What are their challenges?* |
|---|---|
| • Those in their first two years of teaching are provided mentors. (Pages 202)<br>• Teachers want to improve their professional development strategies in collaborative ways. (Pages 202)<br>• Staff seems to have solid trust in the school administration. (Pages 203)<br>• Decisions are usually made with input from all components of school community. Parents are involved in School Site Council as well as the PTA. (Pages 203)<br>• Plans are in place to form a curriculum committee to assist in the implementation of the school vision, goals, and plan. (Page 203)<br>• Some partnerships are in place. (Page 204)<br>• The focus on assessment as a means of following student performance is great. (Page 205)<br>• Staff is using SAT 9 data to assign priorities to schoolwide goals. (Page 205) | |

### *What are some implications for their school improvement plan?*

• Consider presenting staff inservices on the effects of poverty on student achievement.
• Revisit the vision and goals, and then make sure the plan is aligned with the vision.
• Training for instructional assistants should be developed.
• Develop additional strategies that use technology to improve instruction.
• Develop effective peer coaching models, teacher as action researcher, critical friends group, or other strategies to assist teachers with their own professional development, and then alter the teacher evaluation process to coincide with this professional development. This needs to be a part of the plan.
• Develop strategies to increase parent involvement.
• Develop a coordinated school partnership program, and determine an approach to evaluate partnership involvement.
• Make access to data easier for teachers.
• Use data in a systematic and rigorous way.

| Questionnaire Data | |
|---|---|
| *What are their perceptual strengths?* | *What are their perceptual challenges?* |
| *Student questionnaires* (CD Narrative)<br>• All student responses were in agreement or strong agreement both years.<br>• Students were in strong agreement both years with respect to the items related to their families wanting them to do well in school, and believing they can do well in school. (CD Narrative)<br>• Students agreed strongly both years that their teacher believes they can learn and that their teacher is a good teacher.<br>• There were no differences among responses by gender.<br>• There were few differences in responses by grade level. Sixth-grade students were the lowest in 2003.<br>• All but two items for one grade level, sixth grade, were in agreement with the items on the questionnaire.<br>• Open-ended responses show that students like the teachers most of all. They also like their friends, the fun activities, recess, and learning new things. | *Student questionnaires* (CD Narrative)<br>• Student averages dropped slightly across the board in 2003 from where they were in December 2001.<br>• Students were in least agreement with *I have freedom at school, Students at my school treat me with respect, Students at my school are friendly,* and *I have choices in what I learn.*<br>• Sixth-grade students' responses varied the most from the other grade levels. Their lowest were items, *I have choices in what I learn* and *I have freedom at school.*<br>• African-Americans and Asians were in most disagreement with the items, *I have choices in what I learn* and *I have freedom at school.*<br>• African-American students also were lowest (neutral average) with respect to the items: *Students are treated fairly by the people on yard duty,* and *Students are treated fairly by teachers.*<br>• Students wish there was better food and a better playground.<br>• Students commented in the open-ended responses about recess needing to be longer and about teachers and other students needing to be nicer. |
| *Staff questionnaires* (CD Narrative)<br>• Staff questionnaire results were in agreement with all but one item.<br>• Teachers believe that student achievement can increase through effective parent involvement, and they feel that learning can be fun. Teachers also strongly agree that every student can learn, and that student achievement can increase through close personal relationships between student and teacher and providing a safe environment. They believe that it is important to communicate often with parents, that quality work is expected of them, and that they work with administrators who treat them with respect. Further, they believe student achievement can increase through hands-on learning, they love to teach, and they feel that they belong at this school.<br>• There were no differences between staff ethnicities with respect to perceptions of the learning environment.<br>• Staff members with four to six years and seven to ten years of teaching experience were most positive about the item, *I feel learning can be fun.*<br>• Instructional assistants were in strongest agreement with the item, *I love teaching.* | *Staff questionnaires* (CD Narrative)<br>• Staff disagreed with the statement *I believe that community businesses are active in this school.*<br>• Upper-grade teachers responded neutral, while primary grade teachers were in agreement with three items: *I believe student achievement can increase through multi-age classrooms; I believe that rules for student behavior are consistently enforced;* and *I believe that student discipline is administered fairly and appropriately.*<br>• Staff members with seven to ten years of teaching experience were in most disagreement with the item, *I believe that rules for student behavior are consistently enforced.*<br>• Staff members with four to six years of teaching experience were in disagreement with the items, *I believe parents often are invited to visit classrooms,* and *I believe that parent volunteers are used wherever possible.*<br>• Instructional assistants were in least agreement with most items on the staff questionnaire.<br>• Classroom teachers and classified staff responded in disagreement to the item, *I believe that community businesses are active in this school.* |

## Questionnaire Data (Continued)

| *What are their perceptual strengths?* | *What are their perceptual challenges?* |
|---|---|
| *Staff questionnaires* (CD Narrative)<br>• Classified staff responded in strongest agreement to the item, *I believe that it is important to communicate often with parents.*<br>• Teachers implementing *Different Ways of Knowing* (DWOK) curriculum responded in slightly stronger agreement to most items on the questionnaire.<br>• In writing responses to the open-ended questions, staff indicated that the staff and the administration are the greatest strengths of the school. | *Staff questionnaires* (CD Narrative)<br>• Instructional assistants were in disagreement with the items, *I work with teachers who communicate well with each other across grade levels, and I communicate with parents often about their child's progress.*<br>• In the open-ended questionnaire results, staff indicated that they need better use of technology, better communication, a more diverse teaching staff, a full-time assistant principal, a stronger science program, better parent involvement, and a better facility. |
| *Parent questionnaires* (CD Narrative)<br>• Parent responses on the questionnaire were mostly in strong agreement with the items. The items that were not in "strong agreement" were in agreement.<br>• Parents were in strongest agreement to items: *I respect the school's teachers; I support my child's learning at home; I am informed about my child's progress; I respect the school's principal; I feel good about myself as a parent; I feel welcome at my child's school; My child's teacher helps me to help my child learn at home; I know how well my child is progressing in school; Teachers show respect for the students;* and, *I know what my child's teacher expects of my child.*<br>• Not a lot of differences appeared between parents' responses by ethnicity, native language, by number of children in the household, by number of children in the school, or by students of different grade levels.<br>• Parents commented that the strengths of the school are the teachers, the principal, and the support staff.<br>• Parents also like the emphasis on Reading, the after-school programs, the academic programs, and the computer skills their children are learning.<br>• Parents feel there is good communication between teachers and parents concerning the progress of their students. | *Parent questionnaires* (CD Narrative)<br>• The open-ended responses indicate individual parent concern for a variety of issues, nothing dominating, except for the need for more playground and after-school traffic supervision.<br>• Parents believe the school could be better with more supervision, smaller class sizes, more parking, more parent participation, cleaner restrooms, and more Spanish speaking teachers. |

---

### Questionnaire Data (Continued)
### *What are some implications for their school improvement plan?*

---

These comments are, of course, from the outside looking in, which is very different from the inside looking out…

- It would be nice if Blue Bird would administer student, staff, and parent questionnaires every year so they could see progress. When administering the questionnaires, the school needs to try to get more respondents. Students and staff are captive audiences; and, therefore, we should see 100% response rates from both groups. Parent questionnaires can be administered during parent-teacher conferences so as to yield a much higher response rate. Consistently administering the questionnaires will help with understanding the perceptions data over time, and will be another measure of growth.
- Include K-2 students when administering questionnaires.
- All staff members should implement *Different Ways of Knowing* (DWOK).
- Communication across grade levels might need to be improved.
- There is a lot of leverage (strength) in the agreement and strong agreement statements of all the questionnaires that can be used to improve the school and particularly student learning. For instance, students were in strong agreement with the items related to their families wanting them to do well in school, and believing they can do well in school. Students also agreed strongly that their teachers believe they can learn and that their teachers are good teachers. Teachers believe that student achievement can increase through effective parent involvement, and they feel that learning can be fun. Teachers also strongly agree that every student can learn, that student achievement can increase through providing a safe environment. They believe that it is important to communicate often with parents, that quality work is expected of them, that they work with administrators who treat them with respect. Further, they believe student achievement can increase through hands-on learning, they love to teach, and they feel that they belong in this school. Parents respect the school's teachers, they feel they support their child's learning at home, that they are informed about their child's progress, they feel good about themselves as parents, they feel welcome at the school, they feel that their child's teacher helps them help their child learn at home, they know how well their child is progressing in school, they feel teachers show respect for the students, they know what their child's teacher expects of their child, and they respect the school's principal.
- Look at consistent discipline enforcement and supervision. It would behoove staff to look into strategies to improve student behavior.
- Consider training for supervisors on the playground, in the lunchroom, and before and after school, and for instructional assistants.
- Consider some team-building training for instructional assistants and teachers.
- Staff needs to consider strategies to improve parent involvement.
- Can the food be improved? Can the students be involved in determining food choices?
- The use of data to guide instruction should be expanded to subject areas other than Math. Access to data needs to be made easier for teachers. The staff needs to take the data to the next level, including following former students into their next levels of schooling.
- Help for the staff to develop consistent rubrics like the one they are currently using in writing, to be used by all teachers.
- Investigate multi-age classrooms and looping, and how to get parent support.
- Inservice staff on the effects of poverty on student achievement.
- Develop strategies to better serve the needs of English Learners.
- Publicize the school plan by developing a brochure or pamphlet.
- Revisit the vision, goals, and plan.
- Provide more training for instructional assistants.
- Provide training in technology to support the improvement of instruction.
- Develop effective peer coaching models, teacher as action researcher, critical friends group, or other strategies to assist teachers with their own professional development, and then alter the teacher evaluation process to coincide with this professional development.
- Develop a coordinated school partnership program and determine an approach to evaluate partnership involvement.

## HOW ARE WE DOING?

Blue Bird's four years of norm-referenced scores and analyses of student achievement results were comprehensive and very informative. Using an equal interval scale, such as the normal curve equivalent (NCE), made it easy to look across subtests, grade levels, and over time. It also made following individual student scores very easy.

| *What are their strengths?* | *What are their challenges?* |
|---|---|
| ◆ All schoolwide subtest averages increased over time, with the exception of the Language subtest averages, which maintained in the last two years. (Figure 9.24) | ◆ Grade six 2002-03 scores were slightly lower than 2001-02 results in all subtests, except Spelling. (Figures 9.25, 9.26, and 9.27) |
| ◆ All 2002-03 subtest averages were higher than, or the same, as the three prior years, in all but grades two and three in Language, grade four in Language Expression and Language Mechanics, and all subtests in grade six. Each of those decreases was extremely small. (Figure 9.25) | ◆ All 2002-03 grade level scores were higher than four years ago, with the exception of grade six subtests and grade two Math Procedures. All grade six language subtest 2002-03 scores were slightly lower than 1999-00 scores. (Figures 9.25, 9.26, and 9.27) |
| ◆ With respect to the Reading subtests, all averages were higher each year for grades two through four. Grade five Reading Vocabulary and Total Reading dropped slightly in 2001-02, with 2002-03 being their highest scoring year. Total Reading scores improved every year at grade six. (Figure 9.26) | ◆ Language subtest scores dipped slightly in 2000-01 in grade two, although up from the previous two years, prior to 2001-02. (Figure 9.25) |
| ◆ All Math subtests at all grade levels, except grade two, increased in 2002-03. (Figure 9.27) | ◆ Grade six Reading subtests were slightly down in Reading Comprehension in 2002-03 (although essentially the same). (Figure 9.26) |
| ◆ Grades three and four Math subtest scores increased every year in a nice progression. (Figure 9.27) | ◆ Grade two Math subtest scores decreased from the previous year in 2000-01 and in 2002-03. (Figure 9.27) |
| ◆ Females generally scored slightly higher than the males at all grade levels in all subtests, except for Math. About one-half of the time the male scores were slightly higher. (Figure 9.28 and CD) | ◆ Males generally scored slightly lower than females at all grade levels in all subtests, except for Math. About one-half of the time the male scores were slightly higher. (Figure 9.28 and CD) |
| ◆ Following cohorts over time, one can see improvement in most subtests over time. (Figures 9.29 and 9.30) | ◆ The cohort scores dipped in grade four 1999-00, grade five in 2002-03, grade three 2002-03, and grade six in 2002-03 for males for some of the Language subtests. (Figures 9.29 and 9.30) |
| ◆ Most Reading subtests improved for both genders for almost all the cohorts. (Figures 9.29 and 9.30) | ◆ Grade three 2002-03 cohort scores are lower for both genders in Reading. (Figures 9.33 and 9.34) |
| ◆ Most Math subtests improved for both genders for almost all the cohorts. (CD) | ◆ Fifth-grade female cohorts lost ground in Math in 2002-03. (CD) |
| ◆ The decile graphs show improvement for every Language, Reading, and Math subtest. (Figure 9.35) | ◆ Grade five 2002-03 males scored lower in Reading Comprehension and Total Reading. (Figure 9.30) |
| ◆ For the demographics (i.e., high percentage of free/reduced lunch students) that this school is working with, they are doing a very good job. (Figures 9.12 and 9.13) | |

## *What are some implications for their school improvement plan?*

Look long and hard at the SAT 9 results to see how the standards are not being implemented consistently across all grade levels. Data will be able to tell much of the story that will help Blue Bird improve.

### WHAT ARE THE GAPS?

Even though tremendous progress has been made in increasing the numbers of students achieving above 50 NCE in all the subtests in the last three years, all subtests point to gaps. Reading subtests stand out as the school's greatest gaps.

### What are the root causes of the gaps?

After a quick look at the gaps and digging deeper, one comes up with the idea that there are many contributing causes, with one major root cause. The major root cause in this case has to be the way some teachers are teaching. The major differences in results center on whom the students had as teachers. Some teachers are making progress, no matter who they have as students. The progress that has been made over time shows that when teaching strategies improve, so do the scores of students.

### Implications for the Blue Bird Elementary School Plan

Studying the data and pulling together the implications for the continuous school improvement plan derived from the data, one would want to see the following strategies and activities appear in the Blue Bird continuous school improvement plan, and then implemented.

*Strategies to:*
- consider presenting staff inservices on the effects of poverty on student achievement.
- work with the students who are absent, and their parents.
- implement a schoolwide discipline plan with total staff engagement.
- bring up the scores of African-American and Hispanic students, English Learners, and students living in poverty.
- develop consistent rubrics to be used by all teachers for students.
- increase parent involvement.
- get partnerships in a systematic manner.
- evaluate partnership involvement.
- use data to guide instruction in all areas.

*Professional development training for:*
- working with English Learning students.
- working with families living in poverty.
- new and emergency-credentialed teachers with mentoring.
- analyzing and utilizing data and student work.
  - * The use of data to guide instruction should be expanded to subject areas other than Math. Access to data needs to be made easier for teachers. The staff needs to take the data to the next level, including following former students into their next levels of schooling.
- learning how to use technology as a means to improve instruction.
- developing effective peer coaching models, teacher as action researcher, critical friends group, or other strategies to assist teachers with their own professional development, and then alter the teacher evaluation process to coincide with this professional development.
- DWOK for all staff?
- supervisors of the playground, the lunchroom, and before and after school.
- teaching to and implementing the standards.

*Reorganize the school to:*
- spread veteran teachers across all grade levels, so as not to leave any grade level with too many novice teachers.
- revisit the mission, vision, and plan for the school.
- improve communication of teachers across grade levels.
- bring in partners to assist with the implementation of student learning standards in a systematic fashion.
- publicize the school plan by developing a brochure or pamphlet.
- make sure at least one teacher at each grade level speaks Spanish.

*Annually:*
- administer the student, staff, and parent questionnaires.
- schedule time to assess on the *Continuous Improvement Continuums* and determine next steps, preferably twice a year.
- set aside time to study the student achievement results as soon as possible when the SAT 9 results come in.
- systematically and deeply review the gaps and root causes.

*Other things:*
- start believing all students can learn.
- the school must be ready for increases in enrollment and possibly even higher free/reduced lunch percentages.
- the school will need to continue to hire teachers for English Learners.
- maybe establish a student advisory group to improve the school from the perspective of the students (issues like food, behavior, learning…).
- need to investigate multi-age classrooms and looping, and how to gain parent support for these methods if they look like good strategies for Blue Bird students.
- develop a coordinated school partnership program.

## Summary

Blue Bird Elementary School analyzed its data—from demographics to deciles to cohort analyses of their norm-referenced test scores. The analyses helped staff see what they need to do to improve student learning. The implications for the school improvement plan will help staff create a continuous school improvement plan similar to Little River's, presented in Figure 8.3. The implementation of such a comprehensive plan will help each teacher improve everything she/he does for the students.

## On the CD Related to this Chapter

▼ Study Questions Related to Example Two (Ch9Qs.pdf)

These study questions will help you better understand the information provided in Chapter 9. This file can be printed for use with staffs.

▼ *What I Saw in Example Two* (Ch9Saw.pdf)

*What I Saw in Example Two* is a file, organized by the student learning study questions, that summarizes what I saw in the student learning data provided by Blue Bird Elementary School.

▼ Demographic Graphing Templates for Blue Bird School (DemogCh9.xls)

All of the *Microsoft Excel* files that were used to create the demographic graphs in the Blue Bird example (Chapter 9) appear on the CD. Use these templates by putting your data in the data table and changing the title/labels to reflect your data. Your graphs will build automatically.

▼ Demographic Data Table Templates for Blue Bird Elementary School (DemogCh9.doc)

All of the *Microsoft Word* files that were used to create the demographic data tables in the Blue Bird example (Chapter 9) appear on the CD. Use these templates by putting your data in the data table and changing the title/labels to reflect your data.

▼ *School Data Profile Template* (BBProfil.doc)

This *Microsoft Word* file provides a template for creating your own school data profile like the one for example two: *Blue Bird Elementary School.*

▼ *Education for the Future* Perception Questionnaires used by Example Two, Blue Bird Elementary School:

   ◆ *Education for the Future Student Questionnaire* (BBStudnt.pdf)
   ◆ *Education for the Future Staff Questionnaire* (BBStaff.pdf)
   ◆ *Education for the Future Parent Questionnaire* (BBParent.pdf)

▼ Full narratives of Questionnaire Results for Example Two, Blue Bird Elementary School:

   ◆ *Blue Bird Student Questionnaire Results* (StuNarr2.pdf)
   ◆ *Blue Bird Staff Questionnaire Results* (StfNarr2.pdf)
   ◆ *Blue Bird Parent Questionnaire Results* (ParNarr2.pdf)

▼ *Blue Bird Elementary School Baseline CIC Results* (BBBase.pdf)

This read-only file is the summary of Blue Bird's baseline assessment on the *School Portfolio Continuous Improvement Continuums.*

▼ *Continuous Improvement Continuums* Graphic (CICs.pdf)

This read-only file is of the seven *School Portfolio Continuous Improvement Continuums.* These can be printed out as is or enlarged to put on the wall to use during staff assessments.

▼ *Continuous Improvement Continuum* Tools

These files are tools for assessing on the CICs and for writing the CIC report.

◆ *Continuous Improvement Continuums Self-Assessment Activity* (ACTCIC.pdf)

Assessing on the *Continuous Improvement Continuums* will help staffs see where their systems are right now with respect to continuous improvement and ultimately show they are making progress over time. The discussion has major implications for the *Continuous School Improvement (CSI) Plan.*

◆ *Coming to Consensus* (Consenss.pdf)

This read-only file provides strategies for coming to consensus.

◆ *Continuous Improvement Continuums Report Example* (ExReprt1.pdf)

This read-only file shows a real school's assessment on the *School Portfolio Continuous Improvement Continuums,* as an example.

◆ *Continuous Improvement Continuums Report Example for Follow-Up Years* (ExReprt2.pdf)

This read-only file shows a real school's assessment on the *School Portfolio Continuous Improvement Continuums* over time, as an example.

◆ *Continuous Improvement Continuums Baseline Report Template* (ReptTemp.doc)

This *Microsoft Word* file provides a template for writing your school's report of its assessment on the *School Portfolio Continuous Improvement Continuums.*

◆ *Continuous Improvement Continuums* Graphing Templates (CICGraph.xls)

This *Microsoft Excel* file is a template for graphing your assessments on the seven *School Portfolio Continuous Improvement Continuums.*

▼ Student Achievement Graphing Templates for Blue Bird (SA1Ch9.xls and SA2Ch9.xls)

All of the *Microsoft Excel* files that were used to create the student achievement graphs in the Blue Bird example (Chapter 9) appear on the CD. Use these templates by putting your data in the data table and changing the title/labels to reflect your data. Your graphs will build automatically. This file also explains how to use the templates.

▼ Student Achievement Data Table Templates for Blue Bird Elementary School (SACh9.doc)

All of the *Microsoft Word* files that were used to create the student achievement data tables in the Blue Bird example (Chapter 9) appear on the CD. Use these templates by putting your data in the data table and changing the title/labels to reflect your data.

▼ *Blue Bird Elementary School Gap Analyses Graphing Templates* (BBGaps.xls)

All of the *Microsoft Excel* files that were used to create the gap analyses graphs in the Blue Bird example (Chapter 9) appear on the CD. Use these templates by putting your data in the data table and changing the title/labels to reflect your data. Your graphs will build automatically. This file also explains how to use the templates.

▼ *Blue Bird Elementary School Gap Analyses Data Table Templates* (BBGaps.doc)

All of the *Microsoft Word* files that were used to create the gap analyses data tables in the Blue Bird example (Chapter 9) appear on the CD. Use these templates by putting your data in the data table and changing the title/labels to reflect your data.

▼ *Root Causes Activity* (ACTRoot.pdf)

Root causes are the real causes of our educational problems. We need to find out what they are so we can eliminate the true cause and not just address the symptom. This activity asks staff teams to review and analyze data and ask probing questions to uncover the root cause(s).

▼ *Gap Analysis and Objectives Activity* (ACTGap.pdf)

The purpose of this activity is to look closely at differences between current results and where the school wants to be in the future. It is this gap analysis that gets translated into objectives that guide the development of the action plan.

# Analyzing the Data:
## *Conclusions and Recommendations*

Chapter 10

The main purpose of *Using Data to Improve Student Learning in Elementary Schools* is to show two sets of analyses, using a continuous school improvement planning model to understand, explain, and continuously improve learning for all students in elementary schools.

In this book, analyses of two sets of data have been presented. Many of you might consider the analyses to be massive. However, these two examples were created using only state assessments, some perceptions, some demographics, and very little process data. The data shown here and on the CD, therefore, are not exhaustive. More comprehensive data analyses would use other measures of student learning in addition to state assessments, such as grades, authentic assessments, and more process measures such as degree of program or process implementation. Additionally, comprehensive data analyses would have multiple years of data—ideally, we want to follow students throughout their K-12 education experiences. This is not very realistic for all schools and districts at this point in time. Three years of consistent measures are good—five years are better. Most schools have plenty of data. Most do not need to gather more data—where effort is needed is in organizing, graphing, analyzing, and using what they already have.

## What the Examples Show

From the examples, I hope you can see how much a person can learn about a school through data—even when only little data are available. I hope you can also see that one person alone cannot do all the data analysis. Everybody sees something different in the results, so many perspectives are necessary and valuable.

The demographic analyses of these two schools showed us that we could get a very good understanding of the context of education for their students. To me, it was almost shocking how much the implications for improvement were detected in the demographic data. The way the school organizes itself to provide for its students is shown in the demographic data, and it tells a story. My hope is that school personnel reviewing these data will take the time to comprehensively analyze their own system's demographic data. There are times when others must read about your organization. Remember how easy it was, when reviewing these schools' data, to start "making up" parts of the story when it was not complete. Your best defense against others drawing incorrect or incomplete assumptions about your school is to provide complete analyses.

With regard to perceptions data, we viewed two different types of perceptual data—questionnaire data and *Continuous Improvement Continuum* assessments. These two data types helped each school see itself from different perspectives. A major caution in looking at the questionnaire results is to make sure one does not over-interpret differences in subgroups—even though a gap in averages appears, there might not be a *real* difference if both averages indicate agreement. It just might be the degree of the agreement that is different. Real differences would show agreement-disagreement. We are not concerned with looking for "significant differences." We want to know about "educational or perceptual differences," because these differences are significant in the learning of students.

The *Continuous Improvement Continuums* are powerful self-analysis tools. These assessments help whole staffs talk the same talk and walk the same walk. Over time, they show staffs they are making improvement, which keeps them moving ahead.

In analyzing student learning results, our examples displayed two different types of test analyses, *criterion-referenced* and *norm-referenced.*

Little River used its state criterion-referenced test (CRT) to evaluate processes. Needless to say, data for one grade level do not give enough information to understand the impact of processes throughout the school. We do not know about the educational experiences of students before this grade level that contributed to the grade level results. We also do not know how well the students did after that particular grade level. One can see through this example, however, that analyzing data for even one grade level can give powerful information about how students are taught and which students are not being reached.

Blue Bird used a norm-referenced test (NRT) at every grade level over time. Normal Curve Equivalent (NCE) scores, that have the same range (1 to 99) and the same average (50) for every grade level and subtest, can provide extremely valuable information for looking at the system of education for students at a school site. If a school is doing what it is supposed to be doing for its students, cohort averages should show increases each year. Analyzing by teacher and grade level, we also know that NCE averages will remain approximately the same if teachers are not provided with quality professional development to help them reflect on their own results and work differently.

As far as gap analyses are concerned, both examples were able to indicate gaps—regardless of whether the test used was criterion referenced or norm referenced. Neither example was able to find *one* root cause, however, which is very common. Having the data available by teacher enabled us to see the results of each classroom for each subgroup of students. Just when we thought that student background was the cause of our results, we found teachers who got positive results from students with these backgrounds. This leads us to want to look deeper into the data by teacher. We need to track student performance of various teachers over time to determine if student performance in their classes is consistent from year to year.

Neither example was really able to analyze processes, other than the few mentioned above. Ultimately, we want to be able to organize the data and understand the impact of teaching methodologies, curriculum, and programs. One simple way to begin to do that would be to describe the curriculum instructional strategies used, by year, under the graphic.

## Data Warehouses

Done well, data analysis is a massive activity requiring the technical support of knowledgeable people and a data warehouse. Districts are just now coming on board with acquiring data warehouses that will enable the storage of a large number of data elements, and the analysis of data quickly, easily, accurately, and meaningfully. (See *Designing and Using Databases for School Improvement* [Bernhardt, 2000].) On the CD is an article entitled *Databases Can Help Teachers with Standards Implementation* (Bernhardt, 1999), summarizing how databases can help with standards implementation.

School districts or schools that do not have such a tool right now must begin looking and preparing to buy a data warehouse, because they need one. It simply is no longer an option not to have one. When looking for a database or data warehouse, districts need to keep at least six considerations in mind:

1. *Accessibility at different levels.* We would like the data stored at the district, possibly even regional or state levels, and have it accessible from the school and classroom levels. Small rural districts can form consortia.

2. *Build graphs automatically.* We want to be able to look over the data tables to check for accuracy; however, we want the data analysis tool to build graphs as well. Because we want staffs to review the data, it is wise to put the data in picture form so everyone can see the resulting information in the same way. Trends are often easier to detect in graphs than in tables. However, sometimes we need tables to display the data.

3. *Disaggregation on the fly.* When performing analyses that are starting to show interesting data, we want to be able to analyze quickly and easily at the next deeper levels. The easier and quicker this is to do, the deeper one can get into the data, and the more likely we are to get to root causes.

4. *Point and click or drag and drop technology that is intuitive.* We want anyone to be able to use the database without requiring a manual every time it is used.

5. *The ability to create standard reports with a click of a button.* Some reports have to be created every year, such as a School Accountability Report Card or a Title 1 report. If the same information is required each year, the programming should allow one merely to push a button the next year to create the report without spending a lot of time on it.

6. *The ability to follow cohorts.* Following the same groups of students as they progress through their educational careers will provide a great deal of information about one's school processes.

For the analyses in this book, I used a data warehouse tool called *EASE-E Data Analyzer* by *TetraData (www.tetradata.com)*. With this tool, I am able to analyze an entire district's data and all of its schools at the same time, as quickly and easily as analyzing one school. I do the analyses for all the schools at the same time, and then use graphing templates, such as the ones provided on the accompanying CD, to build the graphs quickly and easily. (Point of clarification: *EASE-E* builds graphs. I use graphing templates such as those on the accompanying CD when I perform analyses for multiple schools at the same time—where one graph would be inadequate.) Teachers and administrators can also access specific school and classroom data from this warehouse.

Because of their commitment to help make data analysis easier, especially for schools, *TetraData* has included the analyses made in this work as standard queries and the school profiles as standard reports. In other words, if you own *EASE-E Data Analyzer,* you will be able to create a school report similar to Little River's, with a few clicks of buttons. You will have to verify that what you named as elements are similar to those in this study.

## Who Does the Data Analysis Work?

For the types of data analyses shown here in the examples, or described above as comprehensive data analyses, it would be ideal if someone at the district level did the major analyses. With a good strong data analysis tool, the district person can analyze the data for all the schools, at all grade levels, for all the subtests, disaggregated by demographics, in one query. A clerk can then copy and paste the individual results into charting templates, perhaps even into the templates provided on the CD with this book.

With a strong data analysis tool, standard queries and standard reports, such as a school report card, can be created for each of the schools by one person. Our passion with data analysis is getting the results into the hands of teachers and giving them professional development in understanding the results and the time to study the *results* of the analyses, instead of having them use their time performing the analyses. In our ideal world, at minimum, teachers would start the school year with historical data on each student in their class(es). They would have the demographic data and would know what the students know and what they need to know. Also in our ideal world, teachers would be using ongoing measurements in their classrooms to make sure all students are progressing and mastering the standards/outcomes.

Let's say your district does not have a data warehouse and provides only the state assessment results on paper; you can still use these data in meaningful ways. At minimum, schools can use the templates on the CD to graph the content and average student learning scores over time. If there have been positive improvements in the school, you should see increases in scores. If the school is making a positive impact on students, student cohort scores should increase over time.

## The Role of the Administrator

Research shows that there are three preconditions to school/district performance improvement: instructional coherence, a shared vision for school improvement, and data-driven decision making. Data are necessary, but not sufficient. All three—instructional coherence, a shared vision, and data-driven decision making—must work together. We believe the link for these three preconditions is the administrator. The administrator must lead the way through challenging processes through the study of school results, inspiring the shared vision, enabling others to act through planning, plan implementation, professional development, and partnerships, modeling the way through consistent actions, and encouraging the heart by reminding teachers of the purpose of the school, why they got into teaching in the first place, and celebrating successes (Kouzes & Posner, 2002). A school's performance cannot improve without the building administrator(s) being totally dedicated to and engaged in this process.

## Evaluation

Just a word about evaluation. *Continuous Improvement and Evaluation* is required to assess the alignment of all parts of the system to the vision and to check the results the learning organization is getting compared to what is being implemented. If schools or districts conduct the analyses described in this book, they will have a fairly comprehensive evaluation. An evaluation does not have to be different from data analysis. You might organize an evaluation around school goals, objectives, or even purpose and vision, by asking the basic question, *What do we have as evidence that we are doing these things?* This might take reorganizing the data already analyzed, or simply answering questions, using the data already analyzed. 

*A school's performance cannot improve without the building administrator(s) being totally dedicated to and engaged in this process.*

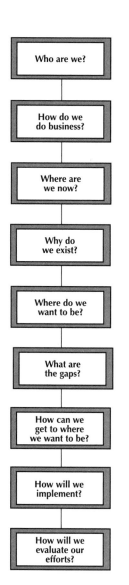

Who are we?

How do we do business?

Where are we now?

Why do we exist?

Where do we want to be?

What are the gaps?

How can we get to where we want to be?

How will we implement?

How will we evaluate our efforts?

## Summary: Review of Steps in Using Data to Improve Student Learning in Elementary Schools

Continuous school improvement planning for increasing student learning can be organized through answering a series of logical questions.

One of the first questions we want to answer is *Who are we?* Demographic data can answer this question. The answers set the context for the school, have huge implications for the direction the continuous school improvement plan will take, and can help explain how the school gets the results it is getting. In fact, there is no way any school can understand another number without the context.

The second question, *How do we do business?*, tells us about perceptions of the learning environment from student, staff, and parent perspectives. Understanding these perceptions can help a school know what is possible and what is appropriate, needed, and doable in the continuous school improvement plan.

Answering the question, *How are we doing?* takes the data analysis work into the student learning realm. Analyzing required norm-referenced and/or criterion-referenced tests is an excellent way to begin answering this question. Looking across all measures can be useful and informative—another way to think about what students know and are able to do, giving us a glimpse of *how* students learn.

Gap analyses are critical for answering the question, *What are the gaps?* Gap analyses help schools see the differences between where they are (current results) and where they want to be (vision and goals). To be effective, gap analyses must dig layers deep into the data to truly understand the results and to begin to uncover root causes.

A root cause, as used in this continuous school improvement planning model, refers to the deep underlying reason for the occurrence of a specific situation, the gap. While a symptom may become evident from a needs assessment or gap analysis—the symptom (low student scores) is not the cause. To find a root cause, one often has to ask *why* at least five levels down to uncover the root reason for the symptom. Root causes are not easy to uncover, but the information that is uncovered in the process of uncovering root causes is well worth the effort.

With the strengths, challenges, gap analyses, and root cause analyses complete, one can integrate findings to create a continuous school improvement plan that is informed by the data, and that will lead to student achievement increases. Additionally, a continuous school improvement plan based on data will eliminate root causes.

A continuous school improvement plan to eliminate root causes can answer the question, *How will we get there?* A continuous school improvement plan focused on data lays out the strategies and activities to implement. Required professional development, a leadership structure, a design for partnerships with parents, communities, and businesses, and the evaluation of the plan are vital components of the plan.

Gather your schoolwide data, graph it in a manner similar to the examples in this book; this will get a good look at where your school is right now. To understand what to improve in your system, you have to know as much about your systems as you possibly can, study your demographic data, and your perceptual and student learning results, along with your current processes.

Time and time again, the differences in results by classroom or by school come down to the fact that some teachers are teaching to the standards and some are not. I can almost guarantee that if all teachers in your school know what the students know when they start a grade level and subject area, focus their effective instructional strategies on teaching what they want students to know and be able to do to meet the standards, measure in an ongoing fashion to know if the students are improving, student learning results for all students will increase in a very short period of time.

## Final Notes

In the past, the usual way typical school personnel dealt with schoolwide data was to analyze the dickens out of their annual state assessment results, develop a plan to increase the lowest scores, and then wait for the next year's results to come out to know if their plan made a difference. Many found they could improve their assessment results in that area, only to discover that other subject-area scores declined. With *No Child Left Behind*, this approach is no longer plausible. To move all students to proficiency, school personnel must have a complete understanding of the whole system the students experience and work on improving the system that creates the results.

In our examples, we started with demographic and perceptual data, which gave us a view of the system that student learning data alone cannot give. There were definite student learning issues that would be missed had we only looked at student learning results. My recommendations for getting student learning increases at the schoolwide level include (not in any particular order):

▼ Gather and analyze your demographic data to understand clearly the students you are serving and who is teaching them, by grade level and by content area.

▼ Listen to the *voices* of students, parents, and staff
through questionnaires.

▼ Analyze your student achievement results by subgroups, by
grade level, and by following cohorts.

▼ Align your curriculum and instructional strategies to meet
content standards.

▼ Incorporate into all teaching ongoing assessments related to
standards acquisition (e.g., diagnostics, benchmarking, grade level
indicators).

The data are not the hardest part of creating this scenario. Getting staffs to work
together to share and implement this vision takes strong and consistent
leadership from the school administrator(s) and leadership teams, as well as the
district leadership teams.

Best wishes to you as you continuously improve your systems for the students.
You are creating the future in which the next generation will live.

## On the CD Related to this Chapter

▼ *Databases Can Help Teachers with Standards Implementation* (Dbases.pdf)
This read-only article, by Victoria L. Bernhardt, describes how databases
can help with standards implementation.

▼ *Evaluating a Program Activity* (ACTEval.pdf)
The purpose of this activity is to get many people involved in creating a
comprehensive evaluation design to determine the impact of a program
and to know how to improve the program.

# Appendix A
## *Overview of the CD Contents*

The Appendix provides a list of the files as they appear on the accompanying CD. These files are listed by section, along with a description of the file's content and file type. (This list appears as the Index file [Index.pdf] on the CD.)

▼ **WHAT DATA ARE IMPORTANT?**

The files in this section support Chapter 2 in the book and provide an overview of what data are important in understanding if a school is effectively carrying out its purpose and assessing if *all* students are learning.

Multiple Measures of Data Graphic         MMgraphc.pdf      Acrobat Reader

This is Figure 2.1 in a PDF (portable document file) for printing.

Summary of Data Intersections         IntrscTbl.pdf      Acrobat Reader

This is Figure 2.2 in a PDF for your use with staff.

Data Discovery Activity         ACTDiscv.pdf      Acrobat Reader

The purpose of this activity is to look closely at examples of data and to discover specific information and patterns of information, both individually and as a group.

Intersections Activity         ACTIntrs.pdf      Acrobat Reader

The purpose of this activity is to motivate school improvement teams to think about the questions they can answer when they cross different data variables. It is also designed to help teams focus their data-gathering efforts so they are not collecting everything and anything.

Creating Intersections Activity         ACTCreat.pdf      Acrobat Reader

This activity is similar to the *Intersections Activity*. The purpose is to have participants "grow" their intersections.

Data Analysis Presentation         DASlides.ppt      Microsoft PowerPoint

This *Microsoft PowerPoint* presentation is an overview to use with your staffs in getting started with data analysis. The script of the presentation can be found under "view notes" and by setting the print option to "notes pages." Handouts can be created by setting the print option to "handouts" (three slides to a page).

### Articles

These read-only articles, by Victoria L. Bernhardt, will be useful in workshops or in getting started on data with staff.

Multiple Measures         MMeasure.pdf      Acrobat Reader

This article by Victoria L. Bernhardt, in read-only format, summarizes why, and what, data are important to continuous school improvement.

Intersections: New Routes Open when One
    Type of Data Crosses Another         Intersct.pdf      Acrobat Reader

This article by Victoria L. Bernhardt, in read-only format, published in the *Journal of Staff Development* (Winter 2000), discusses how much richer your data analyses can be when you intersect multiple data variables.

No Schools Left Behind         NoSchls.pdf      Acrobat Reader

This article by Victoria L. Bernhardt, in read-only format, published in *Educational Leadership* (February 2003), summarizes how to improve learning for *all* students.

Study Questions Related to *What Data are Important?*         Ch2Qs.pdf      Acrobat Reader

These study questions will help you better understand the information provided in Chapter 2. This file can be printed for use with staffs as they think through the data questions they want to answer and the data they will need to gather to answer the questions.

## ▼ GETTING STARTED ON DATA ANALYSIS FOR CONTINUOUS SCHOOL IMPROVEMENT

The files in this section support Chapter 3 in the book and provide an overview of how a school can get started with comprehensive data analysis work.

| | | |
|---|---|---|
| Continuous School Improvement Planning via the School Portfolio Graphic | CSIPlang.pdf | Acrobat Reader |

This read-only graphic displays the questions that can be answered to create a continuous school improvement plan. The data that can answer the questions, and where the answers would appear in the school portfolio, also appear on the graphic. In the book, it is Figure 3.1.

| | | |
|---|---|---|
| Continuous School Improvement Planning via the School Portfolio Description | CSIdscr.pdf | Acrobat Reader |

This read-only file shows Figure 3.1, along with its description.

| | | |
|---|---|---|
| School Portfolio Presentation | SPSlides.ppt | Microsoft PowerPoint |

This *Microsoft PowerPoint* presentation is an overview to use with your staffs in getting started on the school portfolio. The script of the presentation can be found under "view notes" and by setting the print option to "notes pages." Handouts can be created by setting the print option to "handouts" (three slides to a page).

| | | |
|---|---|---|
| Study Questions Related to *Getting Started* | Ch3Qs.pdf | Acrobat Reader |

These study questions will help you better understand the information provided in Chapter 3. This file can be printed for use with staffs as you begin continuous school improvement planning. Answering the questions will help staff determine the data needed to answer the questions discussed in this chapter.

## ▼ ANALYZING THE DATA: *WHO ARE WE?*

The files in this section support Chapter 4 in the book and are tools to create a demographic profile of your school in order to answer the question, *Who are we?*

| | | |
|---|---|---|
| Study Questions Related to *Who Are We?* | Ch4Qs.pdf | Acrobat Reader |

These study questions will help you better understand the information provided in Chapter 4. This file can be printed for use with staffs as you begin setting the context of your school by answering the question, *Who are we?*

| | | |
|---|---|---|
| Demographic Graphing Templates | ElemDemog.xls | Microsoft Excel |

All of the *Microsoft Excel* files that were used to create the demographic graphs in the Little River example in Chapter 4 appear on the CD in this section. Use these templates by putting your data in the data table and changing the title/labels to reflect your data. Your graphs will build automatically.

| | | |
|---|---|---|
| Demographic Data Table Templates | ElemDemog.doc | Microsoft Word |

All of the *Microsoft Word* files that were used to create the demographic data tables in the Little River example in Chapter 4 appear on the CD in this section. Use these templates by putting your data in the data table and changing the title/labels to reflect your data.

| | | |
|---|---|---|
| School Data Profile Template | ElemProfil.doc | Microsoft Word |

This *Microsoft Word* file provides a template for creating your own school data profile like the one for example one: *Little River Elementary School,* using the graphing and table templates provided.

| | | |
|---|---|---|
| School Profile | ProfilSc.doc | Microsoft Word |

The *School Profile* is a template for gathering and organizing data about your school, prior to graphing. Please adjust the profile to add data elements you feel are important for describing the context of your school. This information is then graphed and written into a narrative form. If creating a school portfolio, the data graphs and narrative would appear in *Information and Analysis.* (If you already have your data organized and just need to graph it, you might want to skip this step and use the graphing templates, described on the previous page.)

| Community Profile | ProfilCo.doc | Microsoft Word |

The *Community Profile* is a template for gathering and organizing data about your community, prior to graphing. Please adjust the profile to add data elements you feel are important for describing the context of your community. It is important to describe how the community has changed over time, and how it is expected to change in the near future. This information is then graphed and written into a narrative form. If creating a school portfolio, the data graphs and narrative would appear in *Information and Analysis*. (If you already have your data organized and just need to graph it, you might want to skip this step and use the graphing templates, described on the previous page.)

| Administrator Profile | ProfilAd.doc | Microsoft Word |

The *Administrator Profile* is a template for gathering and organizing data about your school administrators, prior to graphing. Please adjust the profile to fully describe your administrators. This information is then graphed and written into a narrative form. If creating a school portfolio, the data graphs and narrative would appear in *Information and Analysis* and *Leadership* sections. (If you already have your data organized and just need to graph it, you might want to skip this step and use the graphing templates, described on the previous page.)

| Teacher Profile | ProfilTe.doc | Microsoft Word |

The *Teacher Profile* is a template for gathering and organizing data about your school's teachers, prior to graphing. Please adjust the profile to fully describe your teachers. The synthesis of this information is then graphed and written into a narrative form. If creating a school portfolio, the data graphs and narrative would appear in *Information and Analysis*. (If you already have your data organized and just need to graph it, you might want to skip this step and use the graphing templates, described on the previous page.)

| Staff (Other than Teacher) Profile | ProfilSt.doc | Microsoft Word |

The *Staff (Other than Teacher) Profile* is a template for gathering and organizing data about school staff who are not teachers, prior to graphing. Please adjust the profile to fully describe your non-teaching staff. The synthesis of this information is then graphed and written into a narrative form. If creating a school portfolio, the data graphs and narrative would appear in *Information and Analysis*. (If you already have your data organized and just need to graph it, you might want to skip this step and use the graphing templates, described on the previous page.)

| History Gram Activity | ACTHstry.pdf | Acrobat Reader |

A team-building activity that will "write" the history of the school, which could help everyone see what staff has experienced since coming to the school, and how many school improvement initiatives have been started over the years. It is helpful for understanding what it will take to keep this current school improvement effort going.

| Questions to Guide the Analysis of Demographic Data | QsDemogr.doc | Microsoft Word |

This *Microsoft Word* file provides a guide for interpreting your demographic data. Adjust the questions to better reflect the discussion you would like to have with your staff about the gathered demographic data.

| What I Saw in Example One | Ch4Saw.pdf | Acrobat Reader |

*What I Saw in Example One* is a file, organized by the demographic study questions, that summarizes what I saw in the demographic data provided by Little River Elementary School.

| Demographic Data to Gather to Create the Context of the School | DemoData.pdf | Acrobat Reader |

This file defines the types of demographic data that are important to gather to build the context of the school and describe *Who are we?*

The files in this section support Chapter 5 in the book and include tools to help staff understand the organization and climate of the school from the perspective of students, staff, and parents. The resulting analyses can help answer the question, *How do we do business?*

| | | |
|---|---|---|
| Continuous Improvement Continuums Graphic | CICs.pdf | Acrobat Reader |

This read-only file contains the seven *School Portfolio Continuous Improvement Continuums*. These can be printed as is or enlarged for posting individual staff opinions during staff assessments.

| | | |
|---|---|---|
| Continuous Improvement Continuums for Districts | CICsDstrct.pdf | Acrobat Reader |

This read-only file contains the seven *School Portfolio Continuous Improvement Continuums* for assessing the district level. These can be printed as is and enlarged for posting individual staff opinions during staff assessments.

| | | |
|---|---|---|
| Little River Elementary School Baseline CIC Results | LRBase.pdf | Acrobat Reader |

This read-only file is the summary of Little River's baseline assessment on the *School Portfolio Continuous Improvement Continuums*.

### Continuous Improvement Continuum Tools

These files are tools for assessing on the CICs and for writing the CIC report.

| | | |
|---|---|---|
| Continuous Improvement Continuums Self-Assessment Activity | ACTCIC.pdf | Acrobat Reader |

Assessing on the *Continuous Improvement Continuums* will help staffs see where their systems are right now with respect to continuous improvement and ultimately will show they are making progress over time. The discussion has major implications for the *Continuous School Improvement (CSI) Plan.*

| | | |
|---|---|---|
| Coming to Consensus | Consenss.pdf | Acrobat Reader |

This read-only file provides strategies for coming to consensus.

| | | |
|---|---|---|
| Continuous Improvement Continuums Report Example | ExReprt1.pdf | Acrobat Reader |

This read-only file shows a real school's assessment on the *School Portfolio Continuous Improvement Continuums,* as an example.

| | | |
|---|---|---|
| Continuous Improvement Continuums Report Example for Follow-Up Years | ExReprt2.pdf | Acrobat Reader |

This read only file shows a real school's assessment on the *School Portfolio Continuous Improvement Continuums* over time, as an example.

| | | |
|---|---|---|
| Continuous Improvement Continuums Baseline Report Template | ReptTemp.doc | Microsoft Word |

This *Microsoft Word* file provides a template for writing your school's report of its assessment on the *School Portfolio Continuous Improvement Continuums.*

| | | |
|---|---|---|
| Continuous Improvement Continuums Graphing Templates | CICGraph.xls | Microsoft Excel |

This *Microsoft Excel* file is a template for graphing your assessments on the seven *School Portfolio Continuous Improvement Continuums.*

| | | |
|---|---|---|
| Study Questions Related to *How Do We Do Business?* | Ch5Qs.pdf | Acrobat Reader |

These study questions will help you better understand the information provided in Chapter 5. This file can be printed for use with staffs as you answer the question, *How do we do business?,* through analyzing Little River's perceptual data.

| | | |
|---|---|---|
| What I Saw in Example One | Ch5Saw.pdf | Acrobat Reader |

*What I Saw in Example One* is a file, organized by the perceptual study questions, that summarizes what I saw in the perceptual data provided by Little River Elementary School.

| | | |
|---|---|---|
| Analysis of Questionnaire Data Table | QTable.doc | Microsoft Word |

This *Microsoft Word* file is a tabular guide for interpreting your student, staff, and parent questionnaires, independently and interdependently. It will help you see the summary of your results and write the narrative.

## Full Narratives of Questionnaire Results Used in Example One

| | | |
|---|---|---|
| Little River Student Questionnaire Results | StuNarr1.pdf | Acrobat Reader |

This read-only file is the full narrative of student questionnaire results used in example one.

| | | |
|---|---|---|
| Little River Staff Questionnaire Results | StfNarr1.pdf | Acrobat Reader |

This read-only file is the full narrative of staff questionnaire results used in example one.

| | | |
|---|---|---|
| Little River Parent Questionnaire Results | ParNarr1.pdf | Acrobat Reader |

This read-only file is the full narrative of parent questionnaire results used in example one.

## Education for the Future Perception Questionnaires Used in Example One

| | | |
|---|---|---|
| Student Questionnaire | LRStudnt.pdf | Acrobat Reader |

This read-only file is the *Education for the Future* student perception questionnaire used in example one.

| | | |
|---|---|---|
| Staff Questionnaire | LRStaff.pdf | Acrobat Reader |

This read-only file is the *Education for the Future* staff perception questionnaire used in example one.

| | | |
|---|---|---|
| Parent Questionnaire | LRParent.pdf | Acrobat Reader |

This read-only file is the *Education for the Future* parent perception questionnaire used in example one.

| | | |
|---|---|---|
| School IQ Graphing Templates | School IQ Folder | |

*School Improvement Questionnaire Solutions (School IQ)* is a powerful tool for analyzing *Education for the Future* questionnaires. *School IQ* reduces an otherwise technical and complicated process to one that can be navigated with pushbutton ease. There are different versions of *IQ* for each of the eleven standard *Education for the Future* questionnaires. *School IQ* includes online questionnaire templates, all 11 questionnaires in PDF format, the analysis tool, the *School IQ,* and graphing templates.

## Other Popular Education for the Future Questionnaires

| | | |
|---|---|---|
| Student (Kindergarten to Grade 3) Questionnaire | StQKto3.pdf | Acrobat Reader |

This read-only file is the *Education for the Future* perception questionnaire for students in kindergarten through grade three.

| | | |
|---|---|---|
| Student (Grades 1 to 6) Questionnaire | StQ1to6.pdf | Acrobat Reader |

This read-only file is the *Education for the Future* perception questionnaire for students in grades one through six.

| | | |
|---|---|---|
| Student (Grades 6 to 12) Questionnaire | StQ6to12.pdf | Acrobat Reader |

This read-only file is the *Education for the Future* perception questionnaire for students in grades six through twelve.

| | | |
|---|---|---|
| Student (High School) Questionnaire | StQHS.pdf | Acrobat Reader |

This read-only file is the *Education for the Future* perception questionnaire for high school students.

| | | |
|---|---|---|
| Staff Questionnaire | StaffQ.pdf | Acrobat Reader |

This read-only file is the *Education for the Future* perception questionnaire for staff.

| | | |
|---|---|---|
| Administrator Questionnaire | Admin.pdf | Acrobat Reader |

This read-only file is the *Education for the Future* perception questionnaire for administrators.

| | | |
|---|---|---|
| Teacher Predictions of Student Responses (Grades 1-6) Questionnaire | TchPr1.pdf | Acrobat Reader |

This read-only file is the *Education for the Future* perception questionnaire for teachers of students in grades one through six.

| | | |
|---|---|---|
| Teacher Predictions of Student Responses (Grades 6-8) Questionnaire | TchPr2.pdf | Acrobat Reader |

This read-only file is the *Education for the Future* perception questionnaire for teachers of students in grades six through eight.

| Parent Questionnaire | ParntK12.pdf | Acrobat Reader |

This read-only file is the *Education for the Future* perception questionnaire for parents of kindergarten through grade twelve students.

| High School Parent Questionnaire | ParntHS.pdf | Acrobat Reader |

This read-only file is the *Education for the Future* perception questionnaire for parents of high school students.

| Alumni Questionnaire | Alumni.pdf | Acrobat Reader |

This read-only file is the *Education for the Future* perception questionnaire for alumni.

| How to Analyze Open-ended Responses | OEanalz.pdf | Acrobat Reader |

This read-only file discusses how to analyze responses to the open-ended questions on questionnaires.

| Questions to Guide the Analysis of Perceptions Data | PerceptQ.doc | Microsoft Word |

This *Microsoft Word* file is a tabular guide for interpreting your perceptions data. You can change the questions if you like or use the file to write in the responses. It will help you write the narrative for your results.

## ▼ ANALYZING THE DATA: *WHERE ARE WE NOW?*

The tools in this section support Chapter 6 in the book, help staffs determine the results of their current processes, particularly student achievement results, and can help staffs answer the question, *Where are we now?*

| Study Questions Related to *Where Are We Now?* | Ch6Qs.pdf | Acrobat Reader |

These study questions will help you better understand the information provided in Chapter 6. This file can be printed for use with staffs as you begin to explore your own student learning results.

| Arguments For and Against Standardized Testing | TestArgu.pdf | Acrobat Reader |

This table summarizes the most common arguments for and against the use of standardized testing.

| Standardized Test Score Terms | TestTerm.pdf | Acrobat Reader |

This table shows the different standardized testing terms, their most effective uses, and cautions for their uses.

| Arguments For and Against Performance Assessments | PerfArgu.pdf | Acrobat Reader |

This table shows the most common arguments for and against the use of performance assessments.

| Arguments For and Against Teacher Grading | GradeArg.pdf | Acrobat Reader |

This table shows the most common arguments for and against the use of teacher grading.

| Terms Related to Analyzing Student Achievement Results, Descriptively | SAterms1.pdf | Acrobat Reader |

This table shows the different terms related to analyzing student achievement results, descriptively, their most effective uses, and cautions for their uses.

| Terms Related to Analyzing Student Achievement Results, Inferentially | SAterms2.pdf | Acrobat Reader |

This table shows the different terms related to analyzing student achievement results, inferentially, their most effective uses, and cautions for their uses.

| What I Saw in Example One | Ch6Saw.pdf | Acrobat Reader |

*What I Saw in Example One* is a file, organized by the student learning study questions, that summarizes what I saw in the student learning data provided by Little River Elementary School.

| Student Achievement Graphing Templates | ElemSA.xls | Microsoft Excel |

All of the *Microsoft Excel* files that were used to create the student achievement graphs in the Little River example (Chapter 6) appear on the CD. Use these templates by putting your data in the data table and changing the title/labels to reflect your data. The graphs will build automatically. This file also explains how to use the templates.

Student Achievement Data Table Templates        ElemSA.doc      Microsoft Word

All of the *Microsoft Word* files that were used to create the student achievement data tables in the Little River example (Chapter 6) appear on the CD in this section. Use these templates by putting your data in the data table and changing the title/labels to reflect your data.

Questions to Guide the Analysis of Student Achievement Data      QsStachv.doc      Microsoft Word

This *Microsoft Word* file consists of questions to guide the interpretation of your student learning data. You can write your responses into this file.

▼   ANALYZING THE DATA: *WHAT ARE THE GAPS?* AND *WHAT ARE THE ROOT CAUSES OF THE GAPS?*

The tools in this section support Chapter 7 in the book and help staffs analyze their data to determine the gaps and the root causes of the gaps. These files and tools can help answer the questions, *What are the gaps?* and *What are the root causes of the gaps?*

Goal Setting Activity        ACTGoals.pdf      Acrobat Reader

By setting goals, a school can clarify its end targets for the school's vision. This activity will help a school set goals for the future.

Gap Analysis and Objectives Activity        ACTGap.pdf      Acrobat Reader

The purpose of this activity is to look closely at differences between current results and where the school wants to be in the future. It is this gap that gets translated into objectives that guide the development of the action plan.

Root Cause Analysis Activity        ACTRoot.pdf      Acrobat Reader

Root causes are the real causes of our educational problems. We need to find out what they are so we can eliminate the true cause and not just address the symptom. This activity asks staff teams to review and analyze data, and ask probing questions to uncover the root cause(s).

Cause and Effect Analysis Activity        ACTCause.pdf      Acrobat Reader

This activity will help teams determine the relationships and complexities between an effect or problem and all the possible causes.

Problem-Solving Cycle Activity        ACTCycle.pdf      Acrobat Reader

The purpose of the *Problem-Solving Cycle Activity* is to get all staff involved in thinking through a problem before jumping to solutions. This activity can also result in a comprehensive data analysis design.

Study Questions Related to the Gaps and
the Root Causes of the Gaps        Ch7Qs.pdf      Acrobat Reader

These study questions will help you better understand the information provided in Chapter 7. This file can be printed for use with staffs as you analyze their data to determine the gaps and the root causes of the gaps.

What I Saw in Example One        Ch7Saw.pdf      Acrobat Reader

*What I Saw in Example One* is a file, organized by the demographic study questions, that summarizes what I saw in the demographic data provided by Little River Elementary School.

Gap Analyses Data Table Templates        ElemGaps.doc      Microsoft Word

All of the *Microsoft Word* files that were used to create the gap analyses data tables in the Little River example in Chapter 7 appear on the CD in this section. Use these templates by putting your data in the data table and changing the title/labels to reflect your data.

## No Child Left Behind (NCLB) Templates

Table templates for analyzing student learning data for NCLB are provided on the CD .

| | | |
|---|---|---|
| NCLB Language Scores Template | LangTbl.doc | Microsoft Word |

This *Microsoft Word* file is a table template to use in capturing your *No Child Left Behind* (NCLB) Language scores analysis.

| | | |
|---|---|---|
| NCLB Reading Scores Template | ReadTbl.doc | Microsoft Word |

This *Microsoft Word* file is a table template to use in capturing your *No Child Left Behind* (NCLB) Reading scores analysis.

| | | |
|---|---|---|
| NCLB Math Scores Template | MathTbl.doc | Microsoft Word |

This *Microsoft Word* file is a table template to use in capturing your *No Child Left Behind* (NCLB) Math scores analysis.

| | | |
|---|---|---|
| NCLB Student Achievement Reading Results Template | ProfLaEl.doc | Microsoft Word |

This *Microsoft Word* file is a table template to use in summarizing your *No Child Left Behind* (NCLB) disaggregated student achievement Reading proficiency results.

| | | |
|---|---|---|
| NCLB Student Achievement Math Results Template | ProfMaEl.doc | Microsoft Word |

This *Microsoft Word* file is a table template to use in summarizing your *No Child Left Behind* (NCLB) disaggregated student achievement Math proficiency results.

## Group Process Tools and Activities

The files include read-only documents, examples, templates, tools, activities, and strategy recommendations. Many of the group process tools and activities can be used throughout the analysis of data.

| | | |
|---|---|---|
| Affinity Diagram Activity | ACTAfnty.pdf | Acrobat Reader |

The affinity diagram encourages honest reflection on the real underlying root causes of a problem and its solutions, and encourages people to agree on the factors. This activity assists teams in discussing and resolving problems, using a nonjudgmental process.

| | | |
|---|---|---|
| Fishbowl Activity | ACTFish.pdf | Acrobat Reader |

The *Fishbowl Activity* can be used for dynamic group involvement. The most common configuration is an inner ring, which is the discussion group, surrounded by an outer ring, which is the observation group. Just as people observe the fish in the fishbowl, the outer ring observes the inner ring.

| | | |
|---|---|---|
| Forcefield Analysis Activity | ACTForce.pdf | Acrobat Reader |

The *Forcefield Analysis Activity* helps staffs think about the ideal state for the school and the driving and restraining forces regarding that ideal state.

| | | |
|---|---|---|
| Placemat Activity | ACTPlace.pdf | Acrobat Reader |

The *Placemat Activity* was developed to invite participants to share their knowledge about the school portfolio, data, a standard, an instructional strategy, a concept, etc.

| | | |
|---|---|---|
| T-Chart Activity | ACTTChrt.pdf | Acrobat Reader |

A *T-Chart* is a simple tool to organize material into two columns. Use a T-Chart to compare and contrast information or to show relationships. Use it to help people see the opposite dimension of an issue.

| | | |
|---|---|---|
| "X" Marks the Spot Activity | ACTXSpot.pdf | Acrobat Reader |

This activity helps staff understand levels of expertise or degrees of passion about a topic.

| | | |
|---|---|---|
| Quadrant Diagram Activity | ACTQuadr.pdf | Acrobat Reader |

A quadrant diagram is a method to determine which solution best meets two goals at once, such as low cost and high benefit.

## ▼ ANALYZING THE DATA: *HOW CAN WE GET TO WHERE WE WANT TO BE?*

The files in this section support Chapter 8 in the book, helping staffs answer the question, *How can we get to where we want to be?* through comprehensive planning to implement the vision and eliminate the gaps, using powerful professional development, leadership, partnership development, and continuous improvement and evaluation.

| Little River School Plan for Improvement | SchlPlan.pdf | Acrobat Reader |
|---|---|---|

This read-only graphic is the first draft of the Little River Elementary School Plan and is shown as Figure 8.1 in Chapter 8.

| Planning Template | APForm.doc | Microsoft Word |
|---|---|---|

A quality action plan to implement the vision consists of goals, objectives, strategies/actions, persons responsible, resources needed, due dates, and timelines. A template with these components is provided in *Microsoft Word,* ready to be completed.

| Little River Leadership Structure | LeadStruc.pdf | Acrobat Reader |
|---|---|---|

This read-only graphic is the Little River Leadership Structure, created from the overall action plan, and is shown as Figure 8.2 in Chapter 8.

| Little River Professional Development Calendar | PrDevCal.pdf | Acrobat Reader |
|---|---|---|

This read-only graphic is the uncut 2003-04 Fall/Spring Little River Professional Development Calendar.

| Little River Professional Development Calendar Template | PrDevCal.doc | Microsoft Word |
|---|---|---|

This *Microsoft Word* document is a template for creating your school Professional Development Calendar.

| Little River Partnership Plan | PartPlan.pdf | Acrobat Reader |
|---|---|---|

This read-only graphic is the Little River Partnership Plan, created from the overall action plan, and is shown on pages 166-167 in Chapter 8.

| Establishing a Partnership Plan | EstPPlan.pdf | Acrobat Reader |
|---|---|---|

This read-only file describes the steps in creating a partnership plan that will become a part of the continuous school improvement plan.

| Little River Evaluation Plan | EvalPlan.pdf | Acrobat Reader |
|---|---|---|

This read-only graphic, the Little River Evaluation Plan, condenses the measurement column of the action plan into a comprehensive evaluation plan, and is shown as Figure 8.4 in Chapter 8.

| Powerful Professional Development Designs | Designs.pdf | Acrobat Reader |
|---|---|---|

This read-only file describes numerous ways to embed professional development into the learning community.

### *Powerful Professional Development Designs*

Powerful Professional Development Designs are those that are embedded into the daily operations of a staff. They are ongoing and lead to improvement of instruction and increases in student learning.

| Action Research Activity | ACTRsrch.pdf | Acrobat Reader |
|---|---|---|

Teachers and/or administrators raise questions about the best way to improve teaching and learning, systematically study the literature to answer the questions, implement the best approach, and analyze the results.

| Cadres or Action Teams Activity | ACTCdres.pdf | Acrobat Reader |
|---|---|---|

Organizing cadres or teams allows for the delegation of responsibilities so teams of educators can study new approaches, plan for the implementation of new strategies or programs, and get work done without every staff member's involvement.

| Case Studies Activity | ACTCases.pdf | Acrobat Reader |
|---|---|---|

Staff members review case studies of student work, and/or of another teacher's example lessons, which can lead to quality discussions and improved practices.

| Coaching Activity | ACTCoach.pdf | Acrobat Reader |

Teachers form teams of two or three to observe each other, plan together, and to talk and encourage each other in meaningful ways, while reflecting on continuously improving instructional practices.

| Examining Student Data: *Teacher Analysis* | | |
| *of Test Scores Table One* | Table1.doc | Microsoft Word |

Examining student data consists of conversations around individual student data results and the processes that created the results. This approach can be a significant form of professional development when skilled team members facilitate the dialogue.

| Examining Student Work Activity | ACTSWork.pdf | Acrobat Reader |

Examining student work as professional development ensures that what students learn is aligned to the learning standards. It also shows teachers the impact of their actions.

| Example Lessons: *Birds of a Feather Unit Example* | UnitEx.pdf | Acrobat Reader |

Some teachers need to see what a lesson that implements all aspects of the school vision would look like. Providing examples for all teachers to see can reward the teacher who is doing a good job of implementing the vision and provide a template for other teachers. It is very effective to store summary examples in a binder for everyone to peruse at any time.

| Example Lessons: *Unit Template* | UnitTmpl.doc | Microsoft Word |

This template provides the outline for creating instructional units that implement the vision.

| Immersion Activity | ACTImrsn.pdf | Acrobat Reader |

Immersion is a method for getting teachers engaged in different content through hands-on experiences as a learner.

| Journaling Activity | ACTJourn.pdf | Acrobat Reader |

Journal writing helps teachers construct meaning for, and reflect on, what they are teaching and learning.

| Listening to Students Activity | ACTListn.pdf | Acrobat Reader |

Students' perceptions of the learning environment are very important for continuous improvement. Focus groups, interviews, and questionnaires can be used to discover what students are perceiving.

| Needs Assessment: *Professional Development Needs* | | |
| *Related to Technology Example* | TechnEx.pdf | Acrobat Reader |

Needs assessments help staff understand the professional development needs of staff. At the same time, if done well, a tool can lead to quality staff conversations and sharing of knowledge.

| Needs Assessment: *Professional Development Needs* | | |
| *Related to Technology Template* | TechTmpl.doc | Microsoft Word |

This template provides the outline for doing your own professional development needs assessment.

| Networks Activity | ACTNtwrk.pdf | Acrobat Reader |

Purposeful grouping of individuals/schools to further a cause or commitment.

| Partnerships: *Creating Partnerships Activity* | ACTParts.pdf | Acrobat Reader |

Teachers partnering with businesses in the community, scientists, and/or university professors can result in real world applications for student learning and deeper understandings of content for the teacher.

| Process Mapping: *Charting School Processes Activity* | ACTProcs.pdf | Acrobat Reader |

School processes are instruction, curriculum, and assessment strategies used to ensure the learning of all students. Mapping or flowcharting school processes can help staff objectively look at how students are being taught.

| Reflection Log Activity | ACTLog.pdf | Acrobat Reader |

Reflective logs are recordings of key events in the educators' work days to reflect on improvement and/or to share learnings with colleagues.

| Scheduling Activity | ACTSchdl.pdf | Acrobat Reader |

A real test for whether or not a vision is realistic is to have teachers develop a day's schedule. This would tell them immediately if it is doable, or what needs to change in the vision and plan to make it doable.

| School Meetings: *Running Efficient Meetings* | Meetings.pdf | Acrobat Reader |

Staff, department, grade level, and cross-grade level meetings can promote learning through study or sharing best practice, while focusing on the implementation of the vision.

| Self-Assessment: *Teacher Assessment Tool Related to the Central City School Vision* | AssessEx.pdf | Acrobat Reader |

Staff self-assessments on tools to measure progress toward the vision, such as the *Continuous Improvement Continuums,* will help them see where their school is as a system and what needs to improve for better results.

| Self-Assessment: *Teacher Assessment Tool Related to Our School Vision* | AssessEx.doc | Microsoft Word |

This template file for staff self-assessments on tools to measure progress toward the vision, such as the *Continuous Improvement Continuums,* will help them see where their school is as a system and what needs to improve for better results.

| Self-Assessment: *Our School Shared Vision Implementation Rubric Example* | StRubric.pdf | Acrobat Reader |

Staff self-assessments on tools to measure progress toward the vision, such as the *Continuous Improvement Continuums,* will help them see where their school is as a system and what needs to improve for better results.

| Self-Assessment: *Our School Shared Vision Implementation Rubric Template* | StRubric.doc | Microsoft Word |

This template file for staff self-assessments on tools to measure progress toward the vision, such as the *Continuous Improvement Continuums,* will help them see where their school is as a system and what needs to improve for better results.

| Self-Assessment: *Staff-Developed Rubric Activity* | ACTRubric.pdf | Acrobat Reader |

This activity for staff self-assessments on tools to measure progress toward the vision, such as the *Continuous Improvement Continuums,* will help them see where their school is as a system and what needs to improve for better results.

| Shadowing Students Activity | ACTShadw.pdf | Acrobat Reader |

Purposefully following students and systematically recording the students' instructional experiences is a wonderful job-embedded approach to understanding what students are experiencing in school.

| Storyboarding Activity | ACTStory.pdf | Acrobat Reader |

Storyboarding is an activity that will allow participants to share previous knowledge, while reflecting on the topic. It is a structure for facilitating conversations.

| Study Groups Activity | ACTStudy.pdf | Acrobat Reader |

Groups of educators meet to learn new strategies and programs, to review new publications, or to review student work together.

| Teacher Portfolio Activity | ACTTcher.pdf | Acrobat Reader |

Teacher portfolios can be built to tell the story of implementing the vision in the classroom, and its impact on student learning. Portfolios are excellent for reflection, understanding, and showing progress. Portfolios can be used for many things including self-assessment, employment, supervision to replace traditional teacher evaluation, and peer collaboration.

| Train the Trainers Activity | ACTTrain.pdf | Acrobat Reader |

Train the trainers is an approach to saving time and money. Individuals are trained and return to the school or school district to train others.

| Tuning Protocols Activity | ACTTune.pdf | Acrobat Reader |

A tuning protocol is a formal process for reviewing, honoring, and fine-tuning colleagues' work through presentation and reflection.

▼ ANALYZING THE DATA: *EXAMPLE TWO*

The files in this section support Chapter 9 in the book and can help you create a school data profile with the graphing templates and profile template of example two: *Blue Bird Elementary School.*

| Study Questions Related to Example Two | Ch9Qs.pdf | Acrobat Reader |

These study questions will help you better understand the information provided in Chapter 9. This file can be printed for use with staffs.

| What I Saw in Example Two | Ch9Saw.pdf | Acrobat Reader |

*What I Saw in Example Two* is a file, organized by the demographic study questions, that summarizes what I saw in the demographic data provided by Blue Bird Elementary School.

| Demographic Graphing Templates for Blue Bird School | DemogCh9.xls | Microsoft Excel |

All of the *Microsoft Excel* files that were used to create the demographic graphs in the Blue Bird example in Chapter 9 appear on the CD. Use these templates by putting your data in the data table and changing the title/labels to reflect your data. Your graphs will build automatically. This file also explains how to use the templates.

| Demographic Data Table Templates for Blue Bird School | DemogCh9.doc | Microsoft Word |

All of the *Microsoft Word* files that were used to create the demographic data tables in the Blue Bird example in Chapter 9 appear on the CD in this section. Use these templates by putting your data in the data table and changing the title/labels to reflect your data.

| School Data Profile Template | BBProfil.doc | Microsoft Word |

This *Microsoft Word* file provides a template for creating your own school data profile like the one for example two: *Blue Bird Elementary School.*

*Education for the Future Perception Questionnaires Used by Example Two, Blue Bird School*

| Student Questionnaire | BBStudnt.pdf | Acrobat Reader |

This read-only file is the *Education for the Future* student perception questionnaire used in example two.

| Staff Questionnaire | BBStaff.pdf | Acrobat Reader |

This read-only file is the *Education for the Future* staff perception questionnaire used in example two.

| Parent Questionnaire | BBParent.pdf | Acrobat Reader |

This read-only file is the *Education for the Future* parent perception questionnaire used in example two.

*Full Narratives of Questionnaire Results for Example Two, Blue Bird School*

| Blue Bird Student Questionnaire Results | StuNarr2.pdf | Acrobat Reader |

This read-only file is the full narrative of student questionnaire results used in example two.

| Blue Bird Staff Questionnaire Results | StfNarr2.pdf | Acrobat Reader |

This read-only file is the full narrative of staff questionnaire results used in example two.

| Blue Bird Parent Questionnaire Results | ParNarr2.pdf | Acrobat Reader |

This read-only file is the full narrative of parent questionnaire results used in example two.

| Blue Bird Elementary School Baseline CIC Results | BBBase.pdf | Acrobat Reader |

This read-only file is the summary of Little River's baseline assessment on the *School Portfolio Continuous Improvement Continuums*.

| Continuous Improvement Continuums Graphic | CICs.pdf | Acrobat Reader |

This read-only file contains the seven *School Portfolio Continuous Improvement Continuums*. These can be printed as is or enlarged for posting individual staff opinions during staff assessments.

## Continuous Improvement Continuum Tools

These files are tools for assessing on the CICs and for writing the CIC report.

| Continuous Improvement Continuums Self-Assessment Activity | ACTCIC.pdf | Acrobat Reader |

Assessing on the *Continuous Improvement Continuums* will help staffs see where their systems are right now with respect to continuous improvement and ultimately will show they are making progress over time. The discussion has major implications for the *Continuous School Improvement (CSI) Plan*.

| Coming to Consensus | Consenss.pdf | Acrobat Reader |

This read-only file provides strategies for coming to consensus.

| Continuous Improvement Continuums Report Example | ExReprt1.pdf | Acrobat Reader |

This read-only file shows a real school's assessment on the *School Portfolio Continuous Improvement Continuums,* as an example.

| Continuous Improvement Continuums Report Example for Follow-Up Years | ExReprt2.pdf | Acrobat Reader |

This read only file shows a real school's assessment on the *School Portfolio Continuous Improvement Continuums* over time, as an example.

| Continuous Improvement Continuums Baseline Report Template | ReptTemp.doc | Microsoft Word |

This *Microsoft Word* file provides a template for writing your school's report of its assessment on the *School Portfolio Continuous Improvement Continuums*.

| Continuous Improvement Continuums Graphing Templates | CICGraph.xls | Microsoft Excel |

This *Microsoft Excel* file is a template for graphing your assessments on the seven *School Portfolio Continuous Improvement Continuums*.

| Student Achievement Graphing Templates for Blue Bird School | SA1Ch9.xls and SA2Ch9.xls | Microsoft Excel |

All of the *Microsoft Excel* files that were used to create the student achievement graphs in the Blue Bird example in Chapter 9 appear on the CD. Use these templates by putting your data in the data table and changing the title/labels to reflect your data. Your graphs will build automatically. This file also explains how to use the templates.

| Student Achievement Data Table Templates for Blue Bird School | SACh9.doc | Microsoft Word |

All of the *Microsoft Word* files that were used to create the student achievement data tables in the Blue Bird example in Chapter 9 appear on the CD in this section. Use these templates by putting your data in the data table and changing the title/labels to reflect your data.

| Blue Bird School Gap Analysis Graphing Templates | BBGaps.xls | Microsoft Excel |

All of the *Microsoft Excel* files that were used to create the gap analyses graphs in the Blue Bird example in Chapter 9 appear on the CD. Use these templates by putting your data in the data table and changing the title/labels to reflect your data. Your graphs will build automatically. This file also explains how to use the templates.

| Blue Bird School Gap Analysis Data Table Templates | BBGaps.doc | Microsoft Word |

All of the *Microsoft Word* files that were used to create the gap analyses data tables in the Blue Bird example in Chapter 9 appear on the CD in this section. Use these templates by putting your data in the data table and changing the title/labels to reflect your data.

Root Causes Activity                                         ACTRoot.pdf                 Acrobat Reader

Root causes are the real causes of our educational problems. We need to find out what they are so we can eliminate the true cause and not just address the symptom. This activity asks staff teams to review and analyze data, and ask probing questions to uncover the root cause(s).

Gap Analysis and Objectives Activity                         ACTGap.pdf                  Acrobat Reader

The purpose of this activity is to look closely at differences between current results and where the school wants to be in the future. It is this gap analysis that gets translated into objectives that guide the development of the action plan.

▼ ANALYZING THE DATA: *CONCLUSIONS AND RECOMMENDATIONS*

The files in this section support Chapter 10 in the book and help staffs evaluate their programs and processes.

Databases Can Help Teachers with Standards Implementation        Dbases.pdf              Acrobat Reader

This read-only article, by Victoria L. Bernhardt, describes how databases can help with standards implementation.

Evaluating a Program Activity                                ACTEval.pdf                 Acrobat Reader

The purpose of this activity is to get many people involved in creating a comprehensive evaluation design to determine the impact of a program and to know how to improve the program.

# Appendix B
## Continuous Improvement Continuums

These *Education for the Future Continuous Improvement Continuums,* adapted from the *Malcolm Baldrige Award Program for Quality Business Management,* provide an authentic means for measuring schoolwide improvement and growth. Schools use these Continuums as a vehicle for ongoing self-assessment. They use the results of the assessment to acknowledge their accomplishments, to set goals for improvement, and to keep school districts and partners apprised of the progress they have made in their school improvement efforts.

## Understanding the Continuums

These Continuums, extending from *one* to *five* horizontally, represent a continuum of expectations related to school improvement with respect to an *Approach* to the Continuum, *Implementation* of the approach, and the *Outcome* that results from the implementation. A *one* rating, located at the left of each Continuum, represents a school that has not yet begun to improve. *Five,* located at the right of each Continuum, represents a school that is one step removed from "world class quality." The elements between *one* and *five* describe how that Continuum is hypothesized to evolve in a continuously improving school. Each Continuum moves from a reactive mode to a proactive mode—from fire fighting to prevention. The *five* in *outcome* in each Continuum is the target.

Vertically, the *Approach, Implementation,* and *Outcome* statements, for any number one through five, are hypotheses. In other words, the implementation statement describes how the approach might look when implemented, and the outcome is the "pay-off" for implementing the approach. If the hypotheses are accurate, the outcome will not be realized until the approach is actually implemented.

## Using the Continuums

Use the *Continuous Improvement Continuums* (CICs) to understand where your school is with respect to continuous improvement. The results will hopefully provide that sense of urgency needed to spark enthusiasm for your school improvement efforts.

The most beneficial approach to assessing on the Continuums is to gather the entire staff together for the assessment. When assessing on the Continuums for the first time, plan for three hours to complete all seven categories.

Start the assessment by stating or creating the ground rules, setting the tone for a safe and confidential assessment, and explaining why you are doing this. Provide a brief overview of the seven sections, taking each section one at a time, and having each staff member read the related Continuum and make independent assessments of where she/he believes the school is with respect to *Approach, Implementation,* and *Outcome.* We recommend using individual 8 1/2 x 11 copies of the Continuums for individual assessments. Then, have each staff member note where she/he believes the school is with a colorful sticker or marker on a large poster of each Continuum. The markers allow all staff to see how much they are in agreement with one another. If only one color is used for the first assessment, another color can be used for the next assessment, and so forth, to help gauge growth over time, or you can plan to use two different charts for gauging progress over time such as in the photos below.

When all dots or marks have been placed on the enlarged Continuum, look at the agreement or disagreement of the ratings. Starting with *Approach,* have staff discuss why they believe the school is where they rated it. Keep discussing until the larger group comes to consensus on one number that reflects where the school is right now. You might need to make a quick check on where staff is with respect to coming to consensus, using a thumbs up, thumbs down "vote." Keep discussing the facts until consensus is reached. Do not average the results—it does not produce a sense of urgency for improvement. We cannot emphasize this enough! Keep discussing until agreement is reached by everyone on a number that represents where "we" are right now. When that consensus is reached, record the number and move to *Implementation* and then *Outcome.* Determine *Next Steps.* Proceed in the same way through the next six categories.

During the assessments, make sure someone records the discussions of the Continuum assessments. Schools might want to exchange facilitators with a neighboring school or district to have someone external to the school facilitate the assessments. This will enable everyone in the school to participate and provide an unbiased and competent person to lead the consensus-building piece. Assessing over time will help staff see that they are making progress. The decision of how often to assess on the *Continuous Improvement Continuums* is certainly up to the school. We recommend twice a year—about mid-fall and mid-spring—when there is time (or has been time) to implement next steps.

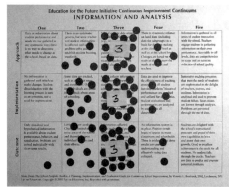

**Fall Assessment**

Using these Continuums will enable you and your school to stay motivated, to shape and maintain your shared vision, and will assist with the continuous improvement of all elements of your school. Take pictures of the resulting charts. Even if your consensus number does not increase, the dots will most probably come together over time showing shifts in whole staff thinking.

Remember that where your school is at any time is just where it is. The important thing is what you do with this information. Continuous improvement is a never-ending process which, when used effectively, will ultimately lead your school toward providing a quality program for all children.

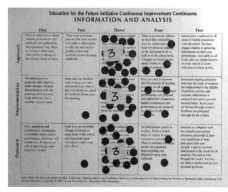

**Spring Assessment**

# School Continuous Improvement Continuums
## INFORMATION AND ANALYSIS

| | One | Two | Three | Four | Five |
|---|---|---|---|---|---|
| **Approach** | Data or information about student performance and needs are not gathered in any systematic way; there is no way to determine what needs to change at the school, based on data. | There is no systematic process, but some teacher and student information is collected and used to problem solve and establish student learning standards. | School collects data related to student performance (e.g., attendance, achievement) and conducts surveys on student, teacher, and parent needs. The information is used to drive the strategic quality plan for school change. | There is systematic reliance on hard data (including data for subgroups) as a basis for decision making at the classroom level as well as at the school level. Changes are based on the study of data to meet the needs of students and teachers. | Information is gathered in all areas of student interaction with the school. Teachers engage students in gathering information on their own performance. Accessible to all levels, data are comprehensive in scope and an accurate reflection of school quality. |
| **Implementation** | No information is gathered with which to make changes. Student dissatisfaction with the learning process is seen as an irritation, not a need for improvement. | Some data are tracked, such as drop-out rates and enrollment. Only a few individuals are asked for feedback about areas of schooling. | School collects information on current and former students (e.g, student achievement and perceptions), analyzes and uses it in conjunction with future trends for planning. Identified areas for improvement are tracked over time. | Data are used to improve the effectiveness of teaching strategies on all student learning. Students' historical performances are graphed and utilized for diagnostics. Student evaluations and performances are analyzed by teachers in all classrooms. | Innovative teaching processes that meet the needs of students are implemented to the delight of teachers, parents, and students. Information is analyzed and used to prevent student failure. Root causes are known through analyses. Problems are prevented through the use of data. |
| **Outcome** | Only anecdotal and hypothetical information is available about student performance, behavior, and satisfaction. Problems are solved individually with short-term results. | Little data are available. Change is limited to some areas of the school and dependent upon individual teachers and their efforts. | Information collected about student and parent needs, assessment, and instructional practices is shared with the school staff and used to plan for change. Information helps staff understand pressing issues, analyze information for "root causes," and track results for improvement. | An information system is in place. Positive trends begin to appear in many classrooms and schoolwide. There is evidence that these results are caused by understanding and effectively using data collected. | Students are delighted with the school's instructional processes and proud of their own capabilities to learn and assess their own growth. Good to excellent achievement is the result for all students. No student falls through the cracks. Teachers use data to predict and prevent potential problems. |

## School Continuous Improvement Continuums
# STUDENT ACHIEVEMENT

| | One | Two | Three | Four | Five |
|---|---|---|---|---|---|
| **Approach** | Instructional and organizational processes critical to student success are not identified. Little distinction of student learning differences is made. Some teachers believe that not all students can achieve. | Some data are collected on student background and performance trends. Learning gaps are noted to direct improvement of instruction. It is known that student learning standards must be identified. | Student learning standards are identified, and a continuum of learning is created throughout the school. Student performance data are collected and compared to the standards in order to analyze how to improve learning for all students. | Data on student achievement are used throughout the school to pursue the improvement of student learning. Teachers collaborate to implement appropriate instruction and assessment strategies for meeting student learning standards articulated across grade levels. All teachers believe that all students can learn. | School makes an effort to exceed student achievement expectations. Innovative instructional changes are made to anticipate learning needs and improve student achievement. Teachers are able to predict characteristics impacting student achievement and to know how to perform from a small set of internal quality measures. |
| **Implementation** | All students are taught the same way. There is no communication with students about their academic needs or learning styles. There are no analyses of how to improve instruction. | Some effort is made to track and analyze student achievement trends on a school-wide basis. Teachers begin to understand the needs and learning gaps of students. | Teachers study effective instruction and assessment strategies to implement standards and to increase their students' learning. Student feedback and analysis of achievement data are used in conjunction with implementation support strategies. | There is a systematic focus on implementing student learning standards and on the improvement of student learning schoolwide. Effective instruction and assessment strategies are implemented in each classroom. Teachers support one another with peer coaching and/or action research focused on implementing strategies that lead to increased achievement and the attainment of the shared vision. | All teachers correlate critical instructional and assessment strategies with objective indicators of quality student achievement. A comparative analysis of actual individual student performance to student learning standards is utilized to adjust teaching strategies to ensure a progression of learning for all students. |
| **Outcome** | There is wide variation in student attitudes and achievement with undesirable results. There is high dissatisfaction among students with learning. Student background is used as an excuse for low student achievement. | There is some evidence that student achievement trends are available to teachers and are being used. There is much effort, but minimal observable results in improving student achievement. | There is an increase in communication between students and teachers regarding student learning. Teachers learn about effective instructional strategies that will implement the shared vision, including student learning standards, and meet the needs of their students. They make some gains. | Increased student achievement is evident schoolwide. Student morale, attendance, and behavior are good. Teachers converse often with each other about preventing student failure. Areas for further attention are clear. | Students and teachers conduct self-assessments to continuously improve performance. Improvements in student achievement are evident and clearly caused by teachers' and students' understandings of individual student learning standards, linked to appropriate and effective instructional and assessment strategies. A continuum of learning results. No students fall through the cracks. |

# School Continuous Improvement Continuums
## QUALITY PLANNING

| | One | Two | Three | Four | Five |
|---|---|---|---|---|---|
| **Approach** | No quality plan or process exists. Data are neither used nor considered important in planning. | The staff realize the importance of a mission, vision, and one comprehensive action plan. Teams develop goals and timelines, and dollars are allocated to begin the process. | A comprehensive school plan to achieve the vision is developed. Plan includes evaluation and continuous improvement. | One focused and integrated schoolwide plan for implementing a continuous improvement process is put into action. All school efforts are focused on the implementation of this plan that represents the achievement of the vision. | A plan for the continuous improvement of the school, with a focus on students, is put into place. There is excellent articulation and integration of all elements in the school due to quality planning. Leadership team ensures all elements are implemented by all appropriate parties. |
| **Implementation** | There is no knowledge of or direction for quality planning. Budget is allocated on an as-needed basis. Many plans exist. | School community begins continuous improvement planning efforts by laying out major steps to a shared vision, by identifying values and beliefs, the purpose of the school, a mission, vision, and student learning standards. | Implementation goals, responsibilities, due dates, and timelines are spelled out. Support structures for implementing the plan are set in place. | The quality management plan is implemented through effective procedures in all areas of the school. Everyone commits to implementing the plan aligned to the vision, mission, and values and beliefs. All share responsibility for accomplishing school goals. | Schoolwide goals, mission, vision, and student learning standards are shared and articulated throughout the school and with feeder schools. The attainment of identified student learning standards is linked to planning and implementation of effective instruction that meets students' needs. Leaders at all levels are developing expertise because planning is the norm. |
| **Outcome** | There is no evidence of comprehensive planning. Staff work is carried out in isolation. A continuum of learning for students is absent. | The school community understands the benefits of working together to implement a comprehensive continuous improvement plan. | There is evidence that the school plan is being implemented in some areas of the school. Improvements are neither systematic nor integrated schoolwide. | A schoolwide plan is known to all. Results from working toward the quality improvement goals are evident throughout the school. Planning is ongoing and inclusive of all stakeholders. | Evidence of effective teaching and learning results in significant improvement of student achievement attributed to quality planning at all levels of the school organization. Teachers and administrators understand and share the school mission and vision. Quality planning is seamless and all demonstrate evidence of accountability. |

Copyright © 1991–2004 Education for the Future Initiative, Chico, CA.

## School Continuous Improvement Continuums
# PROFESSIONAL DEVELOPMENT

| | One | Two | Three | Four | Five |
|---|---|---|---|---|---|
| **Approach** | There is no professional development. Teachers, principals, and staff are seen as interchangeable parts that can be replaced. Professional development is external and usually equated to attending a conference alone. Hierarchy determines "haves" and "have-nots." | The "cafeteria" approach to professional development is used, whereby individual teachers choose what they want to take, without regard to an overall school plan. | The shared vision, school plan, and student needs are used to target focused professional development for all employees. Staff is inserviced on relevant instructional and leadership strategies. | Professional development and data-gathering methods are used by all teachers and are directed toward the goals of the shared vision and the continuous improvement of the school. Teachers have ongoing conversations about student achievement data. Other staff members receive training in their content areas. Systems thinking is considered in all decisions. | Leadership and staff continuously improve all aspects of the learning organization through an innovative, data-driven, and comprehensive continuous improvement process that prevents student failures. Effective job-embedded professional development is ongoing for implementing the vision for student success. Traditional teacher evaluations are replaced by collegial coaching and action research focused on student learning standards. Policies set professional development as a priority budget line-item. Professional development is planned, aligned, and lead to the achievement of student learning standards. |
| **Implementation** | Teacher, principal, and staff performance is controlled and inspected. Performance evaluations are used to detect mistakes. | Teacher professional development is sporadic and unfocused, lacking an approach for implementing new procedures and processes. Some leadership training begins to take place. | Teachers are involved in year-round quality professional development. The school community is trained in shared decision making, team building concepts, effective communication strategies, and data analysis at the classroom level. | Teachers, in teams, continuously set and implement student achievement goals. Leadership considers these goals and provides necessary support structures for collaboration. Teachers utilize effective support approaches as they implement new instruction and assessment strategies. Coaching and feedback structures are in place. Use of new knowledge and skills is evident. | Teams passionately support each other in the pursuit of quality improvement at all levels. Teachers make bold changes in instruction and assessment strategies focused on student learning standards and student learning styles. A teacher as action researcher model is implemented. Staffwide conversations focus on systemic reflection and improvement. Teachers are strong leaders. |
| **Outcome** | No professional growth and no staff or student performance improvement. There exists a high turnover rate of employees, especially administrators. Attitudes and approaches filter down to students. | The effectiveness of professional development is not known or analyzed. Teachers feel helpless about making schoolwide changes. | Teachers, working in teams, feel supported and begin to feel they can make changes. Evidence shows that shared decision making works. | A collegial school is evident. Effective classroom strategies are practiced, articulated schoolwide, are reflective of professional development aimed at ensuring student achievement, and the implementation of the shared vision, that includes student learning standards. | True systemic change and improved student achievement result because teachers are knowledgeable of and implement effective, differentiated teaching strategies for individual student learning gains. Teachers' repertoire of skills are enhanced, and students are achieving. Professional development is driving learning at all levels. |

# School Continuous Improvement Continuums
# LEADERSHIP

| | One | Two | Three | Four | Five |
|---|---|---|---|---|---|
| **Approach** | Principal as decision maker. Decisions are reactive to state, district, and federal mandates. There is no knowledge of continuous improvement. | A shared decision-making structure is put into place and discussions begin on how to achieve a school vision. Most decisions are focused on solving problems and are reactive. | Leadership team is committed to continuous improvement. Leadership seeks inclusion of all school sectors and supports study teams by making time provisions for their work. | Leadership team represents a true shared decision-making structure. Study teams are reconstructed for the implementation of a comprehensive continuous improvement plan. | A strong continuous improvement structure is set into place that allows for input from all sectors of the school, district, and community, ensuring strong communication, flexibility, and refinement of approach and beliefs. The school vision is student focused, based on data, and appropriate for school/community values, and meeting student needs. |
| **Implementation** | Principal makes all decisions, with little or no input from teachers, the community, or students. Leadership inspects for mistakes. | School values and beliefs are identified; the purpose of school is defined; a school mission and student learning standards are developed with representative input. A structure for studying approaches to achieving student learning standards is established. | Leadership team is active on study teams and integrates recommendations from the teams' research and analyses to form a comprehensive plan for continuous improvement within the context of the school mission. Everyone is kept informed. | Decisions about budget and implementation of the vision are made within teams, by the principal, by the leadership team, and by the full staff as appropriate. All decisions are communicated to the leadership team and to the full staff. | The vision is implemented and articulated across all grade levels and into feeder schools. Quality standards are reinforced throughout the school. All members of the school community understand and apply the quality standards. Leadership team has systematic interactions and involvement with district administrators, teachers, parents, community, and students about the school's direction. Necessary resources are available to implement and measure staff learning related to student learning standards. |
| **Outcome** | Decisions lack focus and consistency. There is no evidence of staff commitment to a shared vision. Students and parents do not feel they are being heard. Decision-making process is clear and known. | The mission provides a focus for all school improvement and guides the action to the vision. The school community is committed to continuous improvement. Quality leadership techniques are used sporadically. | Leadership team is seen as committed to planning and quality improvement. Critical areas for improvement are identified. Faculty feel included in shared decision making. | There is evidence that the leadership team listens to all levels of the organization. Implementation of the continuous improvement plan is linked to student learning standards and the guiding principles of the school. Leadership capacities for implementing the vision among teachers are evident. | Site-based management and shared decision making truly exists. Teachers understand and display an intimate knowledge of how the school operates. Teachers support and communicate with each other in the implementation of quality strategies. Teachers implement the vision in their classrooms and can determine how their new approach meets student needs and leads to the attainment of student learning standards. Leaders are standards-driven at all levels. |

# School Continuous Improvement Continuums
## PARTNERSHIP DEVELOPMENT

| | One | Two | Three | Four | Five |
|---|---|---|---|---|---|
| **Approach** | There is no system for input from parents, business, or community. Status quo is desired for managing the school. | Partnerships are sought, but mostly for money and things. | School has knowledge of why partnerships are important and seeks to include businesses and parents in a strategic fashion related to student learning standards for increased student achievement. | School seeks effective win-win business and community partnerships and parent involvement to implement the vision. Desired outcomes are clearly identified. A solid plan for partnership development exists. | Community, parent, and business partnerships become integrated across all student groupings. The benefits of outside involvement are known by all. Parent and business involvement in student learning is refined. Student learning *regularly* takes place beyond the school walls. |
| **Implementation** | Barriers are erected to close out involvement of outsiders. Outsiders are managed for least impact on status quo. | A team is assigned to get partners and to receive input from parents, the community, and business in the school. | Involvement of business, community, and parents begins to take place in some classrooms and after school hours related to the vision. Partners begin to realize how they can support each other in achieving school goals. School staff understand what partners need from the partnership. | There is a systematic utilization of parents, community, and businesses schoolwide. Areas in which the active use of these partnerships benefit student learning are clear. | Partnership development is articulated across all student groupings. Parents, community, business, and educators work together in an innovative fashion to increase student learning and to prepare students for the 21st Century. Partnerships are evaluated for continuous improvement. |
| **Outcome** | There is little or no involvement of parents, business, or community at-large. School is a closed, isolated system. | Much effort is given to establishing partner-ships. Some spotty trends emerge, such as receiving donated equipment. | Some substantial gains are achieved in implementing partnerships. Some student achievement increases can be attributed to this involvement. | Gains in student satisfaction with learning and school are clearly related to partnerships. All partners benefit. | Previously non-achieving students enjoy learning with excellent achievement. Community, business, and home become common places for student learning, while school becomes a place where parents come for further education. Partnerships enhance what the school does for students. |

# School Continuous Improvement Continuums

## CONTINUOUS IMPROVEMENT AND EVALUATION

| | One | Two | Three | Four | Five |
|---|---|---|---|---|---|
| **Approach** | Neither goals nor strategies exist for the evaluation and continuous improvement of the school organization or for elements of the school organization. | The approach to continuous improvement and evaluation is problem solving. If there are no problems, or if solutions can be made quickly, there is no need for improvement or analyses. Changes in parts of the system are not coordinated with all other parts. | Some elements of the school organization are evaluated for effectiveness. Some elements are improved on the basis of the evaluation findings. | All elements of the school's operations are evaluated for improvement and to ensure congruence of the elements with respect to the continuum of learning students experience. | All aspects of the school organization are rigorously evaluated and improved on a continuous basis. Students, and the maintenance of a comprehensive learning continuum for students, become the focus of all aspects of the school improvement process. |
| **Implementation** | With no overall plan for evaluation and continuous improvement, strategies are changed by individual teachers and administrators only when something sparks the need to improve. Reactive decisions and activities are a daily mode of operation. | Isolated changes are made in some areas of the school organization in response to problem incidents. Changes are not preceded by comprehensive analyses, such as an understanding of the root causes of problems. The effectiveness of the elements of the school organization, or changes made to the elements, is not known. | Elements of the school organization are improved on the basis of comprehensive analyses of root causes of problems, client perceptions, and operational effectiveness of processes. | Continuous improvement analyses of student achievement and instructional strategies are rigorously reinforced within each classroom and across learning levels to develop a comprehensive learning continuum for students and to prevent student failure. | Comprehensive continuous improvement becomes the way of doing business at the school. Teachers continuously improve the appropriateness and effectiveness of instructional strategies based on student feedback and performance. All aspects of the school organization are improved to support teachers' efforts. |
| **Outcome** | Individuals struggle with system failure. Finger pointing and blaming others for failure occurs. The effectiveness of strategies is not known. Mistakes are repeated. | Problems are solved only temporarily and few positive changes result. Additionally, unintended and undesirable consequences often appear in other parts of the system. Many aspects of the school are incongruent, keeping the school from reaching its vision. | Evidence of effective improvement strategies is observable. Positive changes are made and maintained due to comprehensive analyses and evaluation. | Teachers become astute at assessing and in predicting the impact of their instructional strategies on individual student achievement. Sustainable improvements in student achievement are evident at all grade levels, due to continuous improvement. | The school becomes a congruent and effective learning organization. Only instruction and assessment strategies that produce quality student achievement are used. A true continuum of learning results for all students and staff. The impact of improvements is increasingly measurable. |

# Glossary of Terms

The Glossary provides brief definitions of data analysis and testing terms used throughout *Using Data to Improve Student Learning in Elementary Schools*.

▼ **Achievement**

The demonstration of student performance measured against learning goals, learning objectives, or standards.

▼ **Accountability**

The act of being responsible to somebody else or to others. It also means capable of being explained.

▼ **Action**

Specific steps, tasks, or activity used to implement a strategy.

▼ **Action Plan**

The part of continuous school improvement planning that describes the tasks that must be performed, when they will be performed, who is responsible, and how much they will cost to implement.

▼ **Action Research**

Teachers and/or administrators raise questions about the best way to improve teaching and learning, systematically study the literature to answer the questions, implement the best approach(es), and analyze the results.

▼ **Affinity Diagram**

A visual picture or chart of reflective thinking. The result is that more participants are likely to deal with problems that emerge.

▼ **Aggregate**

Combining the results of all groups that make up the sample or population.

▼ **Alignment**

An arrangement of groups or forces in relation to one another. In continuous school improvement planning, we align all parts of the system to the vision. With curriculum, we align instruction and materials to student learning standards.

▼ **Analysis of Variance (ANOVA)**

ANOVA is an inferential procedure to determine if there is a significant difference among sample means.

▼ **Anticipated Achievement Scores**

An estimate of the average score for students of similar ages, grade levels, and academic aptitude. It is an estimate of what we would expect an individual student to score on an achievement test.

▼ **Assessment**

Gathering and interpretation of student performance, primarily for the purpose of enhancing learning. Also used for the improvement of a program and/or strategies.

▼ **Authentic Assessment**

Refers to a variety of ways to assess a student's demonstration of knowledge and skills. Authentic assessments may include performances, projects, exhibitions, and portfolios.

### ▼ Benchmark

A standard against which something can be measured or assessed.

### ▼ Brainstorming

The act of listing ideas without judgment. Brainstorming generates creative ideas spontaneously.

### ▼ Cadres or Action Teams

Groups or teams of educators who agree to accept responsibility to study new approaches, plan for the implementation of new strategies or programs, and get work done without every staff member's involvement.

### ▼ Case Studies

Reviewing student's work, and/or another teacher's example lessons, which can lead to quality discussions and improved practices.

### ▼ Cause and Effect

The relationship and complexities between a problem or effect and the possible causes.

### ▼ Coaching

Teachers form teams of two or three to observe each other, plan together, and talk and encourage each other in meaningful ways while reflecting on continuously improving instructional practices.

### ▼ Cognitive Abilities or Skills Index

An age-dependent, normalized standard score based on a student's performance on a cognitive skills test with a mean of 100 and standard deviation of 16. The score indicates a student's overall cognitive ability or academic aptitude relative to students of similar age, without regard to grade level.

### ▼ Cohort

A group of individuals sharing a particular statistical or demographic characteristic, such as the year they were in a specific school grade level. Following cohorts over time helps teachers understand the effects particular circumstances may have on results. Matched cohort studies follow the same individuals over time, and unmatched cohort studies follow the same group over time.

### ▼ Cohort Analysis

The reorganization of grade level data to look at the groups of students progressing through the grades together over time.

### ▼ Collaborative

Working jointly with others, especially in an intellectual endeavor.

### ▼ Comprehensive Action Plan

Defining the specific actions needed to implement the vision, setting forth when the actions will take place, designating who is responsible for accomplishing the action, how much it will cost, and where to get the funds.

### ▼ Confidence Interval

Used in inferential statistics, a range of values that a researcher can estimate, with a certain level of confidence, where the population parameter is located.

### ▼ Consensus

Decision making where a group finds a proposal acceptable enough that all members can support it; no member actively opposes it.

▼ **Continuous**

In the context of continuous school improvement, continuous means the ongoing review of the data, the implementation of the plan, and the progress being made.

▼ **Continuous Improvement**

Keeping the process of planning, implementing, evaluating, and improving alive over time.

▼ **Continuous Improvement and Evaluation**

The section of the school portfolio that assists schools to further understand where they are and what they need to do to move forward in the big picture of continuous school improvement.

▼ **Continuous Improvement Continuums (CICs)**

As developed by *Education for the Future Initiative,* CICs are seven rubrics that represent the theoretical flow of systemic school improvement. The *Continuous Improvement Continuums* take the theory and spirit of continuous school improvement, interweave educational research, and offer practical meaning to the components that must change simultaneously and systematically.

▼ **Continuous School Improvement Plan**

The process of answering the following questions: *Who are we? How do we do business? What are our strengths and areas for improvement? Why do we exist? Where do we want to be? What are the gaps? What are the root causes of the gaps? How can we get to where we want to be? How will we implement? How will we evaluate our efforts?*

▼ **Control Groups**

Control groups serve as a baseline in making comparisons with treatment groups and are necessary when general effectiveness of the treatment is unknown. During an experiment, the control group is studied the same as the experimental groups, except that it does not receive the treatment of interest.

▼ **Correlation**

A statistical analysis that helps one see the relationship of scores in one distribution to scores in another distribution. Correlation coefficients have a range of $-1.0$ to $+1.0$. A correlation of around zero indicates no relationship. Correlations of .8 and higher indicate strong relationships.

▼ **Criteria**

Characteristics or dimensions of student performance.

▼ **Criterion-referenced Tests**

Tests that judge how well a test taker does on an explicit objective, learning goal, or criteria relative to a pre-determined performance level. There is no comparison to any other test takers.

▼ **Culture**

Attitudes, values, beliefs, goals, norms of behavior, and practices that characterize a group.

▼ **Curriculum Development and Implementation**

The way content is designed and delivered. Teachers must think deeply about the content, student-learning standards, and how it must be managed and delivered, or put into practice.

▼ **Curriculum Mapping and Webbing**

Approaches that require teachers to align the curriculum and student learning standards by grade levels, and then across grade levels, to ensure a continuum of learning that makes sense f all students.

### ▼ Data Mining

Techniques for finding patterns and trends in large data sets. The process of automatically extracting valid, useful, previously unknown, and ultimately comprehensible information from large databases. Just doing common data analysis is not data mining.

### ▼ Database

A storage mechanism for data that eliminates redundancy and conflict among multiple data files. Data is entered once and is then available to all programs that need it.

### ▼ Deciles

The values of a variable that divide the frequency distribution into ten equal frequency groups. The ninth decile shows the number (or percentage) of the norming group that scored between 80 and 89 NCE, for example.

### ▼ Demographics

Statistical characteristics of a population, such as average age, number of students in a school, percentages of ethnicities, etc. Disaggregation with demographic data allows us to isolate variations among different subgroups.

### ▼ Derived Score

A score that is attained by performing some kind of mathematical operation on a raw score for comparison within a particular grade (e.g., T-scores, NCE, etc.).

### ▼ Descriptive Statistics

Direct measurement (i.e. mean, median, percent correct) of each member of a group or population. Descriptive statistics can include graphing.

### ▼ Diagnostic

Assessment/evaluation carried out prior to instruction that is designed to determine a student's attitude, skill, or knowledge in order to identify specific student needs.

### ▼ Diagnostic Tests

Usually standardized and normed, diagnostic tests are given before instruction begins to help the instructor(s) understand student learning needs. Many different score types are used with diagnostic tests.

### ▼ Different Ways of Knowing (DWOK)

A standards-based, interdisciplinary, arts-infused curriculum that promotes collaborative learning and higher–order thinking.

### ▼ Disaggregate

Separating the results of different groups that make up the sample or population.

### ▼ Educationally Significant

Gains in student achievement, school, or program results can be considered educationally significant, even though they are not statistically significant.

### ▼ Evaluation

Making judgments about the quality of overall student performance for the purpose of communicating student achievement. Evaluation also is the study of the impact of a program or process.

### ▼ Examining Student Data

Conversations around individual student data results and the processes that created the results. This approach can be a significant form of professional development when skilled team members facilitate the discussions.

### ▼ Exemplars

Models or examples of excellent work that meet stated criteria or levels of performance.

### ▼ Experimental Design

The detailed planning of an experiment, made beforehand, to insure the data collected is appropriate and obtained in a way that will lead to an objective analysis, with valid inferences. Preferably, the design will maximize the amount of information that can be gained, given the amount of effort expended.

### ▼ Formative

Assessments at regular intervals of a student's progress, with accompanying feedback in order to help the student's performance and to provide direction for improvement of a program for individual students or for a whole class.

### ▼ Frequency Distribution

Describes how often observations fall within designated categories. It can be expressed as numbers, percents, and deciles, to name just a few possibilities.

### ▼ Gain Score

The difference between two administrations of the same test. Gain scores are calculated by subtracting the previous score from the most recent score. One can have negative gains, which are actually losses.

### ▼ Gaps

The difference between where the school is now and where the school wants to be in the future. It is this gap that gets translated into goals, objectives, strategies, and actions in the action plan.

### ▼ Goals

Achievements or end results. Goal statements describe the intended outcome of the vision and are stated in terms that are broad, general, abstract, and non-measurable. Schools should have only two or three goals.

### ▼ Grade-level Analysis

Looking at the same grade level over time.

### ▼ Grade-level Equivalent

The grade and month of the school year for which a given score is the actual or estimated average. Based on a 10-month school year, scores would be noted as 3.1 for grade three, first month, 5.10 for grade five, tenth month, etc.

### ▼ Grades

Subjective scores given by teachers to students for performance.

### ▼ Inferential Statistics

Statistical analysis concerned with the measurement of only a sample from a population and then making estimates, or inferences, about the population from which the sample was taken; inferential statistics help generalize the results of data analyses.

▼ **Information and Analysis**

Establishes systematic and rigorous reliance on data for decision making in all parts of the organization. This section of the school portfolio sets the context of the learning organization.

▼ **Intersections**

Analyzing the intersection or overlapping of measures (demographics, perceptions, school processes, student learning) enables schools to predict what they must do to meet the needs of all the students they have, or will have in the future.

▼ **Item Analysis**

Reviewing each item on a test or assessment to determine how many students missed the particular item. A general term for procedures designed to access the usefulness of a test item.

▼ **Latent Trait Scale**

A scaled score obtained through one of several mathematical approaches collectively known as Latent-trait procedures or Item Response Theory. The particular numerical values used in the scale are arbitrary, but higher scores indicate more knowledgeable test takers or more difficult items.

▼ **Learning**

A process of acquiring knowledge, skills, understanding, and/or new behaviors.

▼ **Learning Goal**

A target for learning: a desired skill, knowledge, or behavior.

▼ **Matched Cohorts**

Looking at the same students (individual, not groups) progressing through the grades over time.

▼ **Maximum**

The highest actual score or the highest possible score on a test.

▼ **Mean**

Average score in a set of scores; calculated by summing all the scores and dividing by the total number of scores.

▼ **Means**

Methods, strategies, actions, and processes by which a school plans to improve student achievement.

▼ **Measures**

A way of evaluating something; how we know we have achieved the objective.

▼ **Median**

The score that splits a distribution in half: 50 percent of the scores lie above and 50 percent of the scores lie below the median. If the number of scores is odd, the median is the middle score. If the number of scores is even, one must add the two middle scores and divide by two to calculate the median.

▼ **Minimum**

The lowest score or the lowest possible score on a test.

▼ **Mission**

A brief, clear, and compelling statement that serves to unify an organization's efforts. A mission has a finish line for its achievement and is proactive. A mission should walk the boundary between the possible and impossible.

## ▼ Mode

The score that occurs most frequently in a scoring distribution.

## ▼ Multiple Measures

Using more than one method of assessment, gathered from varying points of view, in order to understand the multifaceted world of school from the perspective of everyone involved.

## ▼ Needs Assessment

Questions that help staff understand their professional development needs. At the same time, if done well, this assessment can lead to quality staff conversations and sharing of knowledge.

## ▼ No Child Left Behind (NCLB)

*The No Child Left Behind Act of 2001* reauthorized the 1965 Elementary and Secondary Education Act. NCLB calls for increased accountability for states, school districts, and schools; choices for parents and students; greater flexibility for states, school districts, and schools regarding Federal education funds; establishing a Reading First initiative to ensure every child can read by end of grade three; and improving the quality of teachers.

## ▼ Normal Curve

The bell-shaped curve of the normal distribution.

## ▼ Normal Curve Equivalent (NCE)

Equivalent scores are standard scores with a mean of 50, a standard deviation of 21.06, and a range of 1 to 99.

## ▼ Normal Distribution

A distribution of scores or other measures that in graphic form has a distinctive bell-shaped appearance. In a normal distribution, the measures are distributed symmetrically about the mean. Cases are concentrated near the mean and decrease in frequency, according to a precise mathematical equation, the farther one departs from the mean. Also known as a normal curve.

## ▼ Normalized Standard Score

A transformation procedure used to make scores from different tests more directly comparable. Not only are the mean and the standard deviation of the raw score distribution changed, as with a linear standard score transformation, but the shape of the distribution is converted to a normal curve. The transformation to a normalized z-score involves two steps: 1) compute the exact percentile rank of the raw score; and 2) determine the corresponding z-score for that exact percentile rank from a table of areas under the normal curve.

## ▼ Norming Group

A representative group of students whose results on a norm-referenced test help create the scoring scales with which others compare their performance. The norming group's results are professed to look like the normal curve.

## ▼ Norm-referenced Test

Any test in which the score acquires additional meaning by comparing it to the scores of people in an identified norming group. A test can be both norm- and criterion-referenced. Most standardized achievement tests are referred to as norm-referenced.

▼ **Norms**

The distribution of test scores and their corresponding percentile ranks, standard scores, or other derived scores of some specified group called the norming group. For example, this may be a national sample of all fourth graders, a national sample of all fourth-grade males, or perhaps all fourth graders in some local district.

▼ **Norms versus Standards**

Norms are not standards. Norms are indicators of what students of similar characteristics did when confronted with the same test items as those taken by students in the norming group. Standards, on the other hand, are arbitrary judgments of what students should be able to do, given a set of test items.

▼ **Objectives**

Goals that are redrafted in terms that are clearly tangible. Objective statements are narrow, specific, concrete, and measurable. When writing objectives, it is important to describe the intended results, rather than the process or means to accomplish them, and state the time frame.

▼ **Observation**

Teacher and observer agree on what is being observed, the type of information to be recorded, when the observation will take place, and how the information will be analyzed. The observee is someone implementing strategies and actions that others want to know. Observer might be a colleague, a supervisor, or a visitor from another location.

▼ **Over Time**

No less than three years.

▼ **Parameter**

A parameter is a population measurement that characterizes one of its features. An example of a parameter is the mode. The mode is the value in the population that occurs most frequently. Other examples of parameters are a population's mean (or average) and its variance.

▼ **Partnerships**

Teachers developing relationships with parents, businesses in the community, scientists, and/or university personnel to help students achieve student learning standards, and to bring about real world applications for student learning and deeper understandings of content.

▼ **Pearson Correlation Coefficient**

The most widely-used correlation coefficient determines the extent to which two variables are proportional to each other; measures the strength and direction of a linear relationship between the x and y variables.

▼ **Percent Correct**

A calculated score implying the percentage of students meeting and exceeding some number, usually a cut score, or a standard. Percent passing equals the number passing the test divided by the number taking the test.

▼ **Percent Proficient**

Percent Proficient, Percent Mastery, or Percent Passing are terms that represent the percentage of students who pass a particular test at a level above a cut score, as defined by the test creators or the test interpreters.

▼ **Percentile**

A point on the normal distribution below which a certain percentage of the scores fall. For example, if 70 percent of the scores fall below a raw score of 56, then the score of 56 is at the 70th percentile. The term *local percentile* indicates that the norm group is obtained locally. The term *national percentile* indicates that the norm group represents a national group.

▼ **Percentile Rank (PR)**

Percentage of students in a norm group (e.g., national or local) whose scores fall below a given score. Range is from 1 to 99. A 50th percentile ranking would mean that 50 percent of the scores in the norming group fall below a specific score.

▼ **Perceptions Data**

Information that reflects opinions and views of questionnaire respondents.

▼ **Performance Assessment**

Refers to assessments that measure skills, knowledge, and ability directly—such as through performance. In other words, if you want students to learn to write, you assess their ability on a writing activity.

▼ **Population**

Statisticians define a population as the entire collection of items that is the focus of concern. Descriptive Statistics describe the characteristics of a given population by measuring each of its items and then summarizing the set of measures in various ways. Inferential Statistics make educated inferences about the characteristics of a population by drawing a random sample and appropriately analyzing the information it provides.

▼ **Process Mapping**

School processes are instruction, curriculum, and assessment strategies used to ensure the learning of all students. Mapping or flowcharting school processes can help staff objectively look at how students are being taught.

▼ **Processes**

Measures that describe what is being done to get results, such as programs, strategies, and practices.

▼ **Professional Development**

Planned activities that help staff members, teachers, and administrators change the manner in which they work, i.e., how they make decisions; gather, analyze, and use data; plan, teach, and monitor achievement; evaluate personnel; and assess the impact of new approaches to instruction and assessment on students.

▼ **Program Evaluation**

The examination of a program to understand its quality and impact.

▼ **Purpose**

The aim of the organization; the reason for existence.

▼ **Quality Planning**

Developing the elements of a strategic plan including a vision, mission, goals, action plan, outcome measures, and strategies for continuous improvement and evaluation. Quality planning is a section of the school portfolio.

### ▼ Quality

A standard for excellence.

### ▼ Quartiles

Three quartiles—Q1, Q2, Q3—divide a distribution into four equal groups (Q1=25th percentile; Q2=50th percentile; Q3=75th percentile).

### ▼ Query

A request one makes to a database that is returned to the desktop. Understanding and knowing how to set up queries or to ask questions of the database is very important to the information discovery process.

### ▼ Range

A measure of the spread between the lowest and the highest scores in a distribution, calculated by subtracting the lowest score from the highest score.

### ▼ Raw Scores

A person's observed score on a test or subtest. The number of questions answered correctly on a test or subtest. A raw score is simply calculated by adding the number of questions answered correctly.

### ▼ Regression

An analysis that results in an equation that describes the nature of the relationship among variables. Simple regressions predict an object's value on a criterion variable when given its value on one predictor variable. Multiple regressions predict an object's value on a criterion variable when given its value on each of several predictor variables.

### ▼ Relational Database

A type of database that allows the connection of several databases to each other. The data and relations between them are stored in table form. Relational databases are powerful because they require few assumptions about how data are related and how they will be extracted from the database.

### ▼ Relationships

Looking at two or more sets of analyses to understand how they are associated or what they mean to each other.

### ▼ Reliability

The consistency with which an assessment measures what it intends to measure.

### ▼ Research

The act of methodically collecting information about a particular subject to discover facts or to develop a plan of action based on the facts discovered.

### ▼ RIT Scale Scores

Named for George Rasch, who developed the theory of this type of measurement, RIT scores are scaled scores that come from a series of tests created by the Northwest Evaluation Association (NWEA). The tests that draw from an item bank are created to align with local curriculum and state standards.

## ▼ Root Cause

As used in the continuous school improvement plan, *root cause* refers to the deep underlying reason for a specific situation. While a symptom may be made evident from a needs assessment or gap analysis—the symptom (low student scores) is not the cause. To find a root cause or causes one often has to ask Why? at least five levels down to uncover the root reasons for the symptom.

## ▼ Rubric

A scoring tool that rates performance according to clearly stated levels of criteria. The scales can be numeric or descriptive.

## ▼ Sample

In statistical terms, a random sample is a set of items that have been drawn from a population in such a way that each time an item is selected, every item in the population has an equal opportunity to appear in the sample. In practical terms, it is not so easy to draw a random sample.

## ▼ Scaled Scores

A mathematical transformation of a raw score. It takes the differences in the difficulty of test forms into consideration and is useful for teaching changes over time.

## ▼ School Improvement Planning

Planning to implement the vision requires studying the research, determining strategies that will work with the students, and determining what the vision would look like, sound like, and feel like when the vision is implemented, and how to get all staff members implementing the vision.

## ▼ School Portfolio

A professional development tool that gathers evidence about the way work is done in the school and a self-assessment tool to ensure the alignment of all parts of the learning organization to the vision. A school portfolio can also serve as a principal portfolio.

## ▼ School Processes

Instruction, curriculum, and assessment strategies used to ensure the learning of all students.

## ▼ Scientifically-based Research

The revised *Elementary and Secondary Education Act,* recently approved by Congress and also known as the *No Child Left Behind Act of 2001,* mandates that educators base school programs and teaching practices on Scientifically Based Research. This includes everything from teaching approaches to drug abuse prevention. Scientifically Based Research means research that involves the application of rigorous, systematic, and objective procedures to obtain reliable and valid knowledge relevant to education activities and programs.

## ▼ Self-assessment

Assessment by the individual performing the activity.

## ▼ Skewed Distribution

Most of the scores are found near one end of the distribution. When most of the scores are grouped at the lower end, it is positively skewed. When most of the scores are grouped at the upper end, it is negatively skewed.

## Standard

A guideline or description that is used as a basis for judgment. Exemplary performance; an objective ideal; a worthy and tangible goal.

## Standard Deviation

Measure of variability in a set of scores. The standard deviation is the square root of the variance. Unlike the variance, the standard deviation is stated in the original units of the variable. Approximately 68 percent of the scores in a normal distribution lie between plus one and minus one standard deviation. The more scores cluster around the mean, the smaller the variance.

## Standard Scores

A group of scores having a desired mean and standard deviation. A z-score is a basic standard score. Other standard scores are computed by first converting a raw score to a z-score (sometimes normalized), multiplying the transformation by the desired standard deviation, and then adding the desired mean to the product. The raw scores are transformed this way for reasons of convenience, comparability, and ease of interpretation.

## Standardized Tests

Tests that are uniform in content, administration, and scoring. Standardized tests can be used for comparing results across classrooms, schools, school districts, and states.

## Standards

Consistent expectations of all learners.

## Standards-based Assessments

A collection of items that indicate how much students know and/or are able to do with respect to specific standards.

## Stanines

A nine-point normalized standard score scale. It divides the normal curve distribution of scores into nine equal points: 1 to 9. The mean of a stanine distribution is 5, and the standard deviation is approximately 2.

## Statistically Significant

Statistical significance indicates that there is at least a 95% probability of the result that did not happen by chance.

## Strategies

Procedures, methods, or techniques to accomplish an objective.

## Student Achievement Data

Information that reflects a level of knowledge, skill, or accomplishment, usually in something that has been explicitly taught.

## Study Groups

Teams or groups of educators meet to learn new strategies or programs, to review new publications, or to review student work together.

## Summative

Assessment or evaluation designed to provide information; used in making judgments about a student's achievement at the end of a period of instruction.

▼ **Symptom**

A symptom is the outward (most visible) indicator of a deeper root cause.

▼ **T-Chart**

Used to compare and contrast information or to show relationships. It is used to help people see the opposite dimension of an issue.

▼ **T-Scores**

A calculated standard score with a mean of 50 and a standard deviation of 10. T-scores are obtained by the following formula: $T = 10z + 50$. T-scores are sometimes normalized.

▼ **Table**

A data structure comprised of rows and columns, like a spreadsheet.

▼ **Teacher Portfolios**

The process and product of documenting a teacher as learner; includes reflections, observations, and evidence. Portfolios can be used for many things, such as, self-assessment, employment, supervision to replace traditional teacher evaluation, and for peer collaboration.

▼ **Tests of Significance**

Procedures that use samples to test claims about population parameters. Significance tests can estimate a population parameter, with a certain amount of confidence, from a sample.

▼ **Triangulation**

The term used for combining three or more student achievement measures to get a more complete picture of student achievement.

▼ **Validity**

The degree to which an assessment strategy measures what it is intended to measure.

▼ **Values and Beliefs**

The core of who we are, what we do, and how we think and feel. Values and beliefs reflect what is important to us; they describe what we think about work and how we think it should operate. Core values and beliefs are the first step in reaching a shared vision.

▼ **Variance**

A measure of the dispersion, or variability, of scores about their mean. The population variance is calculated by taking the average of the squared deviations from the mean—a deviation being defined as an individual score minus the mean.

▼ **Vision**

A specific description of what the learning organization will be like when the mission is achieved. A vision is a mental image. It must be written in practical, concrete terms that everyone can understand and see in the same way.

▼ **z-Scores**

A standard score with a mean of zero and a standard deviation of one. A z-score is obtained by the following formula: z = raw score (x) minus the mean, divided by the standard deviation (sd). A z-score is sometimes normalized.

# References and Resources

The references used in this book, along with other resources that will assist busy school administrators and teachers in continuously improving, appear below.

Airasian, P. W. (1994). *Classroom assessment.* New York, NY: McGraw-Hill, Inc.

Ardovino, J., Hollingsworth, J., & Ybarra, S. (2000). *Multiple measures: Accurate ways to assess student achievement.* Thousand Oaks, CA: Corwin Press, Inc.

Armstrong, J., & Anthes, K. (2001). How data can help: Putting information to work to raise student achievement. In *American School Board Journal*, 38-41.

Arter, J. (1999). *Teaching about performance assessment.* Portland, OR: Northwest Regional Educational Laboratory.

Arter, J., & The Classroom Assessment Team, Laboratory Network Program. (1998). *Improving classroom assessment: A toolkit for professional developers: Alternative Assessment.* Aurora, CO: MCREL.

Arter, J., & Busick, K. (2001). *Practice with student-involved classroom assessment.* Portland, OR: Assessment Training Institute, Inc.

Arter, J., & McTighe, J. (2001). *Scoring rubrics in the classroom: Using performance criteria for assessing and improving student performance.* In Guskey, T.R., & Marzano, R.J. (Series Eds.). *Experts in Assessment.* Thousand Oaks, CA: Corwin Press, Inc.

Aschbacher, P. R., & Herman, J. L. (1991). *Guidelines for effective score reporting.* (CSE Technical Report No. 326). Los Angeles, CA: University of California, Center for Research on Evaluation, Standards and Student Testing (CRESST).

Barth, P., Haycock, K., Jackson, H., Mora, K., Ruiz, P., Robinson, S., & Wilkins, A. (Eds.). (1999). *Dispelling the myth: High poverty schools exceeding expectations.* Washington, DC: Education Trust in Cooperation with the Council of Chief State School Officers and partially funded by the U.S. Department of Education.

Bernhardt, V. L. (2004). *Data analysis for comprehensive schoolwide improvement* (2nd ed.). Larchmont, NY: Eye on Education, Inc.

Bernhardt, V. L. (1998). *Multiple Measures.* Monograph No. 4. California Association for Supervision and Curriculum Development (CASCD).

Bernhardt, V. L. (1999). *The school portfolio: A comprehensive framework for school improvement* (2nd ed.). Larchmont, NY: Eye on Education, Inc.

Bernhardt, V.L. (1999, June). *Databases can help teachers with standards implementation.* Monograph No. 5. California Association for Supervision and Curriculum Development (CASCD).

Bernhardt, V. L. (2000). *Designing and using databases for school improvement.* Larchmont, NY: Eye on Education, Inc.

Bernhardt, V. L. (2000). Intersections: New routes open when one type of data crosses another. *Journal of Staff Development, 21*(1), 33-36.

Bernhardt, V. L. (2002). *The school portfolio toolkit: A planning, implementation, and evaluation guide for continuous school improvement.* Larchmont, NY: Eye on Education, Inc.

Bernhardt, V. L. (2003). No Schools Left Behind. *Educational Leadership, 60*(5), 26-30.

Bernhardt, V. L., von Blanckensee, L., Lauck, M., Rebello, F., Bonilla, G., & Tribbey, M. (2000). *The example school portfolio, A companion to the school portfolio: A comprehensive framework for school improvement.* Larchmont, NY: Eye on Education, Inc.

Blythe, T., & Associates. (1998). *The teaching for understanding guide.* San Francisco, CA: Jossey-Bass, Inc.

Commission on Instructionally Supportive Assessment. (2001). *Building tests to support instruction and accountability.* Available: http://www.aasa.org.

Carr, N. (2001). Making data count: Transforming schooling through data-driven decision making. *American School Board Journal,* 34-37.

Cawelti, G. (Ed.). (1999). *Handbook of research on improving student achievement* (2nd ed.). Arlington, VA: Educational Testing Service.

Clarke, D. (1997). *Constructive assessment in mathematics: Practical steps for classroom teachers.* Berkeley, CA: Key Curriculum Press.

Clune, B., & Webb, N. (2001-02). WCER Highlights. Madison, WS: University of Wisconsin-Madison, Wisconsin Center for Education Research.

Conzemius, A., & O'Neill, J. (2001). *Building shared responsibility for student learning.* Alexandria, VA: Association for Supervision and Curriculum Development.

Creighton, T. B. (2001). *Schools and data: The educator's guide for using data to improve decision-making.* Thousand Oaks, CA: Corwin Press, Inc.

Dann, R. (2002). *Promoting assessment as learning.* New York, NY: RoutledgeFalmer.

Deming, W. E. (1986). *Out of the crisis.* Cambridge, MA: MIT Press.

DuFour, R., & Eaker, R. (1998). *Professional learning communities at work: Best practices for enhancing student achievement.* Bloomington, IN: National Education Service.

Educators in Connecticut's Pomperaug Regional School District 15. (1996). *A teacher's guide to performance-based learning and assessment.* Alexandria, VA: Association for Supervision and Curriculum Development.

English, F. W. (2000). *Deciding what to teach and test: Developing, aligning, and auditing the curriculum.* Thousand Oaks, CA: Corwin Press, Inc.

Falk, B. (2000). *The heart of the matter: Using standards and assessment to learn.* Portsmouth, NH: Heinemann.

Fullan, M. (2001). *Leading a culture of change.* New York, NY: Jossey-Bass/Pfeiffer.

Fullan, M. (2002). *Changing forces with a vengeance.* New York, NY: RoutledgeFalmer.

Glatthorn, A. A. (1999). *Performance standards & authentic learning.* Larchmont, NY: Eye on Education, Inc.

Glatthorn, A. A., & Fontana, J. (Eds.). (2000). *Coping with standards, tests, and accountability: Voices from the classroom.* Washington, DC: National Education Association.

Gredler, M. (1999). *Classroom assessment and learning.* Needham Heights, MA: Allyn & Bacon.

Gupta, K. (1999). *A practical guide to needs assessment.* San Francisco, CA: Jossey-Bass, Inc.

Guskey, T. (2000). *Evaluating professional development.* Thousand Oaks, CA: Corwin Press, Inc.

Guskey, T. R., & Bailey, J. M. (2001). Developing grading and reporting systems for student learning. In Guskey, T.R. & Marzano, R.J. (Series Eds.). *Experts in assessment.* Thousand Oaks, CA: Corwin Press, Inc.

Haladyna, T. M., Nolan, S. B., & Haas, N. S. (1991). Raising standardized achievement test scores and the origins of test score pollutions. *Educational Researcher,* 20(5), 2-7.

Haycock, K. (1999). *Results: Good teaching matters.* Oxford, OH: National Staff Development Council.

Henry, T. (2001, June 11). Lawmakers move to improve literacy, the 'new civil right.' *USA Today,* pp. A1-2.

Herman, J. L., & Golan, S. (1991). *Effects of standardized testing on teachers and learning—another look.* (CSE Technical Report No. 334). Los Angeles, CA: University of California, Center for Research on Evaluation, Standards and Student Testing (CRESST).

Holcomb, E. L. (1999). *Getting excited about data.* Thousand Oaks, CA: Corwin Press, Inc.

Isaac, S., & William, B. M. (1997). *Handbook in research and evaluation for education and the behavioral sciences* (3rd ed.). San Diego, CA: Educational and Industrial Testing Services.

Johnson, D. W., & Johnson, R. T. (2002). *Introduction: Cooperative learning and assessment.* Needham Heights, MA: Allyn & Bacon.

Johnson, R. S. (2002). *Using data to close the achievement gap: How to measure equity in our schools.* Thousand Oaks, CA: Corwin Press, Inc.

Kachigan, S. K. (1991). *Multivariate statistical analysis: A conceptual introduction* (2nd ed.). New York, NY: Radius Press.

Kain, D. L. (1996). *Looking beneath the surface: Teacher collaboration through the lens of grading practices.* Teachers College Record, Summer, 569-587.

Kifer, E. (2000). *Large-scale assessment: Dimensions, dilemmas, and policy.* Thousand Oaks, CA: Corwin Press, Inc.

Killion, J. (2002). *Assessing impact: Evaluating staff development.* Oxford, OH: National Staff Development Council.

Koretz, D., Stecher, B., Klein, S., & McCaffrey, D. (1994). The Vermont portfolio assessment program: Finding and implications. *Educational Measurement: Issues and Practice,* 13(3), 5-16.

Kouzes, J. M., & Posner, B. Z. (2002). *The leadership challenge: How to keep getting extraordinary things done in organizations.* (2nd Ed.). San Francisco, CA: Jossey-Bass Publishers.

Lazear, D. (1998). *The rubrics way: Using MI to assess understanding.* Tucson, AZ: Zephyr Press.

Linn, R. L., Baker, E. L., & Dunbar, S. B. (1991). *Complex, performance-based assessment: Expectations and validation guide.* (CSE Technical Report No. 331). Los Angeles, CA: University of California, Center for Research on Evaluation, Standards and Student Testing (CRESST).

Lissitz, R. W., & Schafer, W. D. (2002). (Eds.). *Assessment in educational reform: Both means and ends.* Needham Heights, MA: Allyn & Bacon.

Marzano, R. J. (2000). *Transforming classroom grading.* Alexandria, VA: Association for Supervision and Curriculum Development.

Marzano, R. J., Pickering, D., & McTighe, J. (1993). *Assess student outcomes: Performance assessment using dimensions of learning model.* Alexandria, VA: Association for Supervision and Curriculum Development.

Marzano, R. J., Pickering, D., & Pollock, J. E. (2001). *Classroom instruction that works: Research-based strategies for increasing student achievement.* Alexandria, VA: Association for Supervision and Curriculum Development.

McMillian, J. H. (2001). *Classroom assessment: Principles and practice for effective instruction* (2nd ed.). Needham Heights, MA: Allyn & Bacon.

McMillian, J. H. (2001). *Essential assessment concepts for teachers and administrators.* In Guskey, T.R. & Marzano, R.J. (Series Eds.). Experts in Assessment. Thousand Oaks, CA: Corwin Press, Inc.

McREL. (1995-2002). *Classroom assessment, grading, and record keeping.* Aurora, CO: Author.

McTighe, J., & Ferrara, S. (1998). *Assessing learning in the classroom.* Washington, DC: National Education Association.

Merrow, J. (2001). *"Good enough" Schools are not good enough.* Lanham, MD: Scarecrow Press.

National Staff Development Council. (2002, October). Scientifically-based research as defined by NCLB. *Results.* Oxford, OH: Author.

Northwest Evaluation Association (NWEA). (2002). Available: http://www.nwea.org.

O'Connor, K. (1999). *The mindful school: How to grade for learning.* Arlington Heights, IL: Skylight Professional Development.

Oosterhof, A. (1999). *Developing and using classroom assessments* (2nd ed.). Englewood Cliffs, NJ: Prentice Hall.

Parsons, B. A. (2002). *Evaluative Inquiry: Using evaluation to promote student success.* Thousand Oaks, CA: Corwin Press, Inc.

Patten, M. L. (1997). *Understanding research methods: An overview of the essentials.* Los Angeles, CA: Pyrczak Publishing.

Payne, R. K., & Magee, D. S. (1999). *Meeting standards and raising test scores when you don't have much time or money.* Highlands, TX: RFT Publishing Company.

Perone, V. (Ed.). (1991). *Expanding student assessment.* Alexandria, VA: Association for Supervision and Curriculum Development.

Popham, W. J. (1999). *Classroom assessment: What teachers need to know* (2nd ed.). Needham Heights, MA: Allyn & Bacon.

Popham, W. J. (2001). Standardized achievement tests: Misnamed and misleading. *Education Week,* 21(3), 46.

Preuss, P. G. (2003). *School leader's guide to root cause analysis: Using data to dissolve problems.* Larchmont, NY: Eye on Education, Inc.

Quellmalz, E., & Burry, J. (1983). Analytic scales for assessing students' expository and narrative writing skills. (CSE Technical Report No. 5). Los Angeles, CA: University of California, Center for Research on Evaluation, Standards and Student Testing (CRESST).

Rogers, S., & Graham, S. (2000). *The high performance toolbox: Succeeding with performance tasks, projects, and assessments* (3rd ed.). Evergreen, CO: Peak Learning Systems.

Sanders, J. R. (2000). *Evaluating school programs: An educator's guide.* Thousand Oaks, CA: Corwin Press, Inc.

Schafer, W. D., & Lissitz, R. W. (1987). Measurement training for school personnel: Recommendations and reality. *Journal of Teacher Education, 38*(3), 57-63.

Schmoker, M. (2001). *The results fieldbook: Practical strategies from dramatically improved schools.* Alexandria, VA: Association for Supervision and Curriculum Development.

Shepard, L. A. (2000). *The role of classroom assessment in teaching and learning.* (CSE Technical Report No. 517). Los Angeles, CA: University of California, Center for Research on Evaluation, Standards and Student Testing (CRESST).

Smith, J. K., Smith, L. F., & DeLisi, R. (2001). *Natural classroom assessment: Designing seamless instruction & assessment.* In Guskey, T.R. & Marzano, R.J. (Series Eds.). Experts in Assessment. Thousand Oaks, CA: Corwin Press, Inc.

Solomon, P. (2002). *The assessment bridge: Positive ways to link tests to learning, standards, and curriculum improvement.* Thousand Oaks, CA: Corwin Press, Inc.

Stiggins, R. J. (2000). *Student-Involved classroom assessment* (3rd ed.). Englewood Cliffs, NJ: Prentice Hall.

Stiggins, R. J. (1999). Assessment, student confidence, and school success. *Phi Delta Kappan,* November, 191-198.

Stigler, J. W., & Hiebert, J. (1999). *The teaching gap: Best ideas from the world's teachers for improving education in the classroom.* New York, NY: The Free Press.

Strong, R. W., Silver, H. F., & Perini. M. J. (2001). *Teaching what matters most: Standards and strategies for raising student achievement.* Alexandria, VA: Association for Supervision and Curriculum Development.

TetraData. (2002). Available: http://www.Tetradata.com.

Trice, A. D. (2000). *A handbook of classroom assessment.* Needham Heights, MA: Allyn & Bacon.

Wahlstrom, D. (1999). *Using data to improve student achievement: A handbook for collecting, analyzing, and using data.* Virginia Beach, VA: Successline Publications.

Wiggins, G. (1998). *Educative assessment: Designing assessments to inform and improve student performance.* San Francisco, CA: Jossey-Bass, Inc.

Wiggins, G., & McTighe, J. (1998). *Understanding by design.* Alexandria, VA: Association for Supervision and Curriculum Development.

Wilson, L. W. (2002). *Better instruction through assessment: What your students are trying to tell you.* Larchmont, NY: Eye on Education, Inc.

Wittrock, M. C., & Baker, E. L. (Eds.). (1991). *Testing and cognition.* Englewood Cliffs, NJ: Prentice Hall.

Worthen, B. R., White, K. R., Fan, X., & Sudweeks, R. R. (1999). *Measurement and assessment in the schools* (2nd ed.). Needham Heights, MA: Allyn & Bacon.

Zemelman, S., Daniels, H., & Hyde, A. (1998). *Best practice: New standards for teaching and learning in America's schools* (2nd ed.). Portsmouth, NH: Heinemann.

# Index

# EYE ON EDUCATION and EDUCATION FOR THE FUTURE INITIATIVE
# END-USER LICENSE AGREEMENT

## READ THIS

You should carefully read these terms and conditions before opening the software packet(s) included with this book ("Book"). This is a license agreement ("Agreement") between you and EYE ON EDUCATION. By opening the accompanying software packet(s), you acknowledge that you have read and accept the following terms and conditions. If you do not agree and do not want to be bound by such terms and conditions, promptly return the Book and the unopened software packet (s) to the place you obtained them for a full refund.

### 1. License Grant

EYE ON EDUCATION grants to you (either an individual or entity) a nonexclusive license to use the software and files (collectively, the "Software") solely for your own personal or business purposes on a single computer (whether a standard computer or a workstation component of a multiuser network). The Software is in use on a computer when it is loaded into temporary memory (RAM) or installed into permanent memory (hard disk, CD-ROM, or other storage device). EYE ON EDUCATION reserves all rights not expressly granted herein.

### 2. Ownership

EYE ON EDUCATION is the owner of all rights, title, and interests, including copyright, in and to the compilation of the Software recorded on the CD-ROM ("Software Media"). Copyright to the individual programs recorded on the Software Media is owned by the author or other authorized copyright owner of each program. Ownership of the Software and all proprietary rights relating thereto remain with EYE ON EDUCATION and its licensers.

### 3. Restrictions On Use and Transfer

(a)   You may only (i) make one copy of the Software for backup or archival purposes, or (ii) transfer the Software to a single hard disk, provided that you keep the original for backup or archival purposes. You may not (i) rent or lease the Software, (ii) copy or reproduce the Software through a LAN or other network system or through any computer subscriber system or bulletin-board system, or (iii) adapt or create derivative works based on the Software.

(b)   You may not reverse engineer, decompile, or disassemble the Software. You may transfer the Software and user documentation on a permanent basis, provided that the transferee agrees to accept the terms and conditions of this Agreement and you retain no copies. If the Software is an update or has been updated, any transfer must include the most recent update and all prior versions.

### 4. Restrictions On Use of Individual Programs

You must follow the individual requirements and restrictions detailed for each individual program on the Software Media. These limitations are contained in the individual license agreements recorded on the Software Media. By opening the Software packet, you will be agreeing to abide by the licenses and restrictions for these individual programs that are detailed on the Software Media. None of the material on this Software Media or listed in this Book may ever be redistributed, in original or modified form, for commercial purposes.

### 5. Limited Warranty

(a)   EDUCATION FOR THE FUTURE INITIATIVE warrants that the Software and Software Media are free from defects in materials and workmanship under normal use for a period of thirty (30) days from the date of purchase of this Book. If EDUCATION FOR THE FUTURE INITIATIVE receives notification within the warranty period of defects in materials or workmanship, EDUCATION FOR THE FUTURE INITIATIVE will replace the defective Software Media.

(b)   **EYE ON EDUCATION, EDUCATION FOR THE FUTURE INITIATIVE, AND THE AUTHOR OF THIS BOOK DISCLAIM OTHER WARRANTIES, EXPRESSED OR IMPLIED, INCLUDING WITHOUT LIMITATION IMPLIED WARRANTIES OF MERCHANTABILITY AND FITNESS FOR A PARTICULAR PURPOSE WITH RESPECT TO THE SOFTWARE AND FILES, AND/OR THE TECHNIQUES DESCRIBED IN THIS BOOK. EYE ON EDUCATION DOES NOT WARRANT THAT THE FUNCTIONS CONTAINED IN THE SOFTWARE WILL MEET YOUR REQUIREMENTS OR THAT THE OPERATION OF THE SOFTWARE WILL BE ERROR FREE.**

(c)   This limited warranty gives you specific legal rights, and you may have other rights that vary from jurisdiction to jurisdiction.

## 6. Remedies

(a)  EYE ON EDUCATION's entire liability and your exclusive remedy for defects in materials and workmanship shall be limited to replacement of the Software Media, which may be returned to EDUCATION FOR THE FUTURE INITIATIVE with a copy of your receipt at the following address: EDUCATION FOR THE FUTURE INITIATIVE, ATTN: Brad Geise, 400 West 1st. St., Chico, CA 95929-0230, or call 1-530-898-4482. Please allow three to four weeks for delivery. This Limited Warranty is void if failure of the Software Media has resulted from accident, abuse, or misapplication. Any replacement Software Media will be warranted for thirty (30) days.

(b)  In no event shall EYE ON EDUCATION, EDUCATION FOR THE FUTURE INITIATIVE, or the author be liable for any damages whatsoever (including without limitation damages for loss of business profits, business interruption, loss of business information, or any other pecuniary loss) arising from the use of or inability to use the Book or the Software, even if EYE ON EDUCATION, EDUCATION FOR THE FUTURE INITIATIVE, or the author has been advised of the possibility of damages.

(c)  Because some jurisdictions do not allow the exclusion or limitation of liability for consequential or incidental damages, the above limitation or exclusion may not apply to you.

## 7. U.S. Government Restriction Rights

Use, duplication, or disclosure of the Software by the U.S. Government is subject to restrictions stated in paragraph ( c ) (1)(ii) of the Rights in Technical Data and Computer Software clause of DFARS 252.227-7013, and in subparagraphs (a) through (d) of the Commercial Computer—Restricted Rights clause at FAR 52. 227–19, and in similar clauses in the NASA FAR supplement, when applicable.

## 8. General

This Agreement constitutes the entire understanding of the parties and revokes and supersedes all prior agreements, oral or written, between them and may not be modified or amended except in writing signed by both parties hereto that specifically refers to this Agreement. This Agreement shall take precedence over any other documents that may be in conflict herewith. If any one or more provisions contained in this Agreement are held by any court or tribunal to be invalid, illegal, or otherwise unenforceable, each and every other provision shall remain in full force and effect.

# INSTALLATION INSTRUCTIONS

**Windows**

**Step 1** Set up a folder on your desktop (or in your documents folder) labeled *Elementary Data Tools* for capturing the files that you wish to download.

**Step 2** Make sure your monitor is set to 800 by 600 or higher to view the entire CD contents. (When you are on the main menu page of the CD and cannot see the top menu bar, your monitor must be moved to a higher setting. Do this by going into *Start / Settings / Control Panel / Display.* Open *Display,* and click on *Settings.* Move the arrow on the screen area to at least 800 by 600 pixels.)

**Step 3** The CD should start automatically. The introduction will run up to the *Main Menu* page. If the CD does *not* start automatically, follow steps 3a. and 3b. below:

  **3a.** Open/Explore *My Computer* and Open/Explore the CD *Elemtary.*

  **3b.** With the CD contents showing, click on *Click Here.exe.* The CD will begin.

**Step 4** After the introduction, you will come to the *Main Menu.* If you do not have *Adobe Reader* v.5 or above, download it by pressing *Adobe Acrobat.* After installing, go back to the *Main Menu.*

**Step 5** By placing your cursor on the section titles, you will be able to see what is on the CD. Click on the section that you want to know more about and read the descriptions of the files in that section.

**Step 6** To download the tools from that section, press the *Download* button.

**Step 7** When *Extract Archive Files* appears, click *Next.*

**Step 9** Note: When *Destination Directory* appears, click *Browse* to locate the folder in which you want the files to download. If you put a folder entitled *Elementary Data Tools* on your desktop, you will see it in the *Desktop Folder.* (This may vary slightly depending upon the version of *Windows* you are using.)

**Step 9** Open *The Elementary Data Tools* folder and click *Next.* The files will extract and ask you if it is okay to download. Click *Yes* and the files will extract into your *Elementary Data Tools* folder. Click *Finish.*

**Step 10** Go back to the *INFO* window. Select the *Back to Main Menu* button to return to the *Main Menu.*

**Step 11** Continue exploring and downloading. You must quit the CD to view the documents that you download.

**Mac**

**Step 1** Create a folder on your desktop (or your hard drive) labeled *Elementary Data Tools* for capturing the files that you wish to download.

**Step 2** Make sure your monitor is set to 800 by 600 or higher to view the entire CD contents. (When you are on the main menu page of the CD and cannot see the top menu bar, your monitor must be moved to a higher setting. Change the settings in the *Monitors Control Panel.*)

**Step 3** The CD will start automatically. The introduction will run up to the *Main Menu* page. If the CD does *not* start automatically, follow steps 3a. and 3b. below:

  **3a.** Open the CD by double-clicking the CD icon on your desktop.

  **3b.** Select the icon for *Classic OS 9* or *OS X,* depending upon which operating system you use. The CD will begin.

**Step 4** By placing your cursor on the section titles, you will be able to see what is on the CD. Click on the section that you want to know more about and read the descriptions of the files.

**Step 5** To download the tools from that section, press the *Download* button.

**Step 6** When a dialog box appears, click *Continue.*

**Step 7** Note: A *Save* window will appear. Locate your *Elementary Data Tools* folder, or if you did not make a folder when you started, create a new folder. Save the section's files to the *Elementary Data Tools* folder.

**Step 8** Go Back to *INFO* window. Select the *Back to Main Menu* button to return to the *Main Menu.*

**Step 9** Continue exploring and downloading. You must quit the CD to view the documents that you download.

Please see our website for more information:

## http://eff.csuchico.edu/home/

To contact *Education for the Future,* call:

(530) 898-4482